US ARMY FIELD MANUAL
5-15

FIELD FORTIFICATIONS

AUGUST, 1968

EDITOR'S NOTE

This volume contains the August, 1968 version of US Army **Field Manual 5-15 – Field Fortifications**. This is an older manual that was superseded in the early 1980's by two manuals **FM 5-102 Countermobility** and **FM 5-103 Survivability**. These two successor manuals are much more concentrated on planning factors for engineers and less so on the nuts and bolts of actually building and emplacing field fortifications. I will release these two manuals as hardcopies also at some future time but I wanted to get this manual out there sooner since it is full of more immediately practical information than either 5-102 or 5-103, which are written much more as planning manuals than something you pull out in the field to find practical information on what you need to build a specific obstacle and/or fortification.

The next manual in this series I will be releasing is FM5-34 Engineer Field Data, which is probably the single most useful engineer manual I know as it is chock full of data useful in both the offense and the defense. 5-34 is a huge manual though at over 600 pages and is jammed full of images and data tables so it will take me much longer to convert from PDF to a format that is printable in the size format I want.

It should be quite obvious from the title why this particular manual would be of use to a dedicated prepper. It describes various methods for preparing both hasty and deliberate fortifications. What it does not describe by and large are methods to construct a fortified permanent position such as the FOBs and COPs established in Iraq and Afghanistan in modern American wars. It also does not address methods of defeating modern night vision and thermal sensing, mainly because man-portable night-vision devices were in their infancy when this manual was written and thermal sights were large vehicle borne devices, not the devices that can be mounted on individual weapons available today. Those caveats aside, all the information in the book is still useful as bullets and bombs are still essentially the same today as 50 years ago, with the exception that precision munitions are more plentiful now than then.

I have modified this copy somewhat by taking a two-column layout and making it a single column layout for easier reading. This caused me to re-order the placement of many of the illustrations and in so doing I have tried to put the accompanying illustration directly after the section of text that describes it. I have also updated the spelling and grammar to reflect current usage and somewhat modified the layout by largely re-interpreting the odd outline format used in Army manuals produced during this time period.

As with all the other US Army manuals I am making available as hardcopies I have also re-numbered the pages to be consecutive throughout the book instead of the weird chapter numbering system the military uses and that I always hated. I have attempted to fix all page references to reflect the new numbering but it is entirely possible that I have missed one or more such references.

My goal in compiling these was to make them available at an affordable price using modern Print-On-Demand (POD) technology. I hope these manuals are instructive. Any typos or other errors in the copy of this book are mine alone. If you discover any typos or incorrect references, please send an email to info@military-history.us with the mistake and which page it is on so I can fix it in subsequent releases.

THE TEXT OF THE MANUAL BEGINS ON THE NEXT PAGE

FM 5-15
FIELD FORTIFICATIONS
DEPARTMENT OF THE ARMY FIELD MANUAL

HEADQUARTERS, DEPARTMENT OF THE ARMY
AUGUST 1968

TABLE OF CONTENTS

CHAPTER 1 – GENERAL

Section I. Introduction

1-1. Purpose

This manual is a training guide for small units in the construction of field fortifications, including protected firing positions for weapons, personnel shelters, and defensive obstacles.

1-2. Scope

a. Fortifications. Detailed information on the construction and progressive development of emplacements, entrenchments, shelters, entanglements, and obstacles under varied climatic conditions is included in the manual. The types of fortifications illustrated and discussed are generally within the capabilities of unskilled personnel. Standard plans, bills of material, construction procedures, and estimated time and labor requirements are furnished.

b. Tools and Equipment. Tools and equipment normally available to combat units together with devices and equipment under development which may be available in the near future are illustrated and discussed.

c. Application. The material contained herein is applicable without modification to both nuclear and nonnuclear warfare.

d. Changes. Users of this manual are encouraged to submit recommended changes or comments to improve the manual. Comments should be keyed to the specific page, paragraph, and line of the text in which the change is recommended. Reasons should be provided for each comment to insure understanding and complete evaluation. Comments should be forwarded direct to the Commandant, U.S. Army Engineer School, Fort Belvoir, Va. 22060.

e. Metric Measures. Dimensions and distances are generally given in centimeters and meters. A conversion table to the English system is furnished in appendix B.

Section II. Basic Considerations

1-3. Use of Field Fortifications

a. On the Offense. During offensive operations, periodic halts may be required to regroup, resupply, or consolidate positions gained. Where the enemy threat is known to include a counterattack capability (or probability), offensive units should seek available cover or should dig hasty emplacements as described in paragraph 2-4a.

b. On the Defense. A defensive position is built around a series of organized and occupied tactical positions. Positions are selected for their natural defensive strength and the observation afforded. Fortification measures include clearing fields of fire, digging weapon emplacements and positions for personnel, strengthening natural obstacles, installing artificial obstacles, and providing camouflage.

c. Fortification Plans. Plans for fortifications not only provide for the desired degree of protection but also for bringing the enemy under the maximum volume of effective fire as early as possible. Fortification plans are usually based on progressive construction; that is, proceeding from open to covered emplacements and shelters to the ultimate protection permissible under the circumstances. Characteristics of personnel and individual weapons emplacements are shown in table 11 Located in Back of Manual

d. Dispersion. The separation of units and individuals is a primary means of increasing protection, particularly from the effects of nuclear weapons. If the area occupied by a unit is doubled, it is less vulnerable to shell fire or the effects of nuclear weapons. Proper dispersion can greatly reduce the requirements for high level of protection from field fortifications. The amount that a unit spreads out depends on the mission, terrain, and the enemy situation. Fortifications, properly employed, can be used in lieu of or to supplement dispersion, but fortifications are particularly important for units that cannot disperse sufficiently to obtain adequate protection.

e. Alternate and Dummy Positions. When time and the situation permit, dummy and alternate positions should be constructed to deceive the enemy and to allow flexibility in the defense.

1-4. Responsibilities

Field fortifications are constructed by personnel of all arms and services. Hasty shelters and emplacements are normally constructed by the combat units occupying the position. Some engineer equipment and supervisory assistance are frequently required to assist the combat units. Fortifications of a more complex character may require construction by engineer troops. Actually, engineers at all echelons of command assist in the preparation of plans and orders and furnish technical advice and assistance in the construction of field fortifications.

1-5. Basic Requirements for Fortifications

a. Employment of Weapons. Emplacements must permit effective use of the weapons for which they are designed. This requirement may limit the protection which can be provided and may influence the design and depth of adjacent shelters.

b. Protection. As far as possible, protection should be provided against hazards except a direct hit or a close nuclear explosion. This means that excavations should be as small as possible consistent with space requirements, so as to obtain maximum protection from the walls against airbursts and limit the effective target area for high trajectory weapons.

c. Simplicity and Economy. The emplacement or shelter should be strong and simple, require as little digging as possible, and be constructed when possible with materials that are immediately available.

d. Progressive Development. Plans for defensive works should allow for progressive development to improve the usefulness of the fortification. Development of fortification can be accomplished in three steps -

    (1) Digging in quickly where speed is the principal consideration and no special tools or materials are required.

(2) Improvising with local materials.

(3) Refining, using stock materials.

e. Concealment. Fortifications should be built so that the completed work can be concealed. It may not be practical to conceal a defensive position completely but it should be concealed enough to prevent the enemy from spotting the position by ground observation. If possible, dummy positions should be constructed at the same time as the actual positions.

f. Ingenuity. A high degree of imagination and ingenuity is essential to assure the best use of available materials as well as the best choice and use of the fortifications constructed.

1-6. Protection from Conventional Weapons

a. Digging In. Protection against conventional weapons is best provided by constructing a thickness of earth and other materials. This is done by digging into the ground so that personnel and equipment offer the smallest target possible to the line of sight of the weapon. This means of protection is effective against direct fire of small arms and horizontally impelled shell fragments. Digging in also provides some protection against artillery, infantry heavy weapons, bombs, and other aerial weapons. Advantage should be taken of all available natural cover, improvement of the position continues until the unit leaves the area.

b. Overhead Cover. Overhead protection is important particularly in the forward areas where the threat includes airburst shelling in addition to the possibility of nuclear attack. Covered firing positions should be built for individual riflemen. Small readily accessible shelters adjacent to weapons emplacements are also necessary. A minimum of 15 to 20 cm of logs, 45 cm (18 in.) sandbags, rock, and dirt, in that order, is required for overhead protection. Any available material may be used but cover should be kept low. However, cover of this type will not protect personnel against direct shell hits. Overhead cover should be strengthened and improved as long as the position is occupied. Only part of the firing position should be covered. Sandbags are placed over the logs to prevent dirt from falling on the occupants.

1-7. Protection from Chemical and Biological Weapons

Open or partially open emplacements afford no protection from chemical or biological attack. Personnel in open emplacements should use the poncho for protection against liquid contamination and the protective mask to provide protection from chemical vapors and biological aerosols. Overhead cover will delay penetration of chemical vapors and biological aerosols, thereby providing additional masking time and protection against direct liquid contamination. Covered emplacements with relatively small apertures and entrance areas which can be closed, provide protection from napalm and flamethrowers.

1-8. Protection from Nuclear Weapons

Fortifications which are effective against modern conventional weapons are in varying measure effective against nuclear weapons. The presence of the nuclear threat does not materially alter the principles outlined above.

a. Thermal Effect. Thermal radiation affects anything that will burn. The thermal effect may be reduced as a potential source of nuclear casualties by thermal shielding. Shielding may be any opaque and noninflammable material which shades the individual from the source of heat. It is normally used as a cover over an excavation and it may be required for shelter entrances or other openings. Personnel should habitually wear complete uniforms. Hands, face, and neck should be covered. Protective clothing will also reduce casualties from burns.

b. Blast. Blast can cause damage by its crushing effect. Blast from a nuclear explosion builds up against an obstruction, so vertical or near vertical faces should be avoided in earthworks above ground level.

c. Earth Shock. Collapse of earthworks, particularly unrevetted excavations, may result from the shock of nuclear explosions. To reduce the risk from this effect, excavations deeper than 1.4 meters (4 ft. 6 in.) should be revetted. For the same reason, overhead cover should not normally exceed 45 cm (18 in.) unless heavy roof supports are constructed.

d. Radiation. The effects of direct gamma radiation can be reduced by keeping the exposed openings of excavations and shelters as small as possible and by increasing the thickness of overhead protection for large shelters to 75 cm (2 ft. 6 in.), supported by heavy roof timbers.

CHAPTER 2 – PERSONNEL & EQUIPMENT PROTECTIVE MEANS

Section I. Principles & Methods

2-1. Materials

a. Natural. Full use is made of all available natural materials such as trees, logs, and brush in constructing and camouflaging emplacements, shelters, and overhead cover. Usually, enough natural material can be found to meet the requirements for hasty or expedient fortifications. Snow and ice may be used in the construction of emplacements and shelters in cold regions.

b. Other Materials,

(1) Manufactured materials, such as pickets, barbed wire, lumber, sandbags, corrugated metal, and other materials for revetting, camouflage, shelter, and concrete construction are supplied by support organizations.

(2) Captured enemy supplies, locally procured material, and demolished buildings are other sources of fortification construction materials.

2-2. Methods of Excavating

a. Handtools. The individual soldier is equipped with an entrenching tool and, if necessary he can use his helmet or bayonet to assist in digging. Pick mattocks, shovels, or machetes are also useful and frequently available for this purpose. In addition, captured enemy equipment may be available. The relative value of each tool depends on the soil and terrain. In arctic areas, a larger quantity of picks and pick mattocks are required to aid in the preparation of emplacements in frozen ground. Entrenching equipment and engineer pioneer tools are illustrated in figures 2-1 and 2-2 respectively.

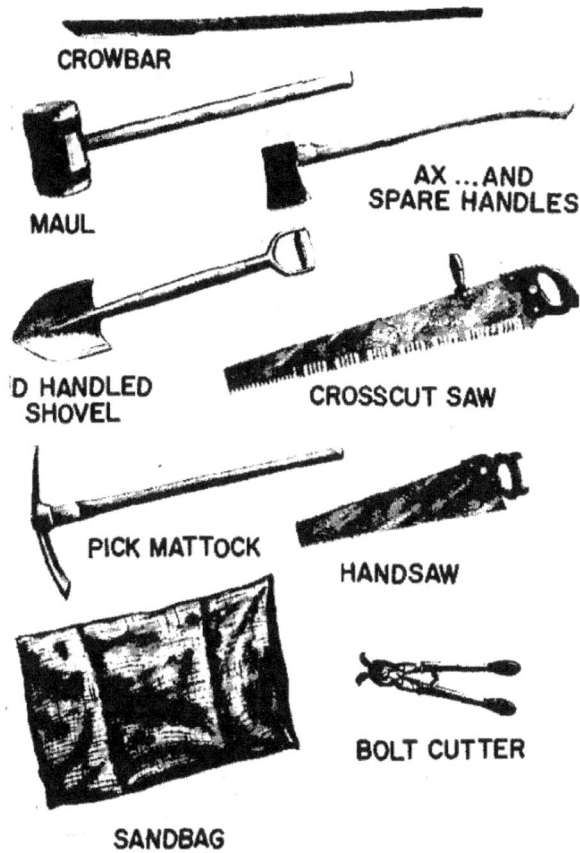

Figure 2-1. Entrenching equipment.

b. Equipment. Relatively narrow cuts with steep or nearly vertical sides required for most emplacements or shelters can be excavated more accurately by hand. However, entrenching machines, backhoes, bulldozers, bucket loaders, and scrapers may be used for larger excavations and trenches where the situation will permit the use of heavy equipment. Usually, these machines cannot dig out the exact shape desired or will dig more earth than necessary, requiring completion of the excavation by hand. Additional revetment material is usually required when machines are used. Distinctive scars on the ground resulting from the use of heavy equipment require more effort for effective camouflage than fortification work performed by hand.

c. Explosives. Many fortification tasks are made easier and accomplished more quickly by using explosive in any type of soil. Special explosive digging aids available include the M2A3 and M3 shaped demolition charges, the foxhole digging and explosive kit, and the earth rod explosive kit set No. 1 (see TM 9-1375-200).

Details on the use of explosives for fortifications and the explosive foxhole digger kit are given in appendix D.

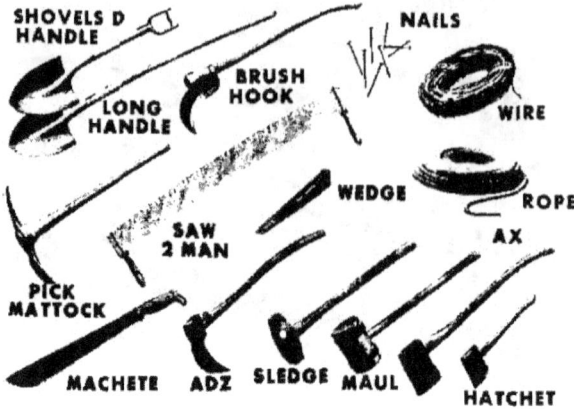

Figure 2-2. Engineer pioneer tools.

2-3. Concealment and Deception

a. Methods. Concealment is of prime importance in constructing defensive works. Concealment can be obtained by -

(1) Careful siting, making maximum use of background to break up outlines.

(2) Strict camouflage discipline throughout all stages of construction, including rigid track discipline and carefully planned disposal of soil.

(3) Intelligent use of natural and artificial camouflage materials. It may not be possible to conceal the position as a whole, but usually it will be possible to prevent pinpointing of individual works by ground observation. Before any excavation is begun, all turf, sod, leaves, snow, or forest humus is removed carefully from both the area to be excavated and from the ground on which excavated soil is to be placed. This material is used to cover the spoil when the work is completed. It is always possible to confuse the enemy by deception, using dummy field-works. Construction of large weapons' emplacements in open country having little or no natural cover can be concealed by camouflage nets suspended from stakes or trees before excavation is started. The net should be suspended high enough above the ground to permit excavation without snagging by equipment or tools. When the excavation is completed and the spoil covered with sod or natural camouflage material, the net is lowered close to the ground so it is inconspicuous from ground observation.

b. Disposal of Soil. Usually excavated soil is much lighter in color and tone than surface soil and must be hidden carefully to prevent disclosure of the fortification (fig. 2-3). Soil may be disposed of by -

(1) Using it to form a parapet if the topsoil is carefully saved and used to cover the parapet Turf, sod, leaves, or litter from under nearby bushes or trees are used to make the parapet resemble its surroundings.
(2) Removing it and carefully hiding it under trees or bushes or in ravines. Care must be taken to avoid revealing tracks.
(3) Collecting and using it, partly camouflaged, to form parapets for dummy positions.
(4) Covering mixed snow and earth from excavated emplacements with a layer of fresh snow to camouflage them.

Figure 2-3. Disposal of soil.

Section II. Individual emplacements

2-4. Types of Emplacements

a. Hasty Emplacements. Hasty emplacements are dug by troops in contact with the enemy, when time and materials are limited. Hasty positions should be supplemented with overhead cover and strengthened as conditions permit. If the situation permits, the small unit leader will verify the sectors of observation and fire for the individual members of the squad from their designated positions before they dig individual foxholes. When the situation is stabilized, even temporarily, positions are selected so they can be connected by trenches later. The emplacements described below provide protection against flat trajectory fire. They are used when there is no natural cover. Hasty positions (fig. 2-4) are good for a short time because they give some protection from direct fire. If the unit remains in the area, they must be developed into well-prepared positions to provide as much protection as possible.

Figure 2-4. Hasty positions in an open field.

(1) Shell crater. A shell or bomb crater of adequate size, 60 to 90 cm wide (2 to 3 ft.), offers immediate cover and concealment and can be quickly made into a hasty position (fig. 2-5). By digging the crater to a steep face on the side toward the enemy, the occupant can provide himself with a firing position. A small crater can later be developed into a foxhole. Craters, even if developed, are susceptible to being overrun by tracked vehicles.

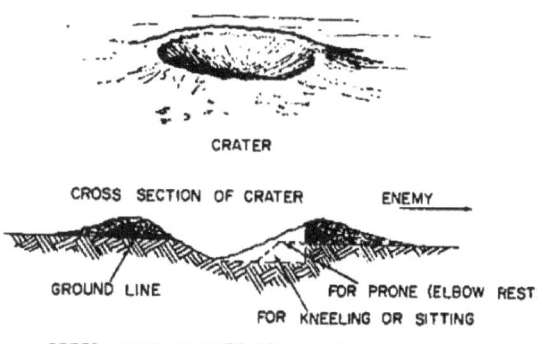

CRATER

CROSS SECTION OF CRATER   ENEMY

GROUND LINE   FOR PRONE (ELBOW REST)

FOR KNEELING OR SITTING

DOTTED LINES INDICATE SPOIL TO REMOVE FOR
IMPROVING CRATER

Figure 2-5. Improved crater.

(2) Skirmisher's trench. This shallow pit type emplacement (fig. 2-6) provides a temporary open prone firing position for the individual soldier. When immediate shelter from heavy enemy fire is required and existing defiladed firing positions are not available, each soldier lies prone or on his side, scrapes the soil with his entrenching tool, and piles it in a low parapet between himself and the enemy. In this manner, a shallow body-length pit can be formed quickly in all but the hardest ground. The trench should be oriented so that it is least vulnerable to enfilade fire. A soldier presents a low silhouette in this type of emplacement and is protected to a limited extent from small arms fire. It can be further developed into a foxhole or a prone emplacement.

Figure 2-6. Skirmisher's trench.

(3) Prone emplacement. This emplacement (fig. 2-7) is a further refinement of the skirmisher's trench. The berm dimension of this emplacement, as shown in the parapet detail, is varied to conform to the position and arm length of the occupant. It serves as a good firing position for a rifleman and provides better protection against small arms or direct fire weapons than the improved crater or skirmisher's trench.

17

(4) Rocks, snow, and ice. Limited protection can be provided by piling up rocks, chunks of ice, or packed snow. Icecrete, formed by mixing dirt and water, is very effective as an arctic building material. A minimum of 30 cm of this material will resist penetration of small arms fire.

b. Foxholes. Foxholes are the individual rifleman's basic defensive position. They afford good protection against enemy small arms fire and can be developed from well-chosen craters, skirmishers' trenches, or prone emplacements. Foxholes should be improved, as time and materials permit, by revetting the sides, adding expedient cover, providing drainage, and excavating a grenade sump to dispose of hand grenades tossed into the hole by the enemy.

(1) One-man foxhole. The overall dimensions and layout of the one-man foxhole are as shown in figure 2-8.

(2) Construction details.

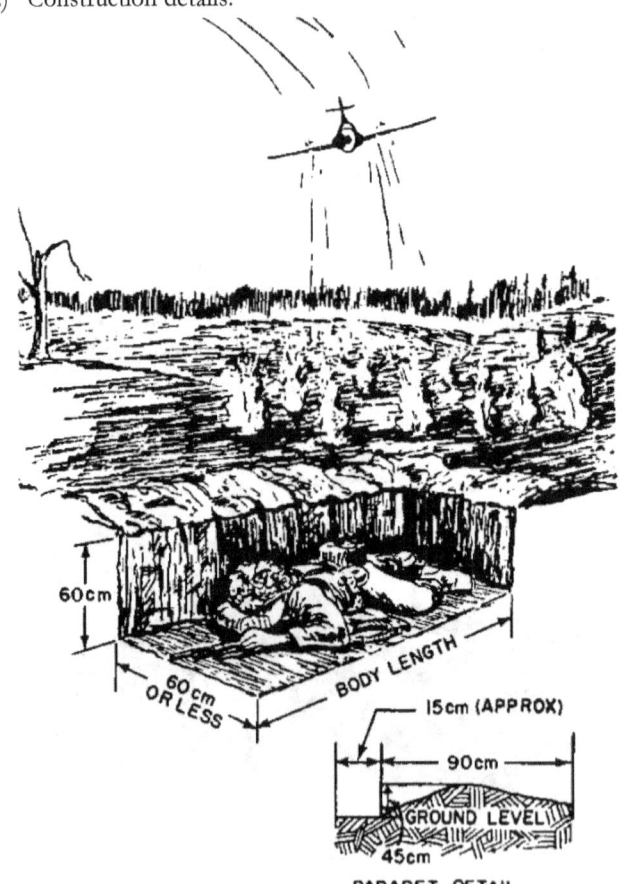

Figure 2-7. Prone emplacement.

(a) Fire step. The depth to the fire step will vary depending on the height of a comfortable firing position for the occupant, usually 105 to 150 cm (31/2 to 5 ft.). The occupant, crouched in a sitting position on the fire step, must have at least 60 cm

18

(2 ft.) of overhead clearance if a tank overruns the foxhole. This will normally provide protection against the crushing action of tanks; however, in loose unstable soils it will be necessary to revet the walls of the foxhole in order to provide this protection.

(b) Water sump. A water sump, 45 by 60 cm (18 in. by 2 ft.) and 45 cm (18 in.) deep below the fire step, is dug at one end of the foxhole to collect water and to accommodate the feet of a seated occupant. One or two layers of large stones are then placed at the bottom of the hole with smaller stones on top up to the level of the ground (fig. 3-9). The sump may simply provide a collecting basin from which water can be bailed.

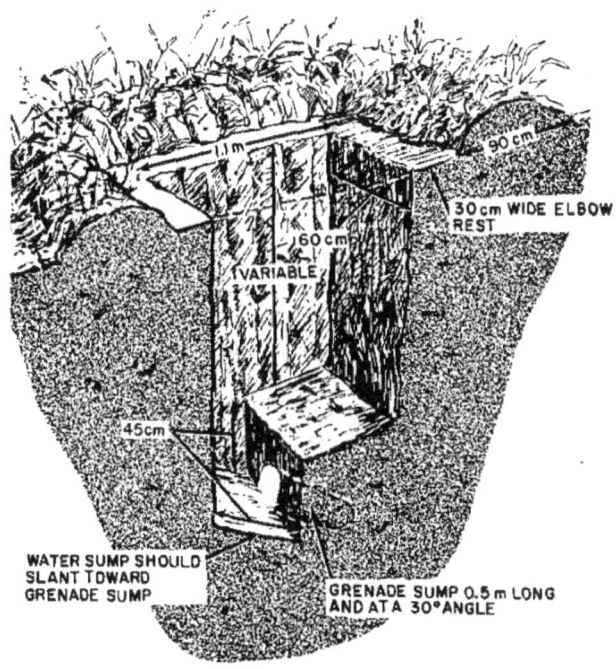

Figure 2-8. One-man foxhole.

(c) Grenade sump. A circular grenade sump 20 cm (8 in. in diameter), 45 cm (18 in.) long, and sloped downward at an angle of 30° is excavated under the fire step beginning at the lower part of the fire step riser. Hand grenades thrown into the foxhole are exploded in this sump, and their fragmentation is restricted to the unoccupied end of the foxhole. For good drainage and to assist in disposing of grenades, the fire step is sloped toward the water sump, and the bottom of the water sump is funneled downward to the grenade sump.

(d) Parapet. If excavated spoil is used as a parapet (fig. 2-7), it should be placed as a layer about 90 cm (3 ft.) wide and 15 cm (6 in.) high all around the foxhole leaving an elbow rest (berm) of original earth about 30 cm (1 ft.) wide next to the foxhole. If sod or topsoil is used to camouflage the parapet, the sod or topsoil should be removed from the foxhole and parapet area, set aside until the parapet is complete, and then placed on top in a natural manner.

(e) Camouflage. Whether or not a parapet is constructed in wooded or brushy type terrain, a foxhole can be camouflaged effectively with natural materials,

19

as shown in figure 2-9. In open or cultivated areas, it may be preferable to omit the parapet, remove the excavated spoil to an inconspicuous place, and improvise a camouflage cover for the foxhole. This can be a light, open frame of branches garnished with grass or other natural foliage to match the surroundings. As an alternate method, the foxhole can be covered with a shelter half, poncho, or other expedient material, and further covered with snow or some other material, according to local terrain conditions (fig. 2-9). The occupant raises one side of the cover for observation or firing.

(f) Overhead Cover. A half-cover (fig. 2-10) over a one-man foxhole provides good protection for the occupant and permits full use of the weapon. Logs, 10 to 15 cm in diameter or 15 cm (6 in.) timbers approximately 1.2 meters (4 ft.) in length, support the earth cover. They should be long enough to extend at least 30 cm (1 ft.) on each side of the foxhole to provide a good bearing surface. Dirt should be removed on each side of the foxhole so that the supporting logs or timbers are even with the ground surface. If the ground is soft and tends to break away, a bearing surface of planks or timbers should be provided for cover supports. Logs or timbers of this size will support an earth cover 30 to 45 cm thick. The walls of the foxhole should be stabilized with revetment material (fig. 2-11) at least under the overhead cover to prevent a cave-in from the added weight of the cover.

① FOXHOLE WITH CAMOUFLAGE COVER IN PLACE

Figure 2-9. Camouflaged one-man foxhole.

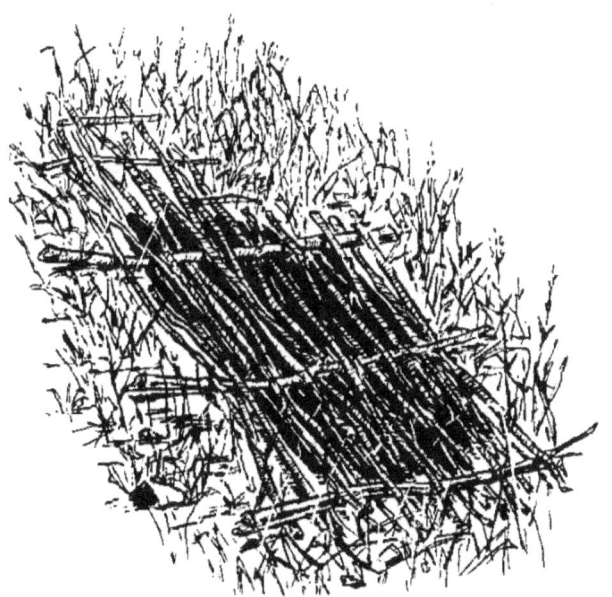

② METHOD OF CONSTRUCTING COVER

Figure 2-9 - Continued.

Figure 2-10. One-man foxhole with half-cover.

(g.) Revetment material. Use of different types of revetting material are shown in figure 2-11. Expedient material, such as brushwood, saplings, sheet metal, or dimensioned lumber should be thin and tough so that it will support the sides of the emplacement when properly staked and tied.

BRUSHWOOD

CHICKEN WIRE AND BURLAP

Figure 2-11. Types of revetting material.

(1) Stakes. Revetment stakes, either metal or wood 1.8 meters (6 ft.) in length, should be spaced not more than 60 cm (2 ft.) apart and driven into the ground 30 to 45 cm.

(2) Anchor stakes. The revetment stakes are held firmly in place by anchor wires of barbed wire or 14-gauge wire attached to anchor stakes (fig. 2-12). Five or six strands of wire should be stretched between the revetment and anchor stakes at ground level and tightened by twisting. The distance between the revetment and anchor stakes should be approximately twice the depth of the excavation. The wire between the stakes should not pass over the parapet in any case.

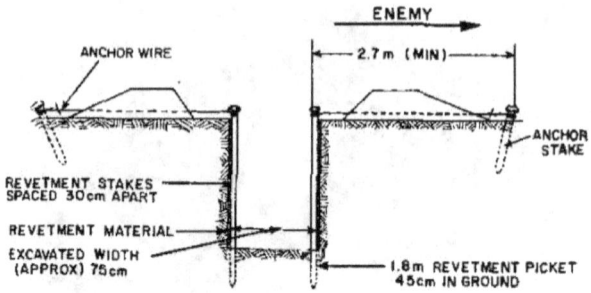

Figure 2-12. Supporting and anchoring revetment.

(3) Open two-man foxhole. In a defensive position, the two-man foxhole (fig. 2-13) is generally preferred to the one-man emplacement.

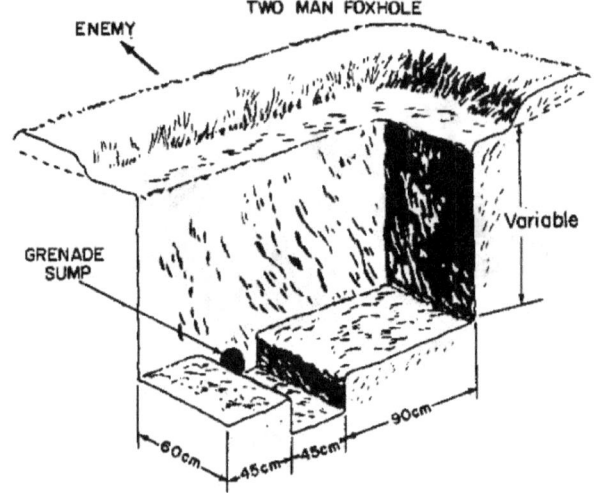

Figure 2-13. Open two-man foxhole.

(a) Advantages.

1. One man can provide protection while the other is digging.
2. It affords relief and rest for the occupants. One man rests while the other observes. In this manner, firing positions can be effectively manned for longer periods of time.
3. If one soldier becomes a casualty, the position is still occupied.
4. The psychological effect of two men together permits positions to be occupied for longer intervals.

(b) Disadvantages.

1. If a direct hit occurs, two men will become casualties instead of one.
2. The area that can be occupied may be reduced significantly.

24

(c) Construction. The two-man foxhole is constructed the same as the one-man foxhole except for the location of the grenade sump which is dug into the face of the foxhole towards the enemy.

(d) Overhead Cover. A substantial overhead cover for a two-man foxhole may be provided by constructing an offset as shown and described in figure 2-14. An alternate method is shown in figure 2-15.

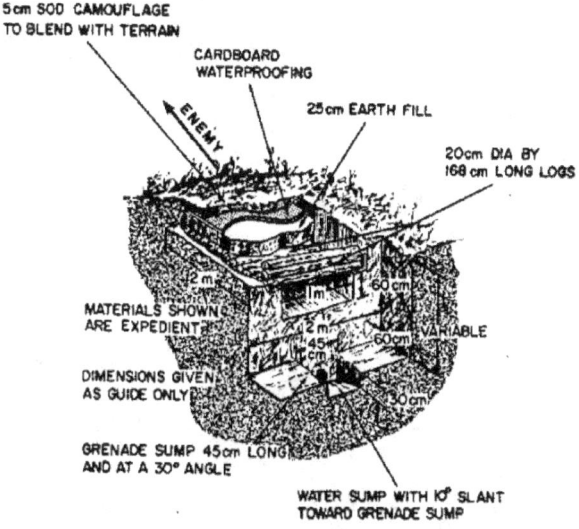

Figure 2-14. Two-man foxhole with offset.

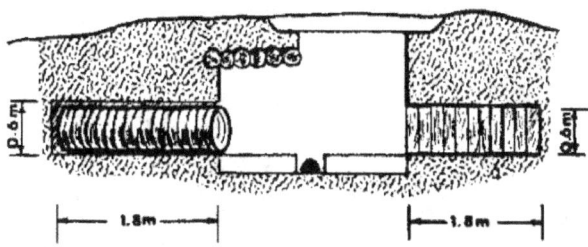

Figure 2-15. Two-man foxhole with offsets constructed of timber and culvert.

2-5. Fields of Fire

a. Principles. There is little opportunity to clear fields of fire when a unit is in contact with the enemy. Individual riflemen and weapons crews must select the best natural positions available. Usually, there is only time to clear areas in the immediate vicinity of the position. However, in preparing defensive positions for expected contact with the enemy, suitable fields of fire are cleared in front of each position. The following principles are pertinent:

(1) Excessive or careless clearing will disclose firing positions (fig. 2-16).

25

(2) In areas organized for close defense, clearing should start near the position and work forward at least 100 meters or to the maximum effective range of the weapon if time permits,

(3) A thin natural screen of vegetation should be left to hide defensive positions.

ORIGINAL TERRAIN

WRONG—AFTER IMPROPER CLEARING

RIGHT—AFTER PROPER CLEARING

Figure 2-16. Clearing fields of fire.

b. Procedure.

(1) Remove the lower branches of large scattered trees in sparsely wooded areas.

(2) In heavy woods, fields of fire may neither be possible nor desirable within the time available. Restrict work to thinning the undergrowth and removing the lower branches of large trees. Clear narrow lanes of fire (fig. 2-17), for automatic weapons.

(3) Thin or remove dense brush since it is never a suitable obstacle and obstructs the field of fire.

(4) Cut weeds when they obstruct the view from firing positions.

26

(5) Remove brush, weeds, and limbs that have been cut to areas where they cannot be used to conceal enemy movements or disclose the position.

(6) Do only a limited amount of clearing at one time. Overestimating the capabilities of the unit in this respect may result in a field of fire improperly cleared which would afford the enemy better concealment and cover than the natural state.

(7) Cut or burn grain, hay, and tall weeds.

WRONG--TOO MUCH CLEARING, DEBRIS NOT REMOVED. ENEMY WILL AVOID

RIGHT—ONLY UNDERBRUSH AND TREES DIRECTLY IN LINE OF FIRE REMOVED. ENEMY SURPRISED

Figure 2-17. Clearing fire lanes.

(8) Whenever possible, check position from the enemy side to be sure that the positions are effectively camouflaged and they are not revealed by clearing fields of fire.

Section III. Crew-served Infantry weapons emplacements

2-6. Principal Considerations

a. Firing Positions. While it is desirable to give maximum protection to personnel and equipment, the principal consideration must be the effective use of the weapon. In offensive combat, infantry weapons are sited wherever natural or existing positions are available or where weapons can be emplaced with a minimum of digging. The positions described in this section are designed for use in all types of terrain that will permit excavation,

b. Protection, Protection of crew-served weapons is provided by emplacements which give some protection to the weapon and crew while in firing positions. As the positions are developed, the emplacements are deepened and provided with half overhead cover, if possible. Then, if the positions are occupied for an extended period of time, shelters adjoining the emplacement or close to it should be built. Characteristics of crew served infantry weapons emplacements are shown in table 2-1, Located in Back of Manual

c. Crew Shelters. Shelters immediately adjoining and opening into emplacements improve the operational capability of the crew, since the men are not exposed when moving between the shelter and the weapon.

2-7. Machinegun Emplacements

a. Pit Type. The gun is emplaced initially in a hasty position (fig. 2-18).

b. Horseshoe Type. The dimensions and layout of the completed emplacement are shown in figure 2-19. The horseshoe shaped trench, about 60 cm wide, is dug along the rear and sides, leaving a chest-high shelf in the center to serve as the gun platform. The spoil from this trench is used to form the parapet, making it at least 1 m wide and low enough to permit all-round fire. This type emplacement permits easy traverse of the gun through an arc of 180°, but the crew cannot fire to the rear effectively.

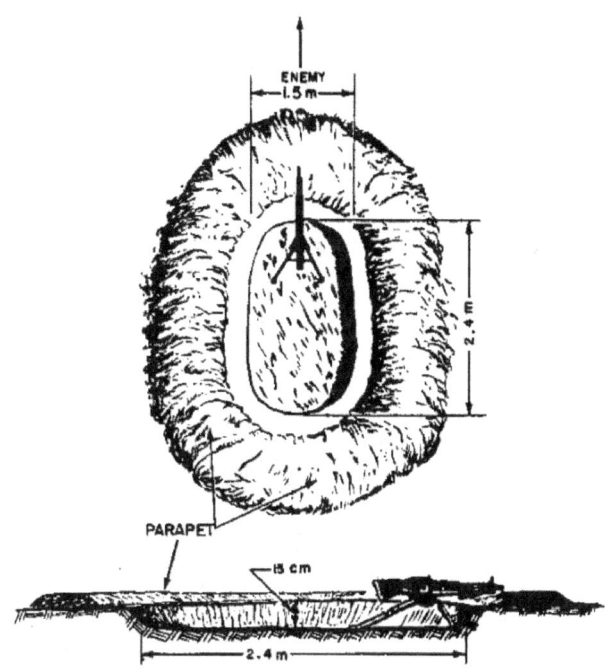

Figure 2-18. Plan view and arose section of machinegun emplacement.

e. Two One-Man Foxhole Type. This emplacement consists of 2 one-man foxholes close to the gun position as illustrated in figure 2-20. The parapet is low enough for all-round fire and good protection for the crew. A foxhole is dug for the gunner at the rear of the gun and another foxhole is dug for the assistant gunner on the left of the gun and 45 cm (18 in.) in front of the gunner's foxhole. The spoil is piled all around the position to form a parapet, care being taken to pile it so as to permit all-round fire of the weapon. Although 360° fire is possible from this position, fire to the front or rear is most effective since the M60 machinegun is fed from the left side.

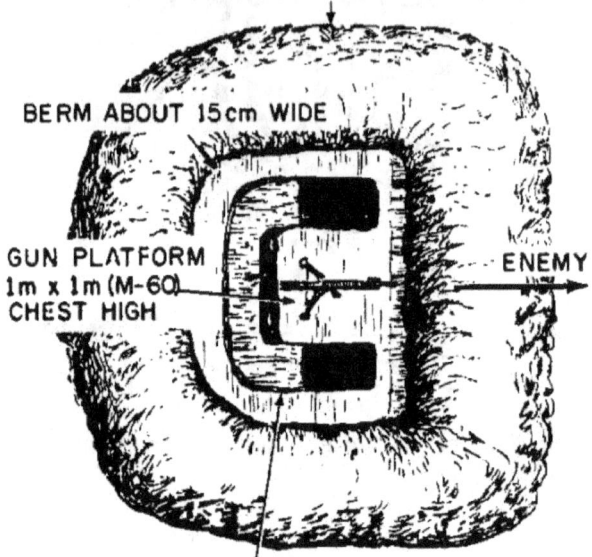

PARAPET 1m WIDE ALL AROUND

BERM ABOUT 15cm WIDE

GUN PLATFORM
1m x 1m (M-60)
CHEST HIGH

ENEMY

DIG HORSESHOE SHAPED
TRENCH 60cm WIDE

Figure 2-19. Horseshoe type emplacement.

2-8. Emplacements for Recoilless Weapons

a. Types. Two types of open emplacements for recoilless weapons are the pit type and the 2 two-man foxhole type.

(1) Pit type: This emplacement is a circular pit about 1.2 meters in diameter and about 1 meter deep depending on the height of the occupants. A parapet should not be constructed for this emplacement because of the backblast. It is large enough for two men and permits the assistant to turn with the traversing weapon, to avoid being behind it when it is fired. The emplacement is shallow enough to permit the rear end of the weapon to clear the top at maximum elevation, thus insuring that the hot backblast of the rockets is not deflected to the occupants. Since this emplacement offers protection for the crew against direct fire weapons only, supplementary personnel emplacements should be provided (1, fig. 2-21).

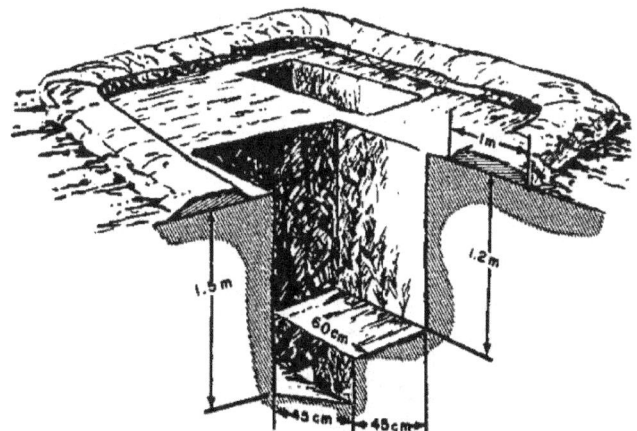

Figure 2-20. Two one-man foxhole type machinegun emplacement.

(2) Two two-man foxhole type. The emplacement shown in 2, figure 2-21 provides limited protection for the crew against nuclear effects and armor except when actually firing.

b. Blast Effects. Due to the backblast effects of the recoilless weapon, it should not be fired from a confined space such as a fully covered emplacement. Because the backblast will reveal the firing position, alternate firing positions with connecting trenches should be constructed if there is sufficient time.

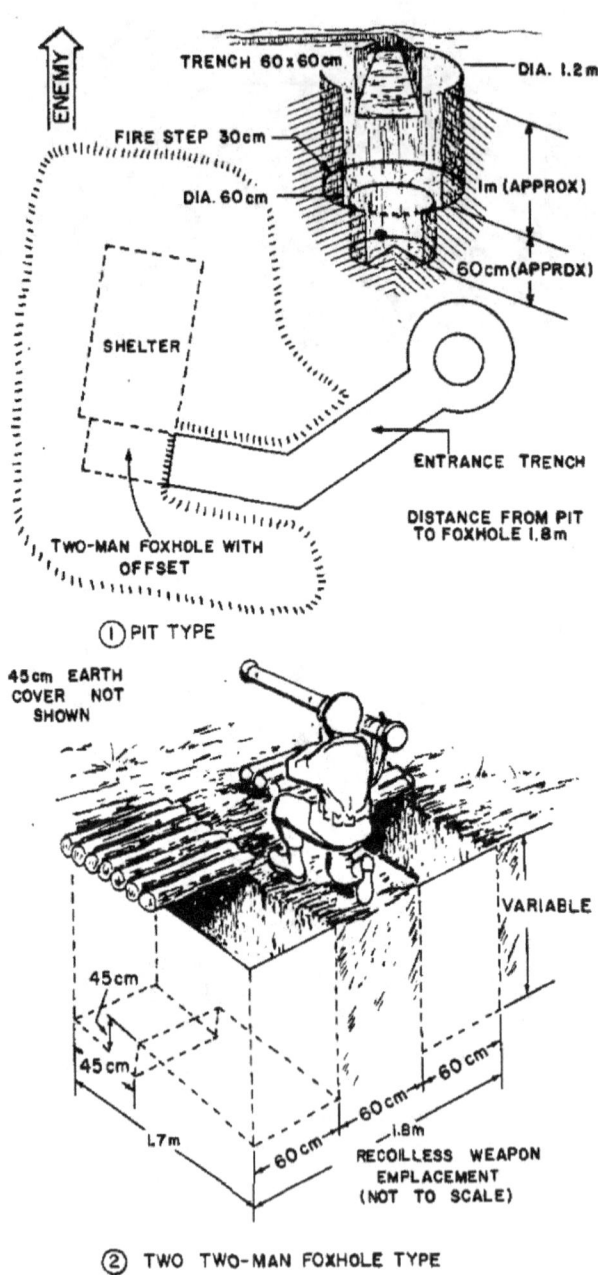

ENEMY

TRENCH 60 x 60 cm — DIA. 1.2 m

FIRE STEP 30 cm

DIA. 60 cm

1 m (APPROX)

60 cm (APPROX)

SHELTER

TWO-MAN FOXHOLE WITH OFFSET

ENTRANCE TRENCH

DISTANCE FROM PIT TO FOXHOLE 1.8 m

① PIT TYPE

45 cm EARTH COVER NOT SHOWN

VARIABLE

45 cm

45 cm

1.7 m

60 cm

60 cm

60 cm

60 cm

1.8 m

RECOILLESS WEAPON EMPLACEMENT (NOT TO SCALE)

② TWO TWO-MAN FOXHOLE TYPE

Figure 2-21. Emplacement for recoilless weapons.

2-9. Mortar Emplacements

32

a. General. The emplacement illustrated in 1, figure 2-22 is circular in shape. The emplacement is excavated to the dimensions shown with the sides of the emplacement sloping inward toward the bottom. The floor slopes to the drainage sump located under the open gap in the parapet. An ammunition ready rack or niche, located so that it is convenient for the gunner, is built into the side of the emplacement. The bottom of the ammunition rack is elevated from the floor of the emplacement. Another ready rack may be constructed in one side of the trench leading to the position. The initial emplacement is revetted using sandbags and the improved emplacement is revetted using corrugated metal. Before constructing the parapet, the mortar is laid for direction of Are by the use of an aiming circle or alternate means. Aiming posts are then normally placed out at a referred deflection of 2,800 mils. The parapet is then constructed, leaving a 1-meter gap for the line of sight. This imaginary line of sight should be so positioned that it is 30 cm from the right edge of the gap. This will allow an approximate 1,500-mil sector of Are without moving any portion of the parapet. The parapet should be not more than 50 cm high and a minimum of 90 cm wide. Dirt should not be placed within 45 cm of the edges of the sighting gap; in order that sandbags positioned here may be removed to provide a greater sector of fire when necessary. An exit trench may be constructed leading to personnel shelters and to other mortar positions.

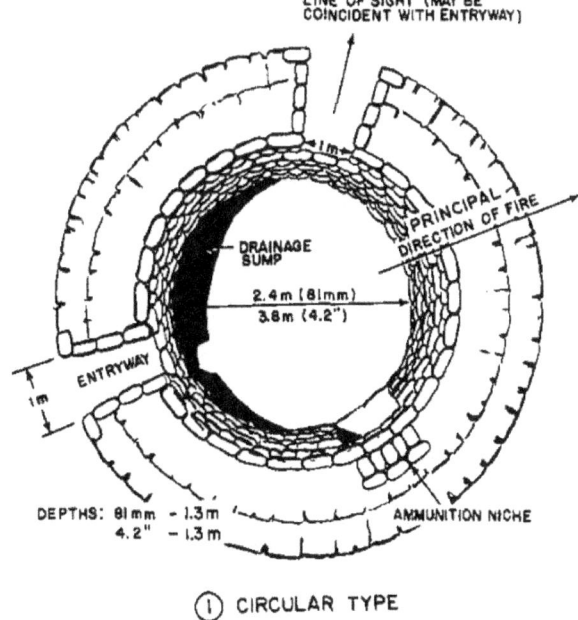

① CIRCULAR TYPE

Figure 2-22. Mortar emplacements.

b, The 81-mm Mortar. A pit type emplacement for the 81-mm mortar is shown in 2, figure 2-22.

c, Emplacement for 4.2-Inch Mortar. The 4.2-inch mortar emplacement is identical to the one described above for the 81-mm mortar except for dimension changes shown in 1, figure 2-22.

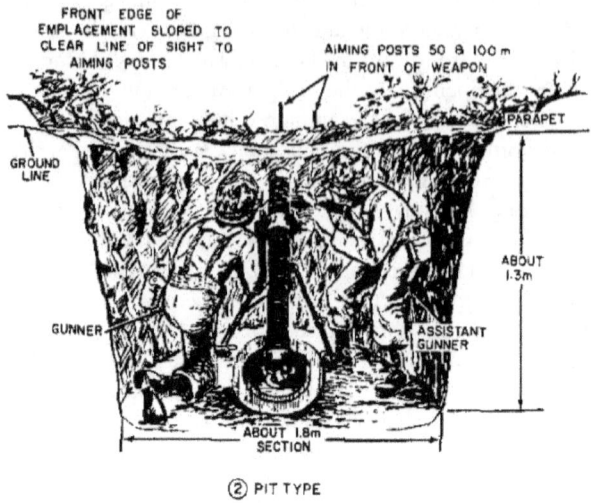

Figure 2-22 - Continued.

2-10. Emplacement for 106-mm Recoilless Rifle

This weapon is often fired from its 14-ton truck mount since the weapon should be mobile and moved to a new position after firing a few rounds. In a defensive operation several open pits should be constructed with concealed routes from these firing positions to a concealed shelter position with overhead cover. The weapon remains in the shelter until needed, then after firing, it is moved to another firing position or back to its shelter. The firing pit should protect the sides and front of the body of the vehicle with the rifle above the parapet level. The rear should be ramped so the vehicle can move out quickly. Emplacements of this type require approximately 30 man-hours to construct since alternate positions are required, so the necessity for using heavy equipment is obvious. Figure 2-23 illustrates an emplacement for the 106-mm recoilless rifle which will permit the weapon muzzle to extend over the parapet to preclude damage to the vehicle from the muzzle blast.

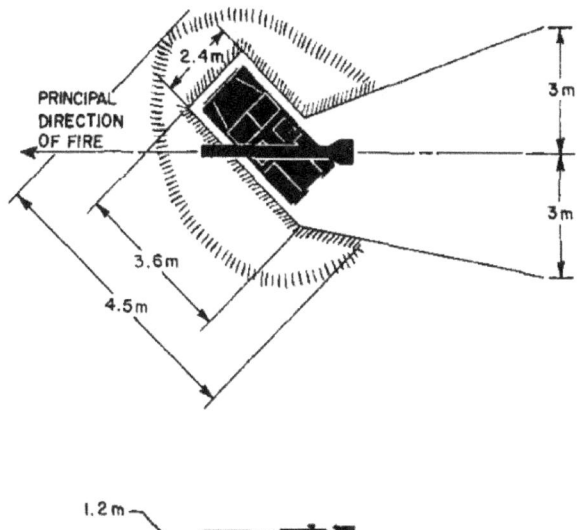

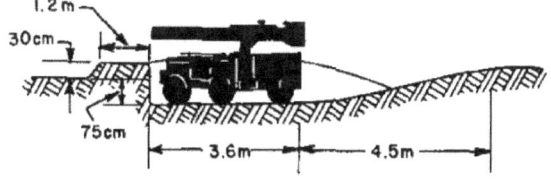

Figure 2-23. Emplacement for 106-mm Recoilless rifle.

Section IV. Vehicle & Artillery Emplacements

2-11. Typical Vehicle Pit

Digging in should be restricted to essential vehicles. Vehicle pits should be as narrow and as short as the vehicle size permits. They should be oriented randomly. All canvas should be removed and the top of the trucks should be at least 30 cm below the top of the surrounding parapet. The excavations should be as shown in table 2-2 and figure 2-24. Use of soil in construction of the parapet reduces the depth of cut necessary to properly protect a vehicle. The parapet should be streamlined and as well compacted as possible. The majority of vehicles should be concealed or camouflaged, with advantage taken of natural features such as woods, defilade, hedgerows, and buildings.

35

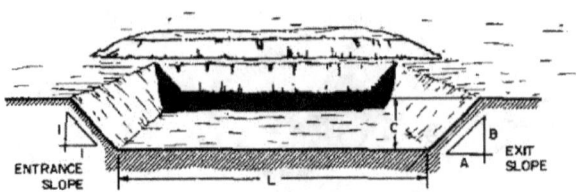

Figure 2-26. Typical vehicle pit.

	¼-ton truck and trailer, canvas down	¾-ton truck and trailer, with radio shelter	2½-ton truck and trailer, canvas down	5-ton truck and trailer, canvas down
Depth of cut (C) _____	0.9 meters	1.8 meters	1.5 meters	1.5 meters
Width of pit _____	2.4 meters	3.0 meters	3.5 meters	3.6 meters
Level length of pit (L) _____	6.0 meters	8.1 meters	10.5 meters	10.8 meters
Thickness of parapet (H) _____	60 cm	75 cm	75 cm	75 cm
Width of parapet (P) _____	1.2 meters	2.4 meters	2.7 meters	2.7 meters
Exit slope (A:B)* _____	1:1	2:1	2:1	2:1
Total excavation _____	19 cubic meters	61 cubic meters	71 cubic meters	76 cubic meters
Equipment hours** _____	0.4	0.8	0.9	0.9

*Entrance slope 1:1.
**For cut and rough parapet construction only, at appropriate rates for D7 or D8 type bulldozers.

Table 2-2. Dimensions of Typical Vehicle Pits

2-12. Towed Artillery Weapons

a. Purpose. Emplacements for artillery weapons must provide maximum flexibility in the delivery of fire and protect the weapon and its crew against the effects of conventional and nuclear weapons.

b. Emplacement for 105and 155-mm Howitzer. Artillery weapons emplacements are constructed so as to allow for continuous improvement in order to provide additional protection and comfort in the event of prolonged occupation. These emplacements are developed in stages as described in (1) through (4) below.

(1) Stage 1. This stage provides open foxholes for the protection of the crew and open emplacements for infantry weapons used to defend the position. Provision is made for only minimum essential shifting of the gun trail and ammunition is stored in the open. Stage-one emplacement for a 105-mm howitzer is illustrated in 1, figure 2-25.

(2) Stage 2. This stage provides trail logs for all around traverse of the weapon, a low parapet to protect the weapon, and covered emplacements for the crew, defensive weapons, and ammunition. Stage-two emplacement for a 105-mm howitzer is illustrated in 2, figure 2-25.

(3) Stage 3. In this stage a parapet revetted on the inside which permits all around direction fire is provided. Work is begun on covered shelters for personnel and ammunition. Stage-three emplacement for a 105-mm howitzer is illustrated in 3, figure 2-25.

(4) Stage 4. In this stage revetment is provided for the ground fighting positions and for the outside and top of the parapet. Overhead cover is also provided for the personnel ready position and the ammunition shelter. Stage-four emplacement for a 105-mm howitzer is illustrated in

4, figure 2-25 and 2, figure 2-26. Dimensions and layout are also shown in figure 2-26.

(5) Use of overhead cover. It is usually difficult to provide overhead cover for artillery weapons. The widths and heights involved make such construction impractical under most conditions. Overhead cover would unduly restrict the firing capability of the weapon. In addition, under most conditions, it is not desirable to excavate an emplacement for the weapon much below ground level or to construct a high all-round parapet for the following reasons:

(a) A high all-round parapet restricts the direct fire capability of the weapon.

(b) An emplacement excavated below ground creates difficulty in rapid removal of the weapon from the emplacement.

c. Accessory Structures.

(1) Ammunition shelters. Sectional shelters as shown in figure 3-13 may be used with overhead cover as ammunition shelters with the types of weapons emplacements discussed above.

(2) Accessory shelters. Ready shelters for personnel and shelters for fire direction centers and switchboards are constructed using standard shelter designs (Ch. 3).

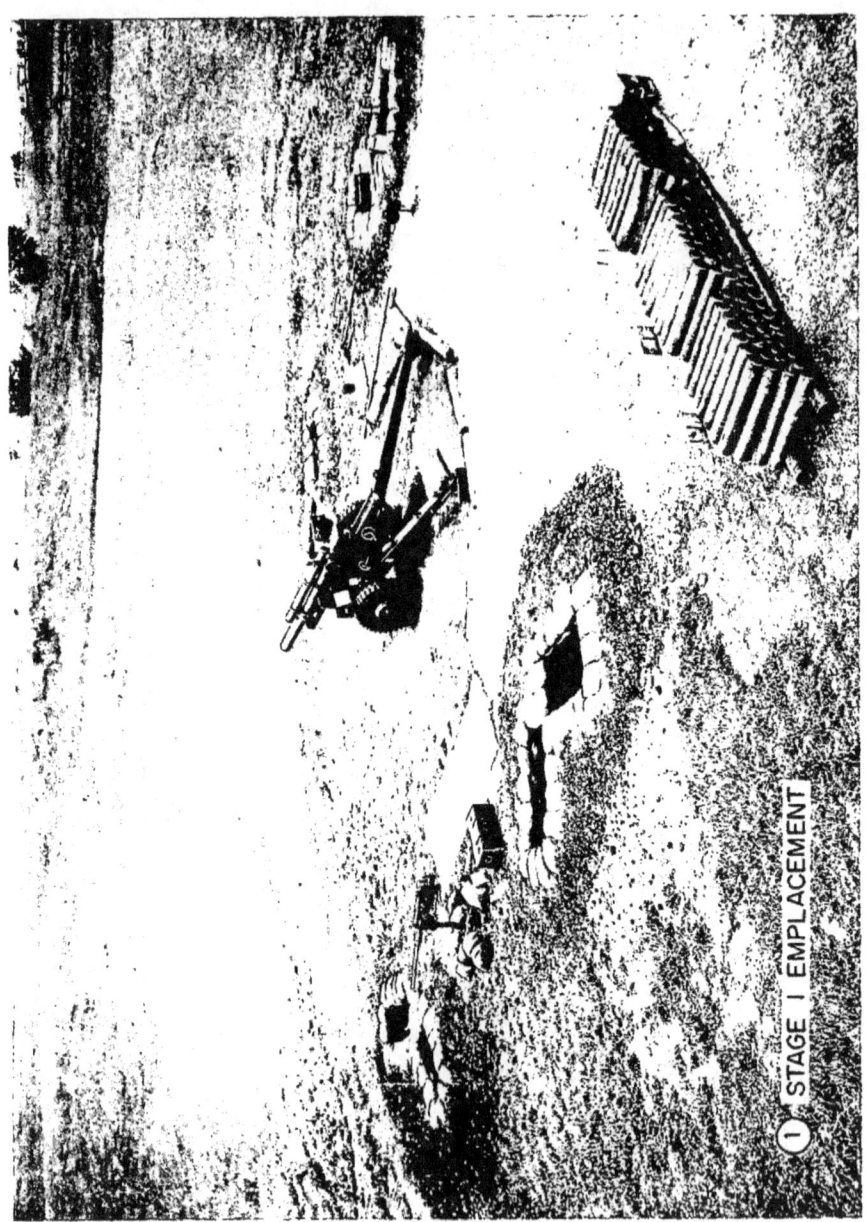

Figure 2-25. Development of 105 mm howitzer emplacement.

Figure 2-25 - Continued.

Figure 2-25 - Continued.

④ COMPLETED EMPLACEMENT

Figure 2-25 - Continued.

41

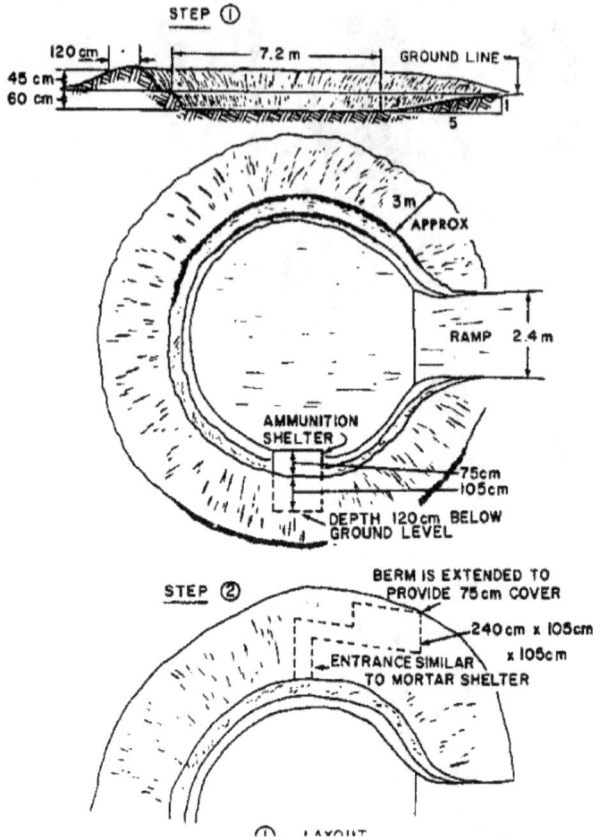

Figure 2-26 - Final stage of development, howitzer emplacement.

42

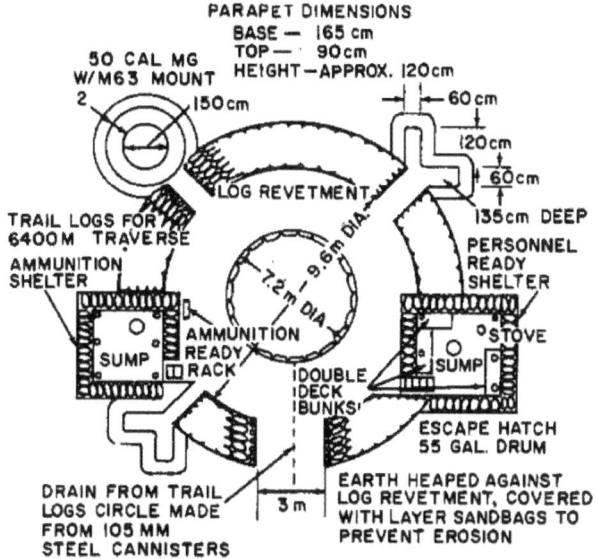

PARAPET DIMENSIONS
BASE — 165 cm
TOP — 90 cm
HEIGHT — APPROX. 120 cm

50 CAL MG
W/M63 MOUNT

2

150 cm

60 cm

120 cm

60 cm

LOG REVETMENT

135 cm DEEP

TRAIL LOGS FOR
6400 M TRAVERSE

AMMUNITION
SHELTER

PERSONNEL
READY
SHELTER

AMMUNITION
READY
RACK

SUMP

9.6 m DIA

7.2 m DIA

STOVE

SUMP

DOUBLE
DECK
BUNKS

ESCAPE HATCH
55 GAL. DRUM

DRAIN FROM TRAIL
LOGS CIRCLE MADE
FROM 105 MM
STEEL CANNISTERS

3 m

EARTH HEAPED AGAINST
LOG REVETMENT, COVERED
WITH LAYER SANDBAGS TO
PREVENT EROSION

② COMPLETED EMPLACEMENT

Figure 2-26 - Continued.

2-13. Self-Propelled Artillery and Tank-Mounted Weapons Emplacement

a. Self-Propelled Artillery. Large caliber self-propelled weapons have a limited traverse without turning the vehicle. For this reason, it is seldom practical to construct emplacements for this type of weapon. When positions for self-propelled weapons are prepared, a sloped ramp is built to facilitate the vehicle's entry into and withdrawal from the gun pit. In extremely cold weather, gravel, saplings, or similar covering may be necessary for the floor of the pit so that the tracks of the vehicles will not freeze to the ground. The rear of the pit and the sloped ramp should be widened sufficiently to permit driving the vehicle in at an angle in order to compensate for the limited traverse of the weapon.

b. Tanks. A tank is emplaced or protected in the same manner as any other vehicle. Natural defilades such as road cuts or ditches are used where available. In open areas, parapets are provided to protect the sides and front of the hull of the vehicle, and the rear is left open. The simplest form of a dug-in position of this type is shown in figure 2-27. Wherever possible, such positions are constructed and occupied during darkness, with all camouflage being completed before dawn. The emplacement normally includes foxhole protection for relief personnel, preferably connected with the emplacement by a short trench. A dug-in emplacement of this type should have the following:

(1) An excavation deep enough to afford protection for the tracks and part of the hull of the vehicle with maximum

thickness of the parapet at the front of the emplacement and the rear left open for entry and exit of vehicle.

(2) Inside dimensions just large enough to permit entry and exit of vehicle.

(3) An inside depth permitting the weapon to depress to its minimum elevation. Tank emplacements must have sufficient space for the storage of ammunition.

(4) Barrel stops, if necessary, to prevent fire into adjacent units.

(5) Provisions for drainage (if possible) and frostproof flooring to prevent tracks from freezing to the ground.

(6) If it is necessary to deliver fire at elevations higher than permitted by the carriage design, the floor must be sloped up in the direction of fire.

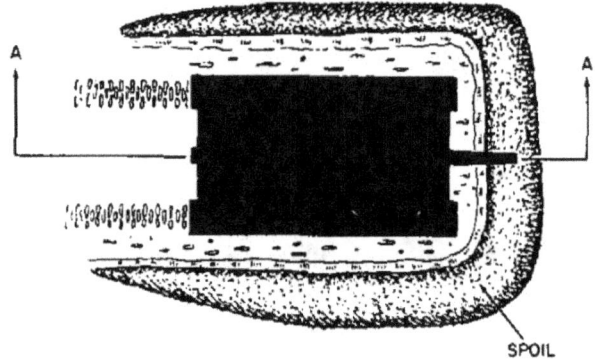

PLAN VIEW

SECTION A-A

CAMOUFLAGE NOT SHOWN

Figure 2-27. Dug-in emplacement for self-propelled weapon.

2-14. Artillery Emplacements in Soft-Ground

The siting of artillery positions in areas where the ground is soft require the construction of pads to preclude differential settlement and thus the relaying of the weapon after each round is fired. Wooden pads can be constructed of two layers of 5-

44

cm lumber with 20x 30-cm radial sleepers (fig. 2-28). The wooden pad distributes the load over a large area with no significant settlement and is flexible and strong enough to withstand the turning and movement of self-propelled weapons. The trail logs are anchored just outside the pad for towed weapons. For self-propelled weapons, the recoil spades can be set in compacted material or a layer of crushed rock just off the pad. A pad of this type does not take long to construct if materials are pre-cut and assembled on the site. Revetments and shelters can be constructed as described in paragraph 2-12.

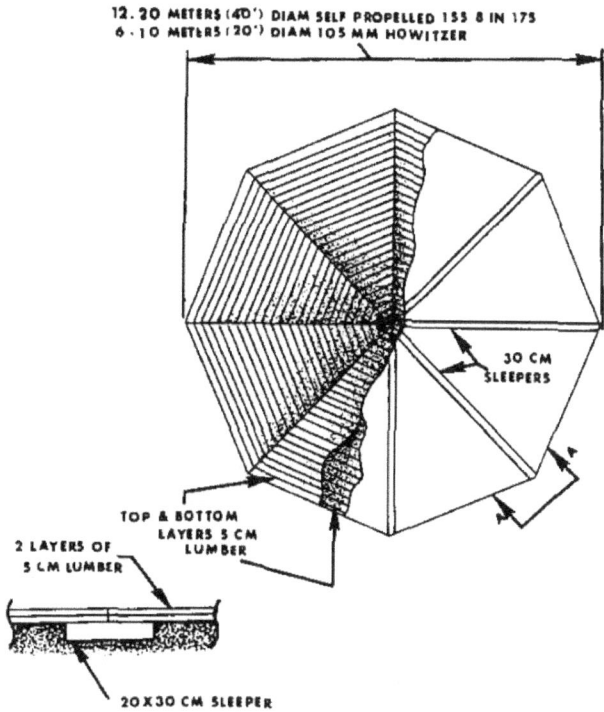

Figure 2-28. Load distribution pad for artillery emplacements in soft ground.

Section V. Aircraft revetments

2-15. Introduction

Often it is necessary to protect parked aircraft from damage by small arms fire, recoilless rifles, and mortar fragments. The most practical type of protective emplacement that can be constructed is the three-sided revetment. Several types are discussed here in general. For exact requirements and design procedures refer to TM 5-330.

2-16. Types of Revetments

a. Sandbag. Revetments constructed with filled sandbags are a practical expedient for fortifications, particularly when equipment is limited to handtools and

45

when skilled supervisory assistance is not available to supervise the construction of other types of structures. The bags can be filled at the construction site with sand hauled to the location, which is preferable, or they can be filled where the sand is available and hauled to the site. The latter procedure increases possible damage to the bags during handling. Sandbags deteriorate rapidly, particularly in damp climates, permitting filler material to run out, causing a consequent reduction of protective characteristics and endangering the stability of the revetment. Shell hits have a similar effect, requiring replacement of bags. Sandbags may be stacked without a retaining wall if the sides of the revetment are sloped approximately 1:4. The substitution of a soil cement mixture, or coating the bags with a cement slurry will partially overcome deterioration of the sandbags, which is the principal disadvantage of this type of fortification.

b. Gravity. This type of revetment is constructed of compacted earthfill placed against a retaining wall (fig. 2-29). The unconfined earth side must have a 1:1 slope or be sloped at the angle of repose. The top of the revetment has a slope of 10:1 to facilitate drainage. To prevent erosion and keep the fill dry, the top and sides are waterproofed using asphalt cutback or cement slurry. Traffic on the revetment must be prohibited in order to preserve the waterproof coating. Sod can be used to prevent erosion, but moisture is allowed to enter the fill and will cause a decrease in protection against penetration by projectiles.

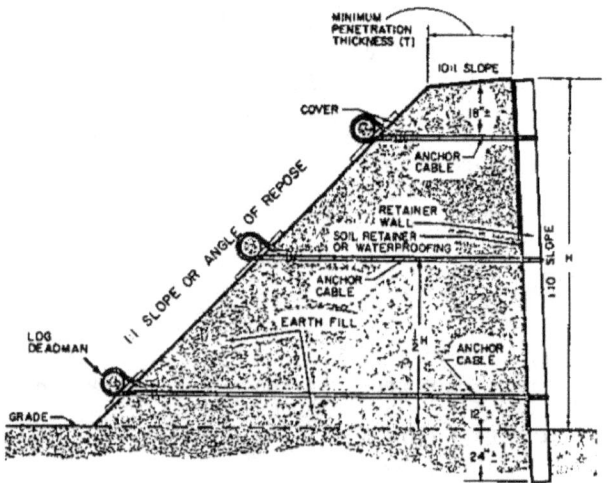

Figure 2-29. Gravity revetment.

c. Earth. The malls of this revetment are constructed entirely of compacted earthfill (fig. 2-30). The sides have a 1:1 slope or sloped at the angle of repose and are covered with a waterproof coating. The top of the revetment should have a 10:1 slope to facilitate drainage.

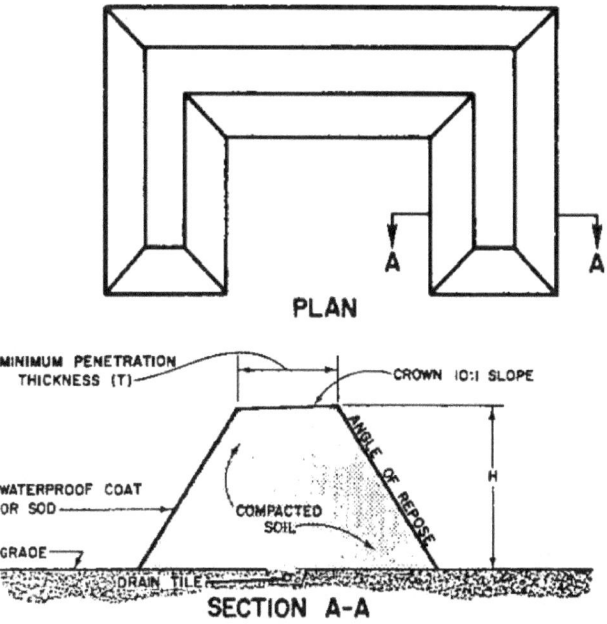

PLAN

MINIMUM PENETRATION
THICKNESS (T)

CROWN 10:1 SLOPE

ANGLE OF REPOSE

WATERPROOF COAT
OR SOD

COMPACTED
SOIL

H

GRADE

DRAIN TILE

SECTION A-A

NOTE :

WATERPROOFING MAY BE ASPHALT CUTBACK OR CEMENT SLURRY.
TRAFFIC ON THE REVETMENT MUST BE PROHIBITED IN ORDER TO
PRESERVE THE WATERPROOF COATING.

Figure 2-30. Earth revetment.

d, Bulkhead. This revetment consists of two retaining walls with earthfill placed between them (fig. 2-31). After both inner and outer wall sections are completed and placed upright, sturdy spacer blocks are used to hold the walls apart at the specified distances while the tie cables are tightened. The filler material is carefully deposited to avoid displacing the spacer blocks. A waterproof cover must be applied to the top of the revetment to keep the fill dry.

e. Free Standing Wall. This revetment can be constructed of either soil cement (fig. 2-32) or reinforced concrete (fig. 2-33). This type of revetment is the most durable but it is the most difficult to construct. Skilled workers and supervisors are required to build the forms, place the reinforcing bars, and place the con

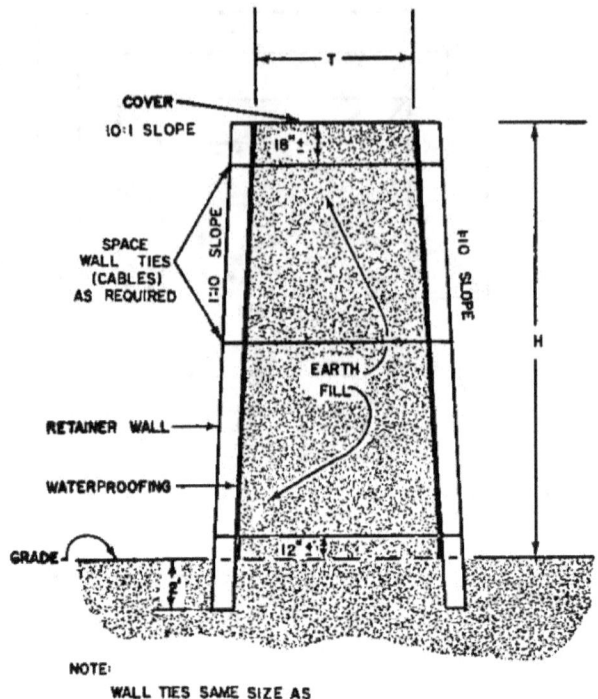

Figure 2-31. Bulkhead revetment.

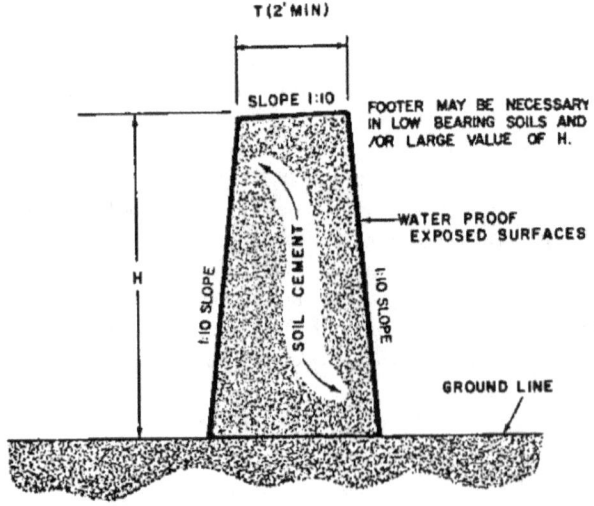

Figure 2-32. Free standing wall-soil cement revetment.

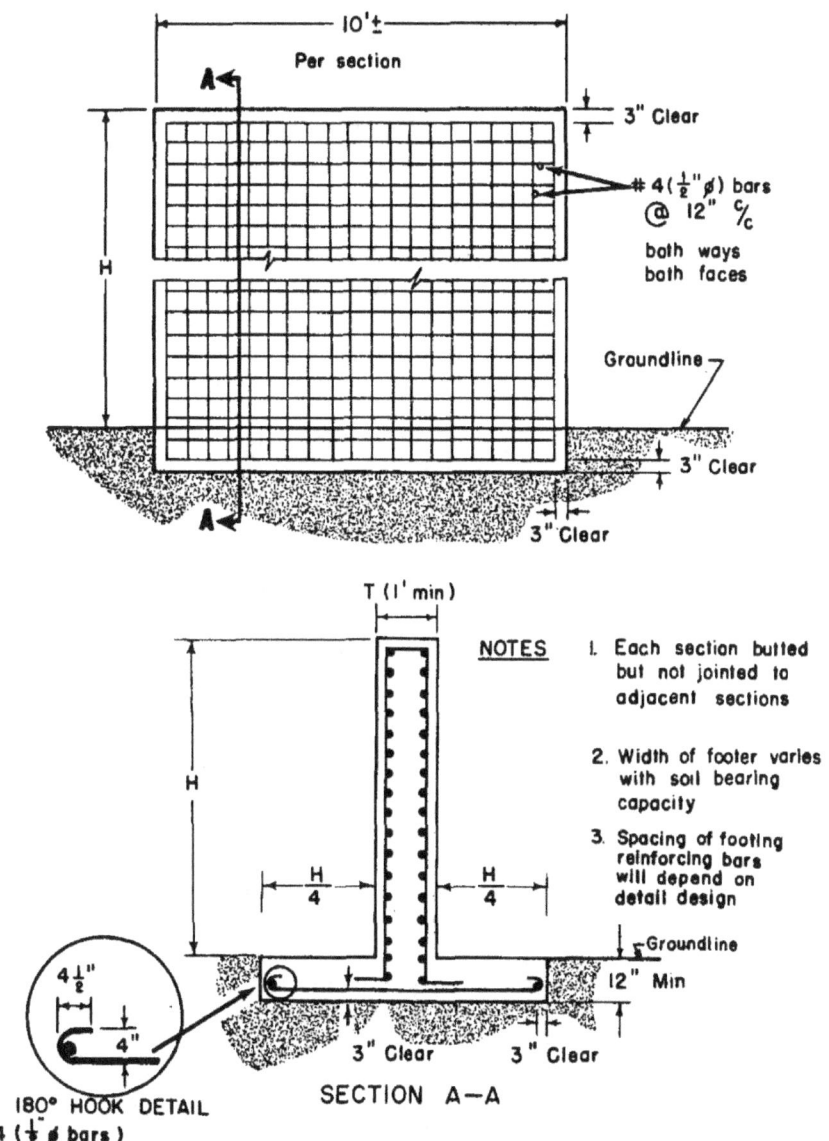

NOTES

1. Each section butted but not jointed to adjacent sections

2. Width of footer varies with soil bearing capacity

3. Spacing of footing reinforcing bars will depend on detail design

Figure 2-33. Free standing wall-reinforced concrete revetments.

CHAPTER 3 – SHELTERS

Section I. Hasty Shelters

3-1. Basic Considerations

a. Protection. Shelters are constructed primarily to protect soldiers, equipment, and supplies from enemy action and the weather. Shelters differ from emplacements because there are usually no provisions for firing weapons from them. However, they are usually constructed near or supplement the fighting positions. When natural shelters such as caves, mines, woods, or tunnels are available, they are used instead of constructing artificial shelters. Caves and tunnels must be carefully inspected by competent persons to determine their suitability and safety. The best shelter is usually the one that will provide the most protection with the least amount of effort. Actually, combat troops that have prepared defensive positions have some shelter in their foxholes or weapon emplacements. Shelters are frequently prepared by troops in support of frontline units. Troops making a temporary halt in inclement weather when moving into positions prepare shelters as do units in bivouacs, assembly areas, rest areas, and static positions.

b. Surface Shelters. The best observation is from this type of shelter and it is easier to enter or leave than an underground shelter. It also 1 requires the least amount of labor to construct, but it is hard to conceal and requires a large amount of cover and revetting material. It provides the least amount of protection from nuclear weapons of the types of shelters discussed in this manual. Surface shelters are seldom used for personnel in forward combat positions unless they can be concealed in woods, on reverse slopes, or among buildings. It may be necessary to use surface shelters when the water level is close to the surface of the ground or when the surface is so hard that digging an underground shelter is impractical.

c. Underground Shelters. Shelters of this type generally provide good protection against radiation because the surrounding earth and overhead cover are effective shields against nuclear radiation.

d. Cut-and-Cover Shelters. These shelters are dug into the ground and backfilled on top with as thick a layer as possible of rocks, logs, sod, and excavated soil. These and cave shelters provide excellent protection from weather and enemy action.

e. Siting. Wherever possible, shelters should be sited on reverse slopes, in woods, or in some form of natural defilade such as ravines, valleys, and other hollows or depressions in the terrain. They should not be in the path of natural drainage lines. All shelters must be camouflaged or concealed.

3-2. Construction

a. Principles. Hasty shelters are constructed with a minimum expenditure of time and labor using available materials. They are ordinarily built above ground or dug in deep snow. Shelters that are completely above ground offer protection against the weather and supplement or replace shelter tents which do not provide room for movement. Hasty shelters are useful in the winter when the ground is frozen, in mountainous country where the ground is too hard for deep digging, in deep snow, and in swampy or marshy ground,

b. Sites for Winter Shelters. Shelter sites that are near wooded areas are the most desirable in winter because these areas are warmer than open fields. They conceal the glow of fires and provide fuel for cooking and heating. In heavy snow tree branches extending to the ground offer some shelter to small units.

① BUILT AROUND A TREE

Figure 3-1. Wigwam.

c. Materials.

(1) Construction. Work on winter shelters should start immediately after the halt so that the men will keep warm. The relaxation and warmth offered by the shelters is usually worth the effort expended in constructing them. Beds of foliage, moss, straw, boards, skis, parkas, or shelter halves may be used as protection against dampness and cold from the ground. Snow should be removed from clothing and equipment before entering the shelter. The entrance of the shelter is located on the side that is least exposed to the wind, is close to the ground and has an upward incline. Plastering the walls with earth and snow reduces the effects of wind. The shelter itself should be as low as possible. The fire is placed low in fire holes and cooking pits.

(2) Insulating. Snow is windproof, so to keep the occupant's body heat from melting the snow, it is necessary only to place a layer of some

51

insulating material such as a shelter half, blanket, or other material between the body and the snow.

3-3. Types

a. Wigwam Shelter. This type of shelter (1, fig. 3-1) may be constructed easily and quickly when the ground is too hard to dig and shelter is required for a short bivouac. It will accommodate three men and provide space for cooking. About 25 evergreen saplings (5 to 7 ½ cm in diameter, 3 meters long) should be cut.

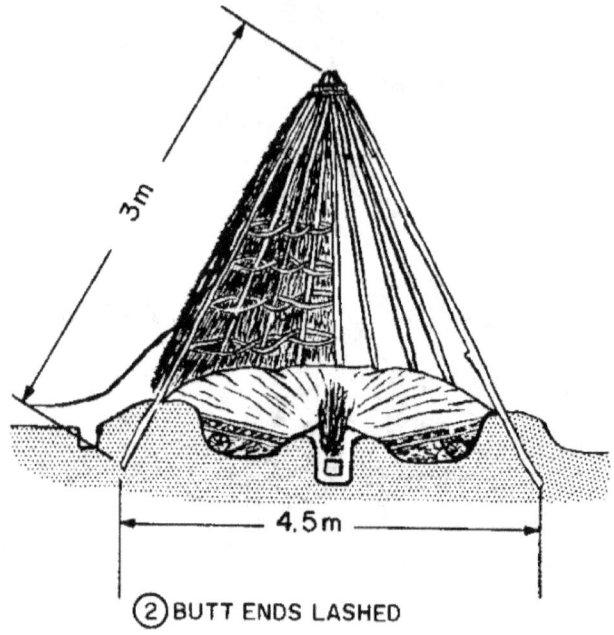

③ BUTT ENDS LASHED

Figure 3-1 - Continued.

Leave the limbs on the saplings, and lean them against a small tree so the butt ends are about 2 meters (7 ft.) up the trunk. Tie the butts together around the tree with a tent rope, wire, or other means. Space the ground end of the saplings about 30 cm (1 ft.) apart, around and about 2 meters from the base of the tree. Then trim the branches off inside the wigwam and bend down on the outside so that they are flat against the saplings. The branches that are trimmed off from the inside may be used to fill in the spaces that are left. Shelter halves wrapped around the outside make it more windproof, especially after it is covered with snow. A wigwam can also be constructed as shown in 2, figure 3-1 by lashing the butt ends of the saplings together instead of leaning them against the tree,

PERSPECTIVE VIEW

SNOW

GROUND
LEVEL

SHELTER HALF
AT ONE OR BOTH
ENDS

SIDE VIEW

Figure 3-2. Lean-to shelter.

b. Lean-to Shelter. This shelter (fig. 3-2) is made of the same material as the wigwam (natural saplings woven together and brush). The saplings are placed against a rock wall, a steep hillside, a deadfall, or some other existing vertical surface, on the leeward side. The ends may be closed with shelter halves or evergreen branches.

c. Two-Man Mountain Shelter. This shelter (fig. 3-3) is useful, particularly in winter or in inclement weather when there is frequent rain or snow. It is basically a hole 2 meters long, 1 meter wide, and 1 meter deep. The hole is covered with 15 to 20 cm diameter logs; then evergreen branches, a shelter half, and local material such as topsoil, leaves, snow, and twigs are added. The floor may be covered with evergreen twigs, a shelter half, or other expedient material. Entrances are provided at both ends if desired. A fire pit may be dug at one end for a small fire or stove. A low earth parapet is built around the emplacement to provide more height for the occupants. This shelter is very similar to an enlarged, roofed, prone shelter (fig. 2-7).

53

Figure 3-3. Two-man mountain shelter.

d. Snow Hole. The snow hole (fig. 3-4) is a simple, one-man emergency shelter for protection against a snow storm in open, snow-covered terrain. It can be made quickly, even without tools. Lying down in snow at least 1 meter deep, the soldier pushes with his feet, digs with his hands, and repeatedly turns over, forming a hole the length of his body and as wide as his shoulders. At a depth of at least 1 meter, the soldier digs in sideways below the surface, filling in the original ditch with the snow that has been dug out until only a small opening remains. This opening may be entirely closed, depending on the enemy situation and the temperature; the smaller the hole, the warmer the shelter.

e. Snow Cave. Snow caves (fig. 3-5) are made by burrowing into a snowdrift and fashioning a room of desirable size. This type of shelter gives good protection from freezing weather and a maximum amount of concealment. The entrance should slope upward for the best protection against the penetration of cold air. Snow caves may be built large enough for several men if the consistency of the snow is such that it will not cave in. Two entrances can be used while the snow is being taken out of the cave; one entrance is refilled with snow when the cave is completed.

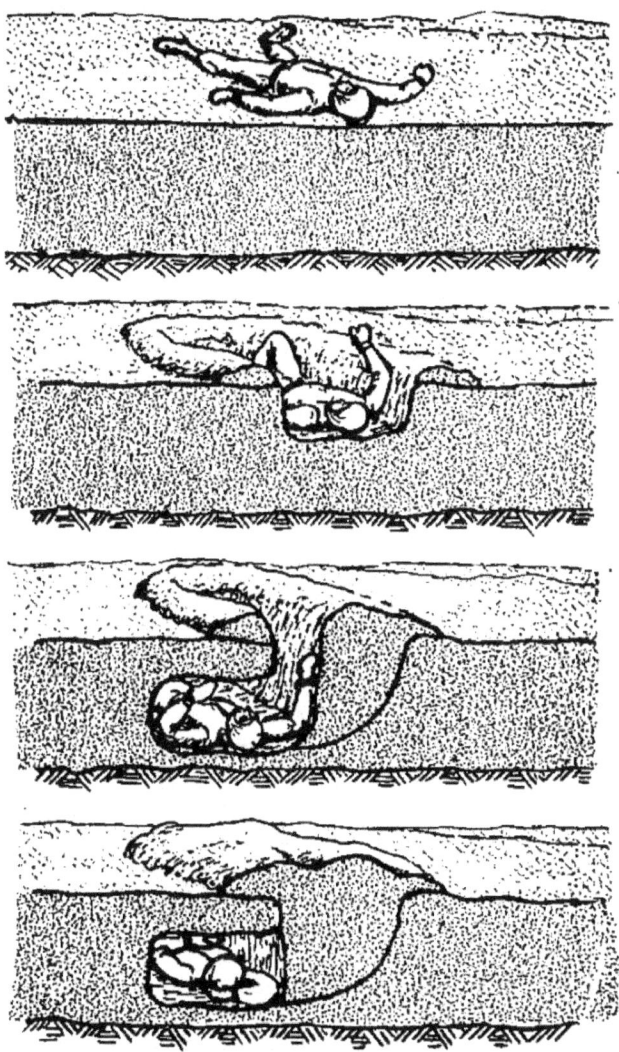

Figure 3-4. Making a snow hole without tools.

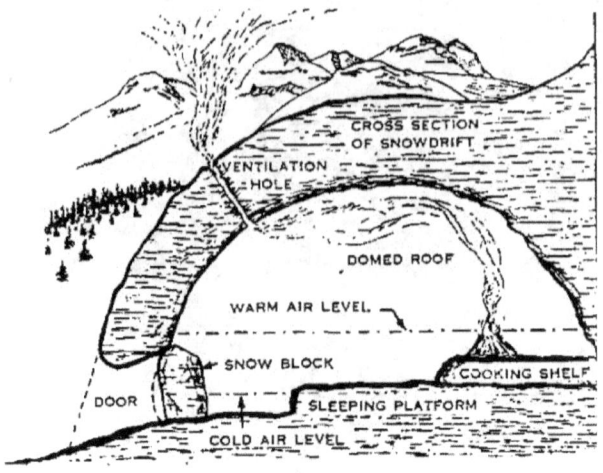

Figure 3-5. Snow cave.

f. Snow pit. The snow pit (fig. 3-6) is dug vertically into the snow with entrenching tools. It is large enough for two or three men. Skis, poles, sticks, branches, shelter halves, and snow are used as roofing. The inside depth of the pit depends upon the depth of the snow, but should be deep enough for kneeling, sitting, and reclining positions. The roof should slope toward one end of the pit. If the snow is not deep enough, the sides of the pit can be made higher by adding snow walls.

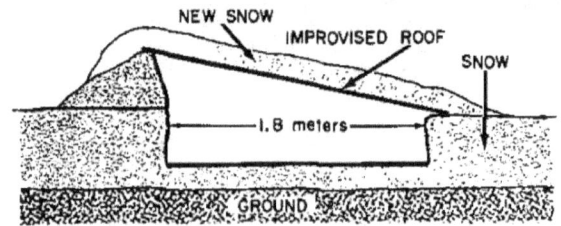

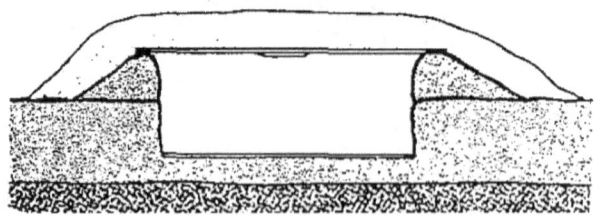

Figure 3-6. Snow pit in shallow snow.

g. Snow house. The size and roof of a snow house are similar to those of a snow pit. The walls consist of snow blocks and may be built to the height of a man. Snow piled on the outside seals the cracks and camouflages the house (fig. 3-7).

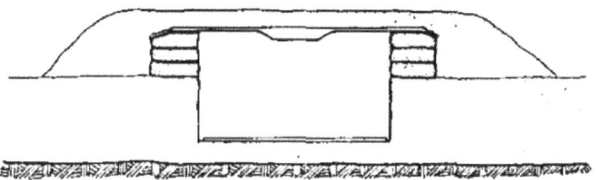

Figure 3-7. Snow house with ice block walls.

3-4. Tropical Shelter

A satisfactory bed and rain shelter (fig. 3-8) may be constructed in a short time from natural materials. The bed itself is made first about 1 meter above the ground. Four forked stakes, about 1.5 meters long and 5 cm in diameter, are driven into the ground. Then, a timber framework lashed together with vines, rope, or wire is placed on the stakes. Stout and pliable reeds, such as bamboo shoots, are laid over the framework and covered with several layers of large, fine ferns. Four longer stakes are driven into the ground alongside the bed stakes for the roof. There must be some pitch to the roof to permit the rain to run off. Leaves for the roofing are laid with the butt ends toward the high end of the shelter.

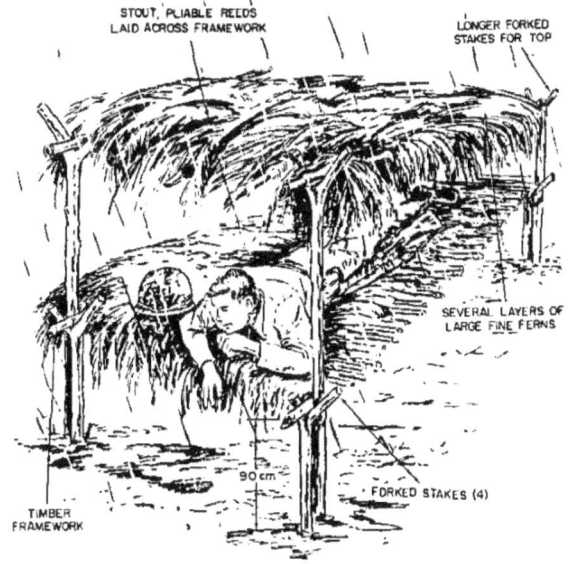

Figure 3-8. Jungle rain shelter.

Section II. Deliberate shelters

3-5. Types

The most effective shelters are deliberate, underground, cut-and-cover or cave shelters. Shelters should be provided with as deep overhead cover as possible. They should be dispersed and have a maximum capacity of 20 to 25 men. Supply shelters may be of any size, depending on location, time, and materials available. The larger the shelter the greater the necessity for easy entrance and exit. Large shelters should have at least two well camouflaged entrances spaced widely apart. The farther away from the frontlines the larger, deeper, and more substantial a shelter may be constructed because of more freedom of movement, easier access to materials and equipment, and more time to spend constructing it.

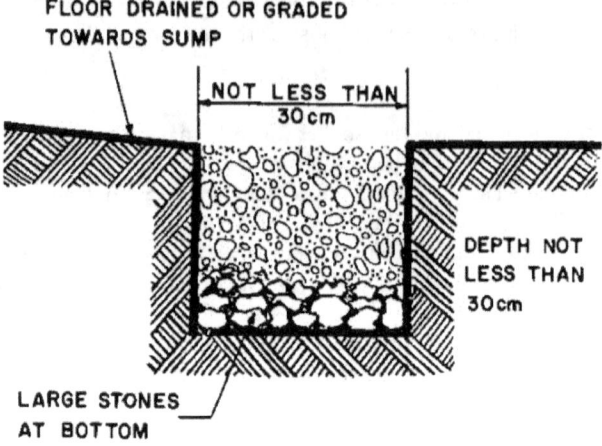

Figure 3-9. Sump for shelter drainage.

3-6. Construction Requirements

a. Drainage. Drainage is an important problem particularly in cut-and-cover and cave shelters. After the shelter is dug, drainage work usually includes keeping the surface and rain water away from the entrance, preventing the water from seeping into the interior by ditching, and removal of water that has collected inside the shelter. The floors of shelters must have a slope of at least 1 percent toward a sump (fig. 3-9) near the entrance, while the entrance should be sloped more steeply toward a ditch or sump outside the shelter (fig. 3-10).

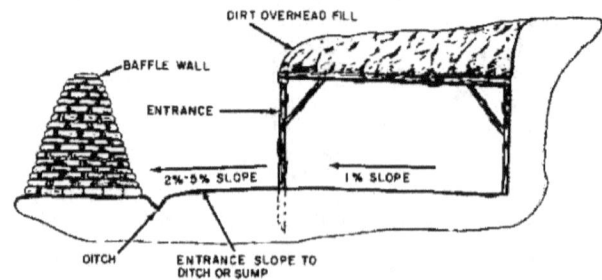

Figure 3-10. Floor and entrance drainage.

b. Ventilation. It is particularly important to ventilate cave shelters, especially if it is necessary to close the entrances during an attack. In surface and cut-and-cover shelters, enough fresh air usually is obtained by keeping entrances open. Vertical shafts bored from within cave shelters are desirable if not absolutely essential. A stovepipe through a shaft assists the circulation of air. Shelters that are not provided with good ventilation should be used only by personnel who are to remain inactive while they are inside. Since an inactive man requires about 1 cubic foot of air per minute, unventilated shelters are limited in capacity. Initial airspace requirements for shelters for not over 12 men are 350 cubic feet per man.

c. Entrance Covering. If gasproof curtains are not available, improvised curtains made of blankets hung on light, sloping frames may be used. They should be nailed securely to the sides and top entrance timbers. Curtains for cave shelters should be placed in horizontal entrances or horizontal approaches to inclines. Windows should be covered with single curtains. All crevices should be caulked with clay, old cloths or sandbags. Flooring or steps in front of gas curtains should be kept clear of mud and refuse. Small, baffled entrances and/or right angle turns will reduce the effects of nuclear blasts and will keep debris from being blown in. Baffle walls may be constructed of sods or sandbags. Materials which may be injurious to the occupants should be avoided.

d. Sanitary Conveniences. Sanitary conveniences should be provided in all but air-raid emergency shelters and surface-type shelters, where latrines are available. Disposal is by burial or chemical treatment. When waterborne sewage facilities are available, disposal can be into septic tanks or drainage into special sewers.

e. Light Security. Blackout curtains should be installed in the entrance to all shelters to prevent light leakage. To be most effective, blackout curtains are hung in pairs so that one shields the other, Blankets, shelter-halves, or similar material may be used for this purpose.

f. Emergency Exits. Emergency exits in larger shelters are desirable in case the main exit is blocked. If possible, the emergency exit should be more blast-resistant than the main entrance. This can be done by making it just large enough to crawl through. Corrugated pipe sections or 55-gallon drums with the ends removed are useful in making this type of exit. A simple emergency exit which is blast resistant can be constructed by sloping a section of corrugated pipe from the shelter up to the surface, bracing a cover against the inside, and filling the section of pipe with gravel. When the inside cover is removed, the gravel will fall into the shelter, and the occupants can crawl through the exit without digging.

3-7. Surface Shelters

A log shelter (fig. 3-11) is constructed in the form of a box braced in every direction. The framework must be strong enough to support a minimum of 45 cm of earth cover and to withstand the concussion of a near-miss of a shell or bomb or the shock of a distant nuclear explosion. The size of the logs used is limited by the size of available logs for the roof supports and by the difficulty of transporting large timbers,

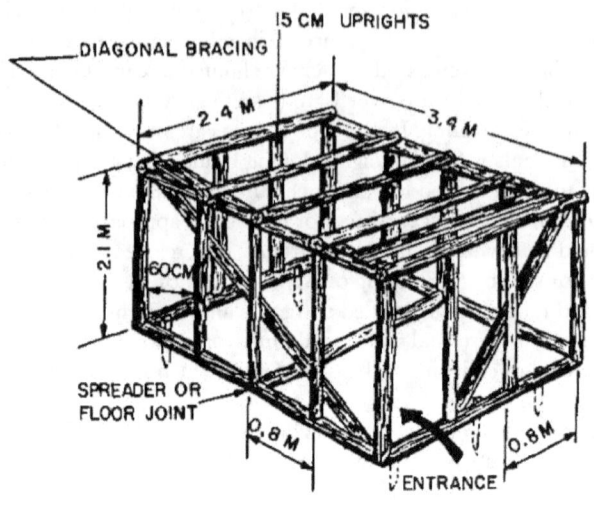

Figure 3-11. Log framed shelter.

a. Size. Shelters 2 to 3 meters wide by 4.2 meters long are suitable for normal use. The shelter shown in figure 3-12 will provide from 1.8 to 2 meters of headroom.

b. Timbers. All timbers should be the same size if possible, approximately 15 to 20 cm in diameter depending on the width of the shelter (table 3-1). The uprights should be approximately 60 cm apart except at the entrance where they may have to be spaced further apart. The roof supports should be spaced the same as the uprights. Holes should be drilled for driftpins at all joints.

c. Bracing. Boards 2.5 by 10 cm (1 in. by 4 in.) in size for the diagonal bracing is nailed to caps, sills, and uprights.

d. Walls. The log shelter frame should be covered with board or saplings and backfilled with approximately 60 cm of earth, or a hollow wall may be constructed around the buildings and filled with dirt.

e. Cover. A roof of planks, sheet metal, or other material is then laid over the roof supports and perpendicular to them to hold a minimum of 45 cm of earth cover.

Size of timber (diameter)		Maximum span when used to support 45 cm of earth		
10 cm	(4 in.).............	1.2 meters	(4	feet)
12.5 cm	(5 in.).........	2.0 meters	(5	feet)
15 cm	(6 in.)............	2.1 meters	(7	feet)
17.5 cm	(7 in.).............	2.7 meters	(9	feet)
20.0 cm	(8 in.)............	3.3 meters	(11	feet)
22.5 cm	(9 in.)............	3.9 meters	(13	feet)

Table 3-1. Size of Roof Supports

3-8. Subsurface Shelters

a. Cut-and-Cover Shelters. The log shelter shown in figure 3-11 is suited to cut-and-cover construction or surface construction. The best location for cut-and-cover shelters is on the reverse slope of a hill, mountain, ridge, or steep bank as shown in figure 3-12. The shelter frame is built in the excavation; the spoil is backfilled around and over the frame to ground level, or somewhat above, and camouflaged. The protection offered depends on the type of construction (size of timbers) and the thickness of the overhead cover. As in the case of a surface shelter of similar construction, approximately 45 cm of earth cover can be supported.

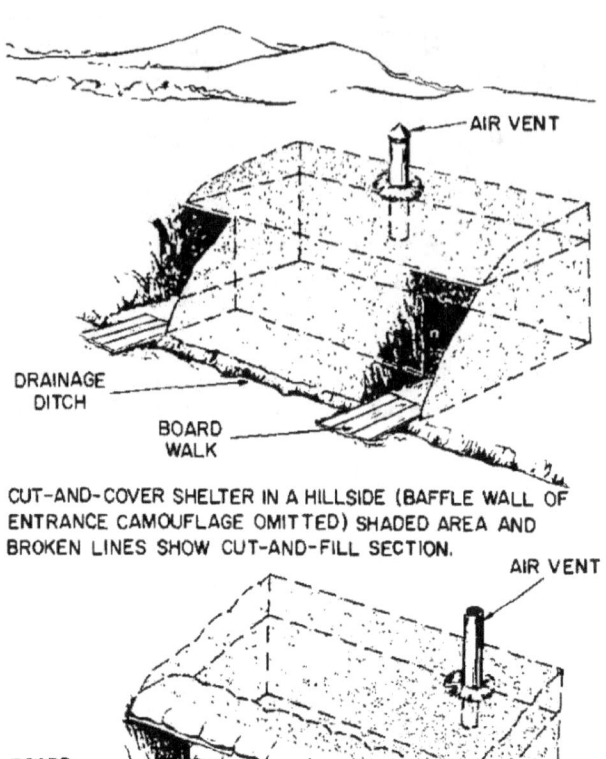

CUT–AND–COVER SHELTER IN A HILLSIDE (BAFFLE WALL OF ENTRANCE CAMOUFLAGE OMITTED) SHADED AREA AND BROKEN LINES SHOW CUT–AND–FILL SECTION.

CUT–AND–COVER SHELTER IN A CUT BANK SHOWING SAND–BAGGED OUTER WALL. SHADED AREA AND BROKEN LINES SHOW AREA OF CUT–AND–FILL.

Figure 3-12. Cut-and-cover shelter.

b. Sectional Shelters. Shelters of the type shown in figure 3-13 are designed so that the 6by 8-foot (1.8 by 2.4 meters) sections may be assembled for use individually or in combinations of two or more sections to provide the required shelter area. The advantages of sectional shelters for the purpose of command posts or aid stations are the flexibility of the shelter area that can be provided, the depth of cover the shelter will support, and the fact that the design lends itself to prefabrication. The principal disadvantage is the degree of skill required in constructing the sections from dimensional lumber of logs of comparable strength, necessitating engineer assistance and supervision.

(1) Siting. The shelter should be sited on a reverse slope for cut-and-cover construction.

(2) Excavation. Assuming that each bent or side unit (fig. 3-13 and table 3-2) is sheathed before installation, the excavated area should be 2.1 meters (7 ft.) wide and 3 meters (10 ft.) long for one section. The additional length of the excavated area will provide working space to install sheathing on the rear unit. The area for the shelter should be excavated to a depth of 3.6 meters (12 ft.) to allow for a laminated roof and 3.2 meters (10 ft. 6 in.) for stringer roof (para 3-9).

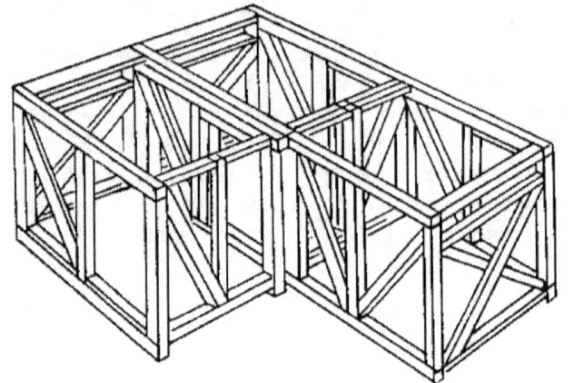

① TYPICAL CONNECTION OF THREE SECTIONS

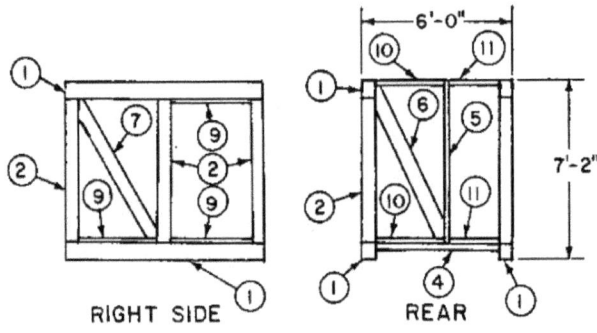

RIGHT SIDE

REAR

② FRAMING DETAILS

Figure 3-13. Sectional shelters.

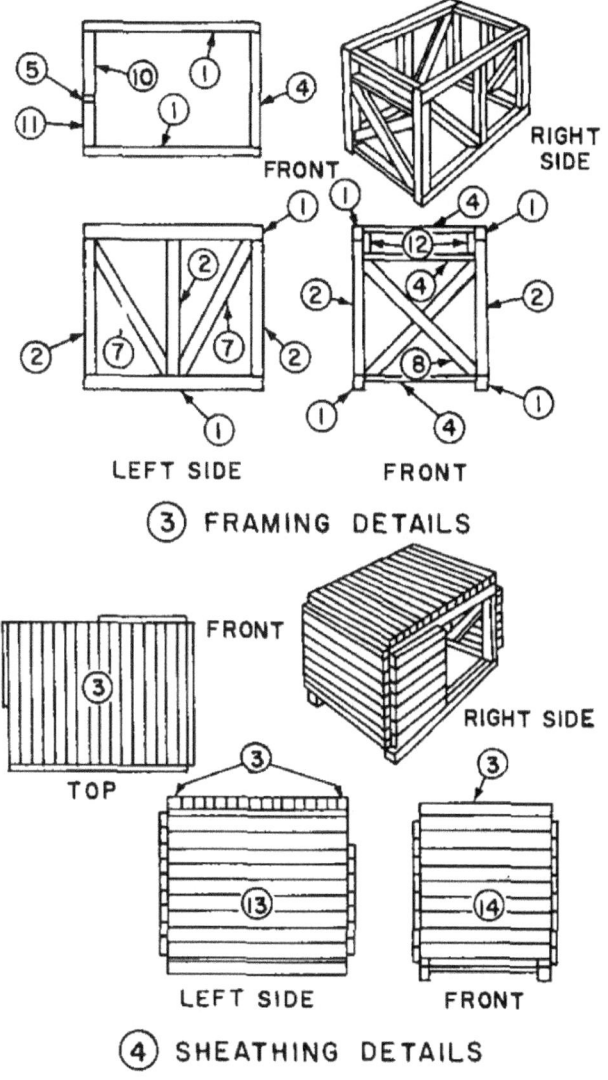

FRONT

RIGHT SIDE

LEFT SIDE

FRONT

③ **FRAMING DETAILS**

FRONT

RIGHT SIDE

TOP

LEFT SIDE

FRONT

④ **SHEATHING DETAILS**

Figure 3-13 - Continued.

(3) Assembly. The two bents or side units may be assembled and sheathed before they are placed in the excavated area. In this manner driftpins are installed in the sills, caps and posts before units are placed in the excavated area. Bracing on the side units as well as the bracing and spreaders on the front and rear units are toenailed.

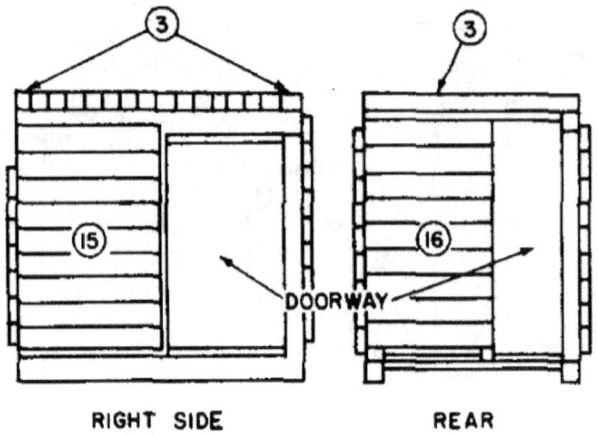

RIGHT SIDE   **REAR**

(5) **SHEATHING DETAILS**

Figure 3-13 - Continued.

(4) Organization of work crews. An engineer squad, or a squad other than engineer under engineer supervision, can be used economically at the worksite to excavate the shelter area, assemble the roofing and cover materials, and construct the overhead cover. Under favorable conditions a trained engineer squad can excavate the area required for the shelter, and install the shelter and overhead cover in 18 to 20 hours. However, if a backhoe or bucket loader is available for the excavation, the time can be reduced to approximately 6 hours.

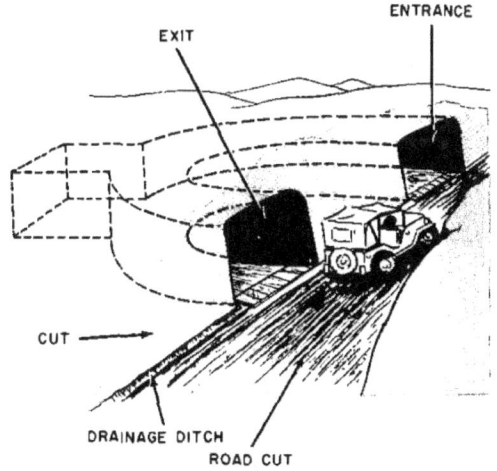

Figure 3-14. Supply cave in a road cut.

(See Metric System conversion table, app. B)

No.	Nomenclature	Rough size	Roof	Front	Right	Left	Rear
		Material list			**Quantities**		
1	Cap or sill	6"x8"x8'0"			2	2	
2	Post	6"x6"x5'10"			3	3	
3	Stringer**	6"x6"x6'0"	16				
4	Spreader	3"x6"x5'0"		2			1
5	Post, door	3"x6"x6'6"					1
6	Brace	*3"x6"x7'0"					1
7	Brace	*3"x6"x6'10"			1	2	
8	Brace	*3"x6"x8'0"		2			
9	Spreader	2"x6"x3'3"			3		
10	Spreader	2"x6"x2'9"					2
11	Spreader	2"x6"x2'0"					2
12	Scab	3"x6"x2'0"					
13	Siding	3"xRWx8'0"				41½SF	
14	Siding	3"xRWx6'0"		36SF			
15	Siding	3"xRWx4'0"			24SF		
16	Siding	3"xRWx3'6"					21SF
17	Roll roofing	100 sq ft roll	6				
18	Driftpin	½"x14"	32		6	6	
19	Nails	60d		8 lb	8 lb	8 lb	8 lb

* Allowance for double cut ends of braces is included in overall length as shown under rough size.
**Laminated wood roof (fig. 3-17) may be substituted if desired.

Table 3-2. BUI of Materials for One 6' x 8' Sectional Shelter with Post, Cap and Stringer Construction - Dimensional Timber.

Size of rectangular timber	Size of round timber required to equal (in inches)
6x6	7
6x8	8
8x8	10
8x10	11
10x10	12
10x12	13
12x12	14

Construction Notes:

67

(1) Any combination of the four types of side panels shown may be used in regard to location and number of doors required.

(2) In the construction of two or more basic units, the exterior wall panels should be based on the number and position of doorways required. Panels to be coupled in the interior of the shelter, forming a double wall, must be of the same type wall construction and provide doorways. Siding is not required on interior walls.

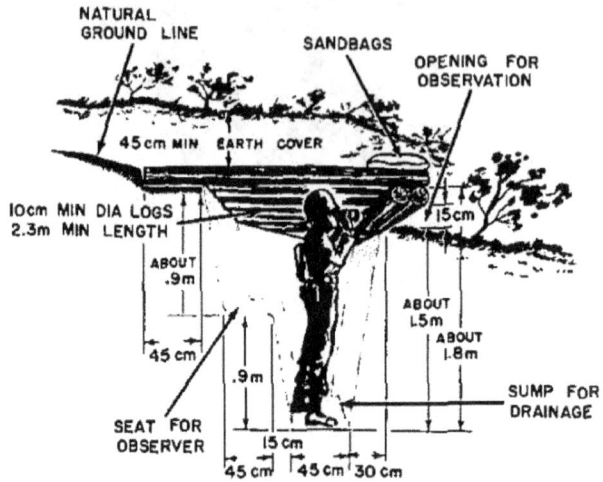

CROSS-SECTIONAL VIEW
(ENTRANCE NOT SHOWN)

Figure 3-15. Observation post.

c. Cave Shelters. Caves are dug in deliberate defensive positions, usually by tunneling into hillsides, cliffs, cuts, or ridges, or excavating into flat ground. Because of the undisturbed overhead cover, a cave is the least conspicuous of all types of shelters if the entrance is covered. One of the best locations for a supply cave entrance is shown in figure 3-14, The disadvantages of cave shelters include limited observation, congested living conditions, small exits, and difficult drainage and ventilation. Their construction is difficult and time consuming. Exits may be blocked or shoring crushed by a direct hit from a conventional weapon or ground shock from a nuclear explosion.

d. Special Use Shelters.

(1) Observation posts. These are located on terrain features offering as good a view as possible of enemy-held areas (fig. 3-15). The ideal observation post has at least one covered route of approach and cover as well as concealment, while offering an unobstructed view of enemy-held ground.

(2) Command posts. Small unit command posts may be located in woods, ravines, in the basements of buildings, or former enemy fortifications. When none of these are available, surface or cut-and-cover shelters previously described may be modified for this purpose.

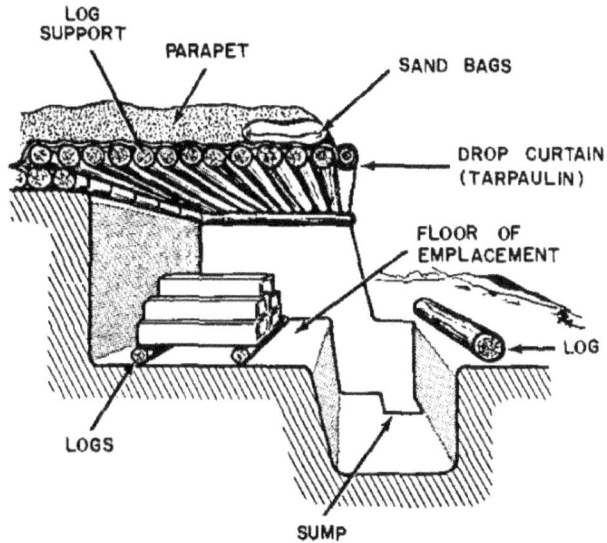

Figure 3-16. Ammunition shelter.

(3) Medical aid stations. Cut-and-cover shelters are especially adaptable as aid stations since they are easily cleaned and ventilated. Suitable sites may be found in pits, quarries, under banks, or in small buildings or ruins.

(4) Ammunition shelters. Ammunition shelters should be located and constructed so that they protect ammunition against the weather and enemy fire. They should be well concealed, and large enough to hold the desired quantity of ammunition close to the firing position. Figure 3-16 shows an ammunition shelter which may be constructed in an emplacement parapet. If it is necessary to construct ammunition shelters above ground, particularly where the water level is close to the surface, a log crib built up with dirt is suitable.

3-9. Heavy Overhead Cover

To provide adequate protection against both penetration and detonation of artillery shells and bombs, a structure would require overhead earth cover so thick as to be impracticable. By combining materials and using them in layers in a logical sequence, the required protection is provided with less excavation and construction effort. Two designs of overhead cover in functional layers which protect against the penetration and explosion from a hit by a 155-mm artillery round are shown in figure 3-17 and described below.

a. Laminated Roof Construction. In this design either five 5cm or seven 2.5cm layers of lumber are used for the laminated roof as shown in 1, figure 3-17.

(1) Dust-proof layer. Tar paper, canvas, or tarpaulins lapped and placed above the laminated roof is used to prevent dust and dirt from shaking down on equipment, weapons, and personnel.

(2) Cushion layer. The cushion layer is intended to absorb the shock of detonation or penetration. Untamped earth is the best material for this purpose and should be at least 30 cm thick. Materials such as loose gravel transmit excessive shock to the layer below and should not be used in the cushion layer. This layer extends on all sides for a distance equal to the depth of the shelter floor below the ground surface or a minimum of 1.5 meters.

(3) Waterproof layer. The waterproof layer is constructed of the same materials as the dustproof layer or similar materials. It is intended to keep moisture from the cushion layer in order to retain the cushioning effect of the soft dry earth, and minimize the dead load the structure must carry.

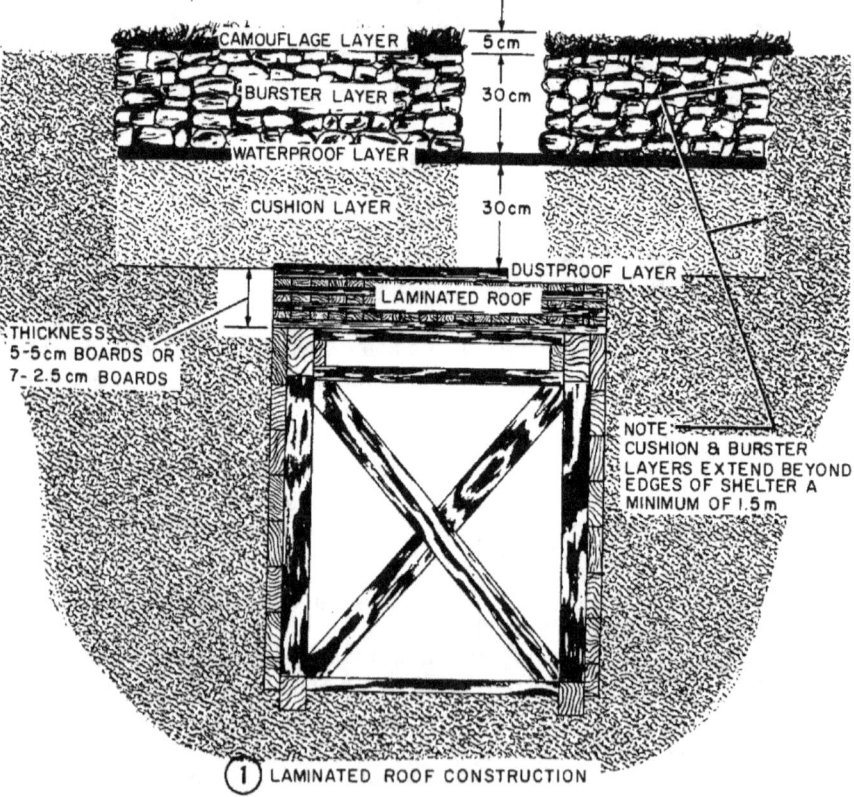

Figure 3-17. Heavy overhead cover.

(4) Burster layer. The burster layer is intended to cause detonation of the projectile before it can penetrate into the lower protective layers. This layer is made of 15 to 20-cm rocks placed in two layers with the joints broken. This layer should be at least 30 cm thick. Irregular-shaped rocks are more effective for this purpose than flat rocks. If rocks are not available, 20-cm logs may be used. They must be wired tightly

together in two layers. The burster layer should extend on each side of the shelter a minimum of 1.5 meters.

(5) Camouflage layer. The burster layer is covered with about 5 cm of untamped earth or sod, as a camouflage layer. A greater thickness of camouflage material will tend to increase the explosive effect.

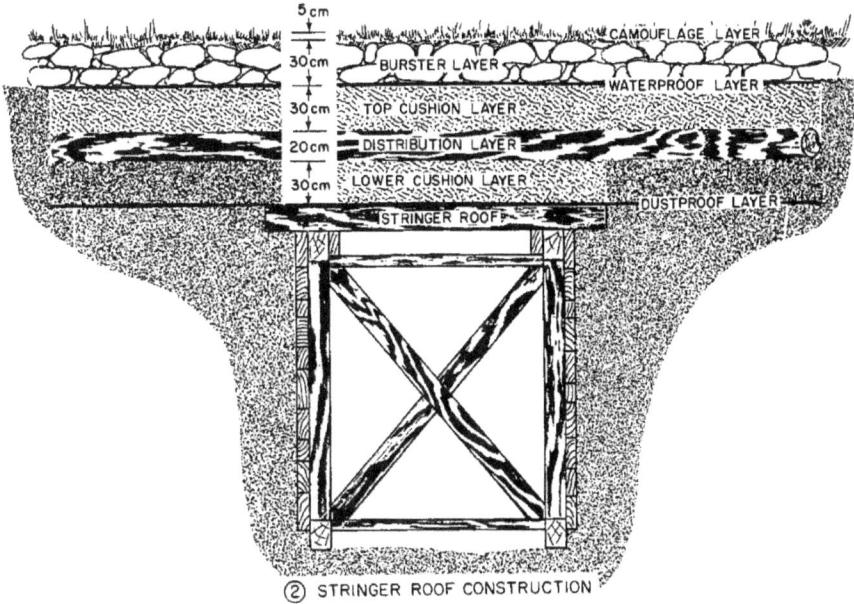

② STRINGER ROOF CONSTRUCTION

Figure 3-17 – Continued.

b. Stringer Roof Construction, Figure 3-17, illustrates stringer roof construction of heavy overhead cover. The construction is similar to laminated roof construction with the addition of-

(1) A lower cushion layer 30 cm thick on top of the dustproof layer. This layer of untamped earth does not extend beyond the sides of the shelter.

(2) A distribution layer consisting 20-cm timbers. This layer extends beyond each side of the shelter a minimum of 1.5 meters and rests on undisturbed earth to transmit part of the load of the top layers to the undisturbed earth on each side of the shelter.

c. Overhead Cover for Fighting Bunker. Figure 3-18 shows the details for the construction of a fighting bunker with heavy overhead cover. The material requirements for the construction of this bunker are found in table 3-3.

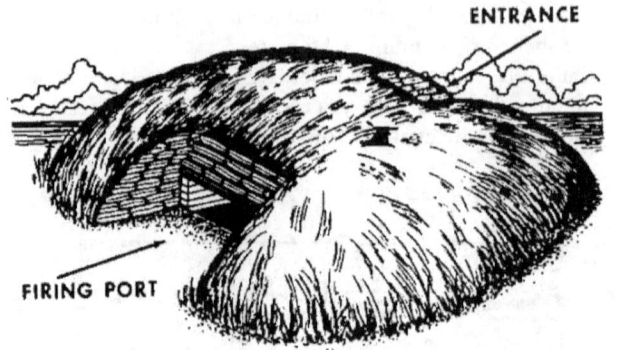

ENTRANCE

FIRING PORT

Figure 3-18. Fighting bunker with heavy overhead cover.

3-10. Support of Overhead Cover

a. Overhead cover is normally supported on the roof of the structure and the resultant load is transmitted through the caps and posts to the foundation on which the structure rests. It may be necessary in some instances, to support the roof directly on the earth outside a revetted position. When this must be done, the roof timber should not bear directly on the earth outside the excavation. The added load may cause the wall to buckle or cave in. Instead, the roof structure is carried on timber sills or foundation logs bedded uniformly in the surface at a safe distance from the cut.

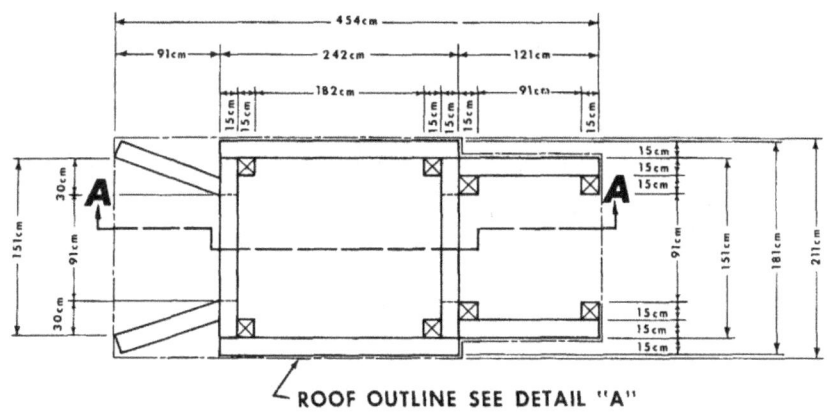

PLAN VIEW

Figure 3-18 - Continued.

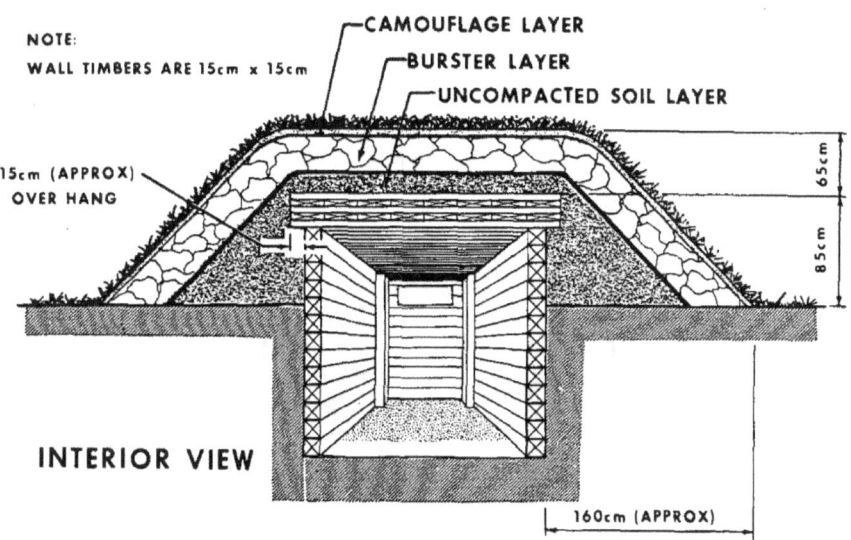

INTERIOR VIEW

Figure 3-18 - Continued.

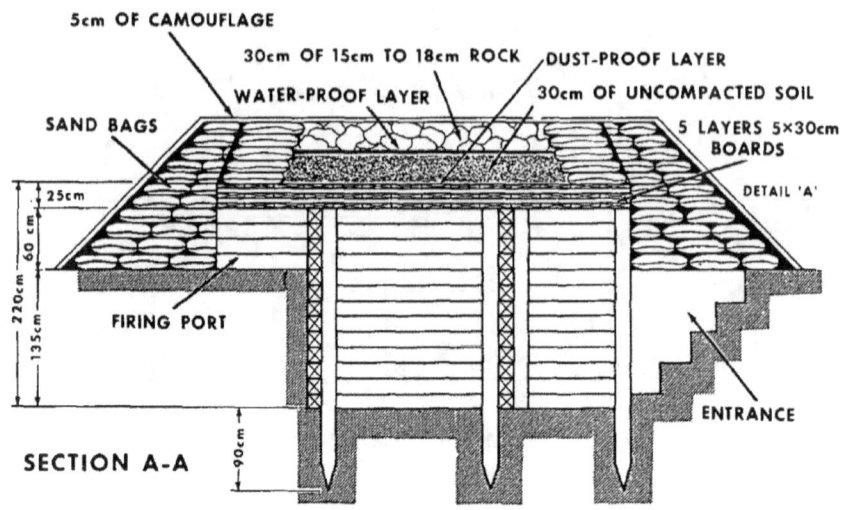

Figure 3-18 - Continued.

No.	Nomenclature	Description	Quantities
1.	Roof	5cm x 30cm x 2.11m-wood	48 pcs
		5cm x 30cm x 4.54m-wood	14 pcs
2.	Sidewalls	15cm x 15cm x 2.42m-wood	26 pcs
3.	Entrance wall	15cm x 15cm x 1.21m-wood	26 pcs
4.	Firing port & entrance door	15cm x 15cm x 30cm -wood	26 pcs
5.	Front & rear walls	15cm x 15cm x 1.51m-wood	13 pcs
6.	Firing port & retaining wall	15cm x 15cm x 1.00m-wood	8 pcs
7.	Side post	15cm x 15cm x 2.85m-wood	6 pcs
		15cm x 15cm x 1.95m-wood	2 pcs
8.	Sandbags		300 ea.
9.	Roofing paper	100 sq ft rolls	8 ea.
10.	Driftpins	½" x 12"	210 ea.
11.	Nails	16d	30 lb

Table 3-3. Bill of Materials, Fighting Bunker.

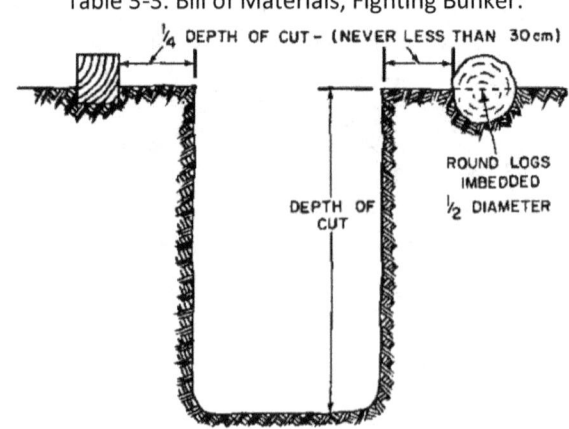

Figure 3-19. Support of overhead cover on earth banks.

b. Laminated planks or stringers are used to support the roof cover.

(1) Table 3-4 shows the thickness of laminated plank roof required to support various thicknesses of earth cover. The planks should extend from support to support in all layers, and adjoining edges should be staggered from one layer to the next.

(2) Table 3-5 shows the spacing of stringers required to support a one-inch plank roof under various thicknesses of earth over various spans. Stringers are 2" x 4" unless otherwise indicated.

(3) The roof designs shown here are not designed to be shellproof, even under a laminated earth and rock cover. The roofs shown with the cover indicated are fragment proof and will give substantial radiation protection, if properly designed entrances are provided.

c. Sandbags are never used to support overhead cover.

(See Metric System conversion table, app B)

Thickness of earth cover in feet	Span width in feet					
	2½	3	3½	4	5	6
1½	1	1	2	2	2	2
2	1	2	2	2	2	3
2½	1	2	2	2	2	3
3	2	2	2	2	3	3
3½	2	2	2	2	3	3
4	2	2	2	2	3	4

Table 3-4. Thickness in Inches of Laminated Wood Required to Support Various Thicknesses of Earth Cover over Various Spans.

(See Metric System conversion table, app B)

Thickness of earth cover in feet	Span width in feet					
	2½	3	3½	4	5	6
1½	40	30	22	16	10	18*
2	33	22	16	12	8/20*	14*
2½	27	18	12	10	16*	10*
3	22	14	10	8/20*	14*	8*
3½	18	12	8/24*	18*	12*	8*
4	16	10	8/20*	16*	10*	7*

*Note. Stringers are 2" by 4" except those marked by an asterisk (*) which are 2" by 6".

Table 3-5. Center to Center Spacing, in Inches, of Wooden Stringers Required to Support a 1-inch Thick Wood Roof with Various Thicknesses of Earth Cover Over Various Spans.

3-11. Fighting Bunker with Light Overhead Cover

When establishing positions in wooded areas, it is very important to provide overhead cover to protect personnel from the shrapnel of tree bursts. A fighting bunker with light overhead cover is shown and described in figure 3-20. The overhead cover will stop fragments from tree and airburst artillery, and it is strong enough to withstand the effects of a direct hit by an 81-mm mortar. If the side openings are closed with sandbags to prevent the entry of grenades, the fields of fire and observation are limited to the front only. This is a serious disadvantage with this type of position. Chicken wire can be placed over the firing apertures to prevent grenades from entering the bunker. The chicken wire should be sloped with a ditch dug at the base to catch grenades as they roll off the wire.

3-12. Buildings as Shelters

a. Protection. Some protection from enemy fire may be achieved for occupants in a building used as a shelter by strengthening the building, by shoring up ceilings, and bracing walls. Men inside buildings are reasonably well protected against thermal effects and radiation unless they are near doors or windows. The principal danger is from falling masonry and from fire in the building.

b. Basic Consideration.

(1) A ground floor or basement is more likely to make a suitable shelter than any other floor. The risk of being trapped must be guarded against. Heavy bars, pieces of pipe, or timbers should be available in each room that is occupied, for use by the occupants in the event the building is demolished.

(2) Small arms fire will not penetrate the walls if they are 45 cm (18 in.) thick. The walls will not usually splinter from small arms fire if they are 30 cm thick. Additional protection can be obtained by building sandbag walls. If sandbags are used inside the building they reduce the useable space, but last longer and are not conspicuous. Care should be exercised in using sandbags above the first floor due to the weight involved.

(3) Window glass should be removed since it gives no thermal protection and is dangerous when shattered. If it is retained as protection from the weather, it should be screened or boarded.

(4) Several exits are necessary.

(5) Provisions for fighting fire should be made.

(6) Blackout arrangements should be made, if not already provided by thermal screening of doors and windows.

c. Use of Weapons. In using a building as a firing position, there are several considerations.

(1) The preparatory work should not disclose the intended use of the building to the enemy.

(2) Weapons must be sited well back from any opening so that neither weapons nor personnel are visible from the outside.

(3) Several firing positions should be available in order to obtain a wide field of fire. The shapes of the openings should not be changed for this purpose.

(4) Any openings other than the normal ones are very conspicuous unless they are close to the ground.

(5) There are no fixed designs for weapons platforms under these circumstances. Platforms must be improvised from materials immediately available. Sandbags should be used sparingly if there is any doubt about the strength of the floor.

d. Utilization of Buildings. Utilization of existing buildings as shelters is discussed in detail in TM 5-311.

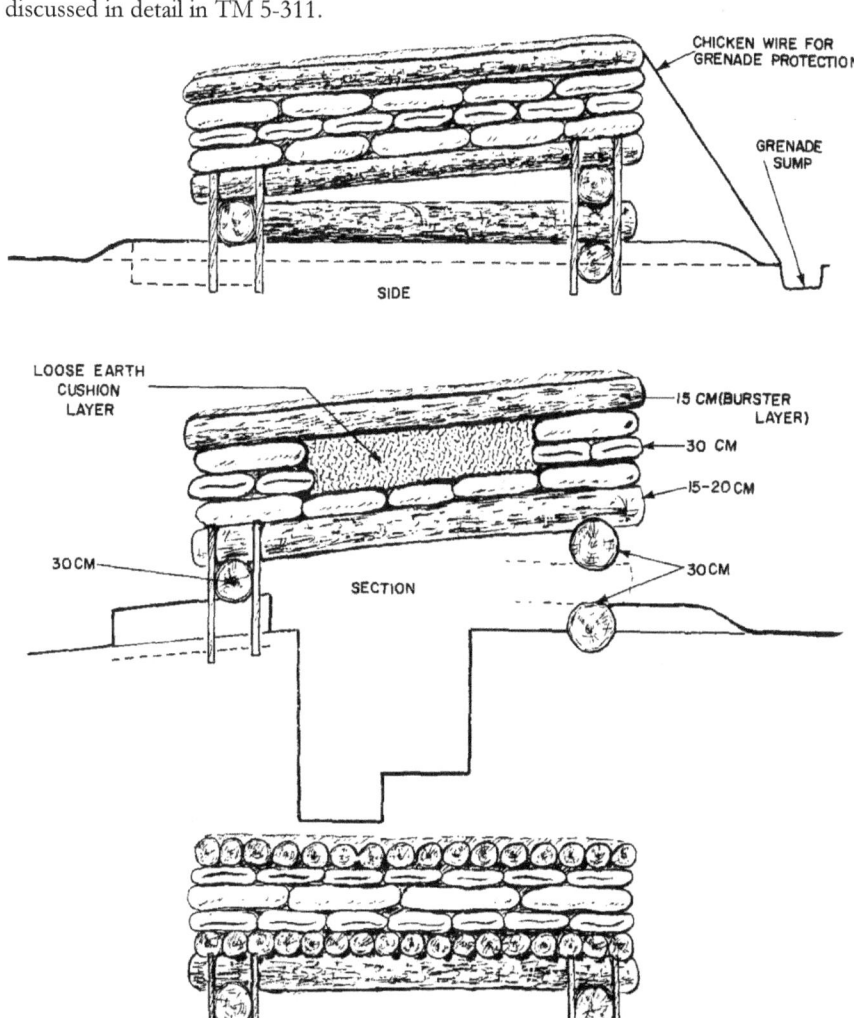

Figure 3-20. Fighting bunker with light overhead cover.

CHAPTER 4 – TRENCHES & FIELDWORKS

Section I. Trenches

4-1. Purpose

a. Defensive Area. Trenches are excavated as fighting positions and to connect individual foxholes, weapons emplacements, and shelters in the progressive development of a defensive area. They provide protection and concealment for personnel moving between fighting positions or in and out of the area. Trenches should be included in the overall layout plan for the defense of a position. The excavation of trenches involves considerable time, effort, and materials and is only justified when an area will be occupied for an extended period. Trenches are usually open excavations but sections may be covered to provide additional protection if the overhead cover does not interfere with the fire mission of the occupying personnel. Trenches are difficult to camouflage and are easily detected, especially from the air.

b. Development. Trenches are developed progressively as is the case for other fighting positions. As they are improved they are dug deeper, from a minimum of 60 cm to approximately 1.7 meters. As a general rule, there is a tendency to excavate deeper for other than fighting trenches to provide more protection or to allow more headroom. Some trenches may also have to be widened to accommodate more traffic including stretchers. It is usually necessary to revet trenches that are more than 1.5 meters deep in any type of soil. In the deeper trenches, some engineer advice or assistance may be necessary in providing adequate drainage.

4-2. Construction

a. Crawl Trench. The crawl trench is used to conceal movement into or within a position and to provide a minimum of protection. Crawl trenches should be 60 to 75 cm deep and about 60 cm wide. This trench is the narrowest practicable for most purposes and of the least width that can be dug without difficulty. It should be zigzagged or winding. The spoil is thrown up onto parapets, normally on each side of the trench. If the trench runs across a forward slope, it is better to throw all the spoil on the enemy side to make a higher parapet.

b. Fighting Trench. In developing a trench system, the outline of the trench is marked out on the ground if time permits; if the digging is to be done at night, the ground is taped. The berm line is indicated about 45 cm from the front edge of the trench. The trench is dug by men working in the same direction (not facing each other or back to back), and far enough apart so that they do not interfere with each other.

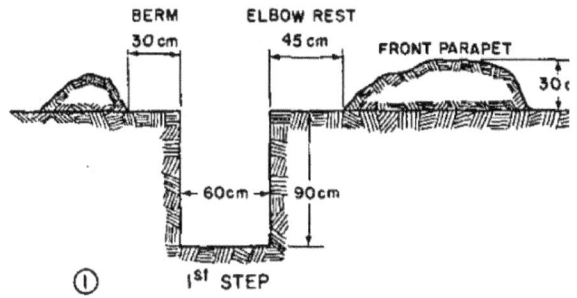

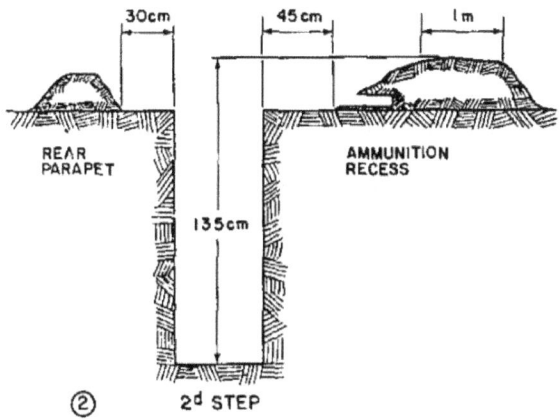

Figure 4-1. Development of a fighting trench.

(1) First step. The trench is dug to a depth of 90 cm (3 ft.) below ground level (1, fig. 4-1). At this point both men are able to fire in either direction, in a kneeling or crouching position. In ordinary soil this step can be completed in approximately 2 hours. The aides of the trench are kept vertical, or as steep as possible. If the soil is not stable, the sides require revetting immediately. Spoil is thrown to each side of the trench in alternate shovelfuls beyond the berm lines until each parapet is about 30 cm high and at least 45 cm wide on the back parapet. The remaining spoil is thrown on the front parapet until it is at least 150 cm wide (fig. 4-1).

(2) Second step. The second step consists of deepening the trench until it is approximately 135 cm deep from the level of the trench parapet (2, fig. 4-1). Normally, the front parapets are 30 cm high and the dirt settles 5 to 10 cm. Parapets are then shaped and camouflaged.

(3) Front parapet. The front parapet must be made according to the lay of the ground and the requirements of the weapon. A front parapet is often unnecessary on a steep forward slope. At most sites a front parapet improves the field of fire and should be constructed as follows:

(1) Height. A convenient height for the front parapet for firing purposes is 23 to 30 cm when the ground is level. It should be higher to fire uphill and the crest should be irregular to aid concealment. The height shown in figure 4-1 is average.

(2) Width. A reasonably bulletproof parapet should be 1 meter in width. Since it is sloped in front and rear, the total width on the bottom will be approximately 2 meters.

(3) Berms. The berm on the front of the trench forms an elbow rest which is usually about 45 cm wide. If an M60 machinegun on a bipod is to be fired, the firing platform should be 90 cm from front to rear.

(4) Rear parapet. The rear parapet is made of spoil that is not required for the front parapet. If the spoil is available, the rear parapet should be higher than the front parapet to prevent silhouetting of soldiers' heads when firing. The rear parapet may be up to 45 cm high and should be at least 45 cm wide at the top, sloped steeply in front. Parapets may be omitted to aid concealment or when ground provides background and protection to the firer's rear.

(5) Concealment. Parapets are finished off by replacing turf or topsoil. The trench and parapets are covered with any available camouflage material, arranged to permit firing.

(6) Drainage. A sump is dug at the lowest point to prevent the floor of the trench from becoming wet and muddy.

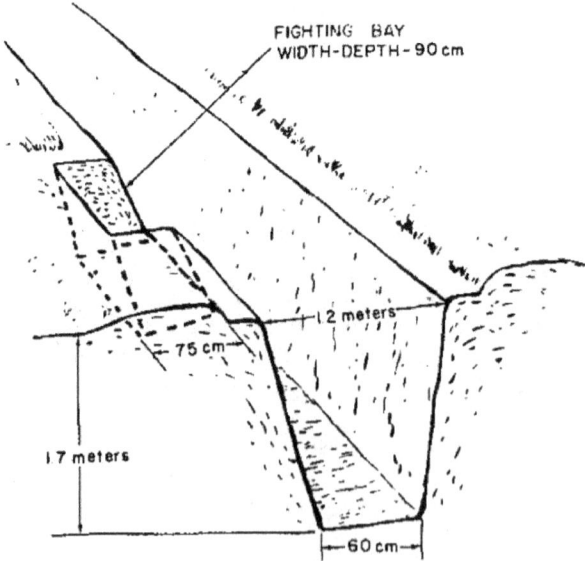

Figure 4-2. Standard trench with fighting bay.

c. Standard Trench. The standard trench is developed from the fighting trench by lowering it to a depth of 1.7 meters (5y 2 ft.) It may be constructed with fighting bay (fig. 4-2) or with a fighting step (fig. 4-3). Fighting positions are constructed on both sides of the trench to provide alternate positions to fight to the rear, to provide step off areas for foot traffic in the trench, and to provide protection against enfilade fire. This trench provides more protection than the fighting trench due to its depth. Additional protection in the form of overhead cover may also be provided. This trench is primarily a fighting position but it can also be used for communications, supply, evacuation, and troop movements.

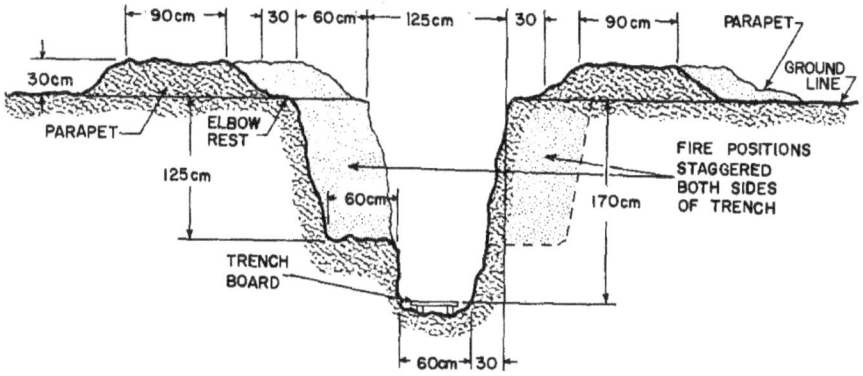

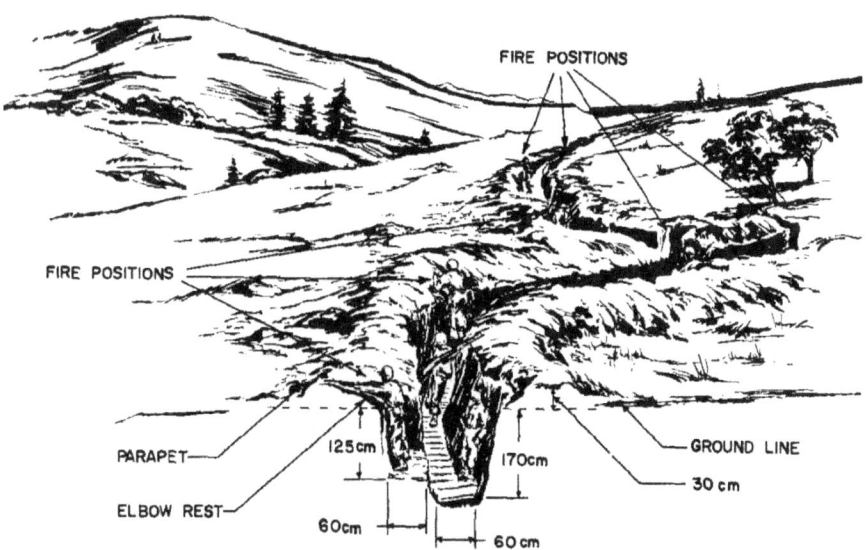

Figure 4-3. Standard trench.

d. Traces. Each trench is constructed to the length required and follows one of the traces described below to simplify construction. Special combinations and modifications may be developed.

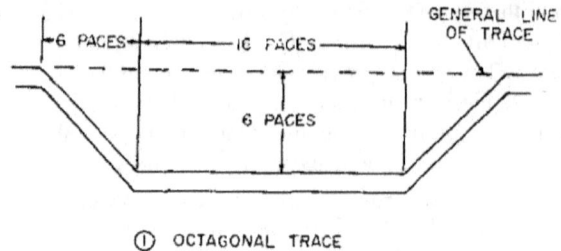

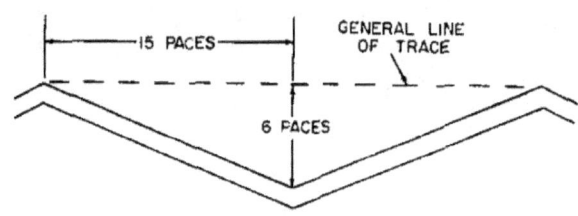

Figure 4-4. Standard trench traces.

(1) Octagonal trace. The octagonal trace (1, fig. 4-4) is excellent for fighting trenches in most situations. The octagonal trace has the following advantages:

    (a) It affords easy communication.

    (b) It affords excellent protection against enfilade fire.

    (c) It facilitates oblique fire along the front.

    (d) It is economical to construct, both in labor and material.

    (e) It can be provided with a continuous fire step. Its chief disadvantage is that its layout lacks simplicity of detail.

(2) Zigzag trace. The zigzag trace (2, fig. 4-4) can provide protection from enfilade fire and shell bursts by the employment of short tangents and by the occupation of alternate tangents. The zigzag trace has the following advantages:

    (a) It is the simplest and easiest to trace, construct, revet, and maintain.

    (b) It may be readily adapted to the terrain.

    (c) It permits both frontal and flanking fire. This trace has no specific disadvantages.

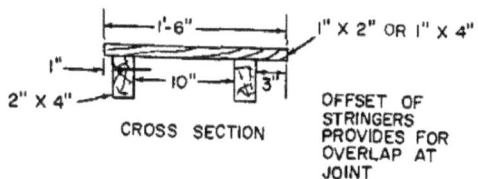

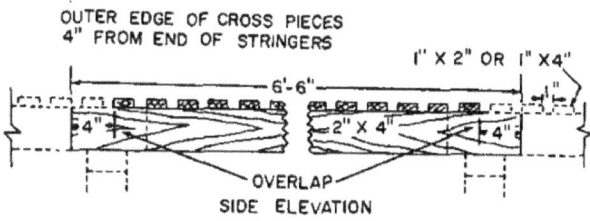

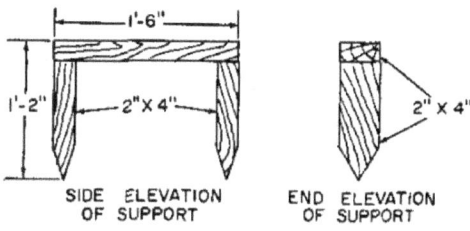

Figure 4-5. Trench board and support.

e. Trench Boards. If the sumps are choked with mud, they will cease to function. When this happens, alternatives include some forms of flooring. Trench boards (fig. 4-5) are the most practical. Timber planks, metal mats, or saplings wired together may also be used.

4-3. Drainage

a. Siting. Emplacements, shelters, and trenches are sited to take advantage of the natural drainage pattern of the ground. They are constructed so as to provide for -
   (1) Exclusion of surface runoff.
   (2) Disposal of direct rainfall or seepage.
   (3) Bypassing or rerouting natural drainage channels if they are intersected by the emplacement or shelter.

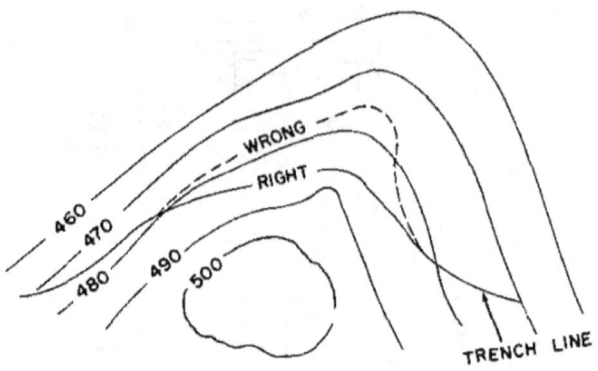

Figure 4-6. Siting to lessen problem of runoff disposal.

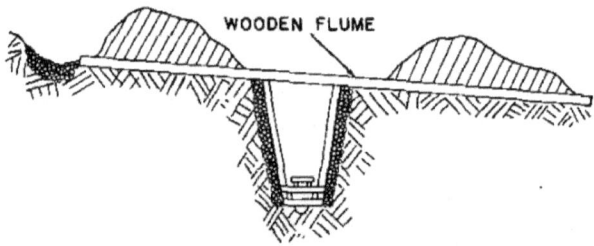

Figure 4-7. Use of open flume to direct water across ditch.

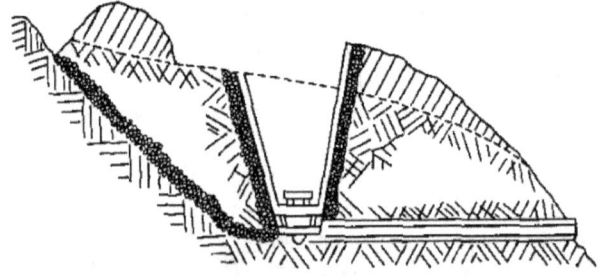

Figure 4-8. Use of undertrench drains.

b. Surface Runoff. Proper siting, as illustrated in figure 4-6, can lessen this problem by locating the emplacement, shelter, or trench in an area not subject to excessive runoff. Surface water may be excluded by excavating interceptor ditches upslope from the emplacement or shelter. It is much easier to prevent surface water from flowing in than to remove it after it is in the excavation. Fortifications should be sited so as to direct the water to natural drainage lines. If this is not possible, the water is conducted across the trench through open flumes developed for the purpose or under the trench using a combination of trench drains and culverts. An application of the open flume method for use with trenches is shown in figure 4-7. A typical undertrench drain is shown in figure 4-8,

c. Direct Rainfall or Seepage. Water collecting within an emplacement or shelter is carried to central points by providing longitudinal slopes in the bottom of the excavation. A very gradual slope of 1 percent is desirable. In trenches the slope is best provided for by fitting the trench to the terrain in such a way that the original surface has a moderate slope, as shown on the contoured layout in figure 4-11. When permitted by the tactical situation, excavation of trenches should commence at the lowest level and progress upward in order to avoid collecting water in the bottom of a partially completed trench. The central collecting points may be either natural drainage lines or sumps below the bottom of the excavation as shown in figure 4-9. Such sumps are located at points where the water will percolate through permeable soil or can be piped, pumped, or bailed out.

Figure 4-9. Drainage sump in bottom of excavation.

4-4. Overhead Cover

a. Light Cover. Expedient overhead cover may be supported as shown in figure 4-10. Logs 15 to 20 cm in diameter should be used to support light earth cover. Saplings laid in a laminated pattern to a depth of 15 to 20 cm may be used as a substitute for the logs. The total thickness of the logs or saplings and the earth cover should be a minimum of 45 cm.

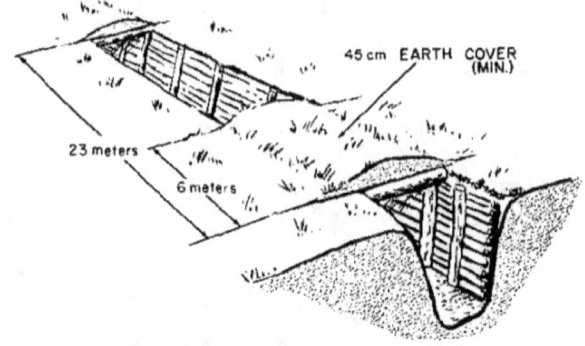

Figure 4-10. Revetted fighting trench with cover.

b. Heavy Cover. If heavy overhead cover is used in the construction of trenches it should be installed in 6 to 12-meter sections and in conjunction with the overhead cover of emplacements and shelters connected by the trenches. Support for heavy overhead cover is provided by post-cap-stringer type structures as shown in figures 4-12 and 4-13. Trenches must be widened and deepened to accommodate these structures in accordance with information contained in the above illustrations. Bills of materials are shown in tables 4-1 and 4-2.

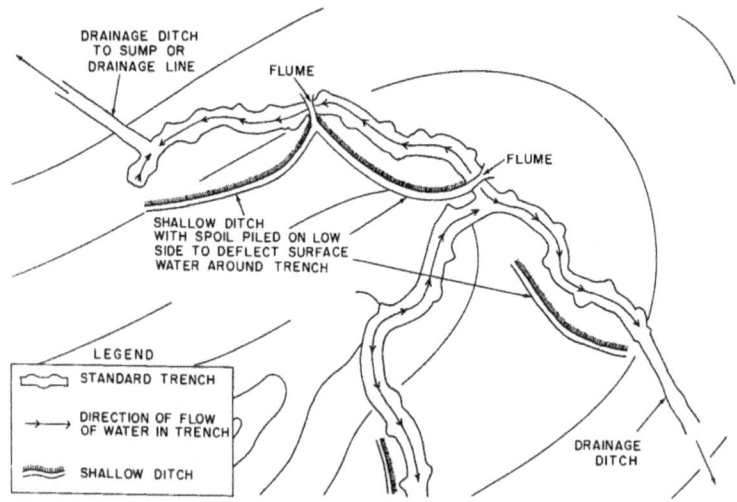

Figure 4-11. Method of sighting trench to provide longitudinal drainage.

4-5. Revetment

a. Wall Sloping. The necessity for revetment may sometimes be avoided or postponed by sloping the walls of the excavation. In most soils a slope of 1:3 or 1 A is sufficient. This method may have to be used temporarily if the soil is loose and no revetting materials are available. However, wall sloping can seriously reduce the protection due to the increased width of the trench at ground level. In any case where wall sloping is used, the walls should be dug vertical first and then sloped. Multiply the height of the wall as in figure 4-14 by the slope to be used 1:4 (1/4). This gives the amount the wall must be cut back at ground level. Then, cut out a section about 30 cm wide for a guide, as shown.

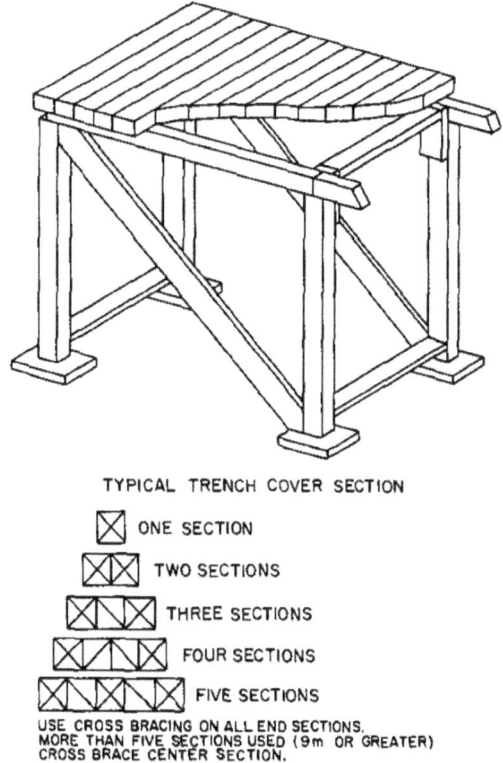

TYPICAL TRENCH COVER SECTION

ONE SECTION

TWO SECTIONS

THREE SECTIONS

FOUR SECTIONS

FIVE SECTIONS

USE CROSS BRACING ON ALL END SECTIONS.
MORE THAN FIVE SECTIONS USED (9m OR GREATER)
CROSS BRACE CENTER SECTION.

Figure 4-12. Trench cover section, dimensioned timber.

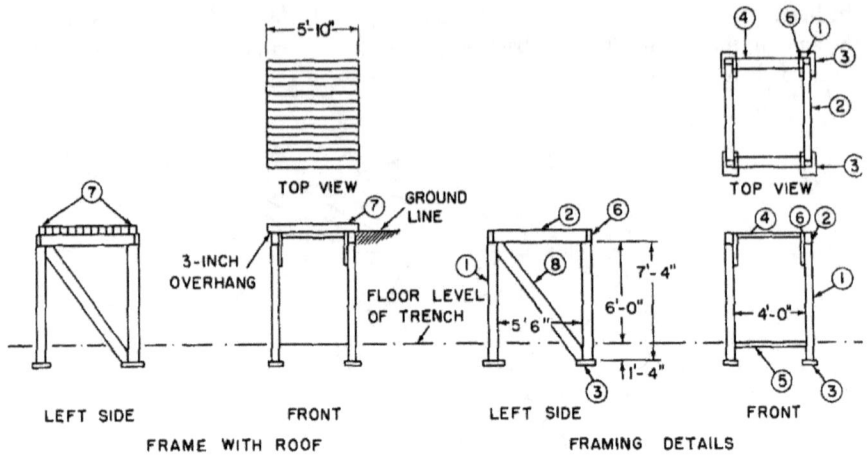

TOP VIEW

3-INCH OVERHANG

GROUND LINE

FLOOR LEVEL OF TRENCH

LEFT SIDE   FRONT

FRAME WITH ROOF

LEFT SIDE   FRONT

FRAMING DETAILS

Figure 4-12 - Continued.

(See Metric System conversion table, app B)

No.	Nomenclature	Size	Basic section as shown	Additional sections when used in series
1	Post	8″ x 8″ x 7′4″	4	2
2	Cap	8″ x 10″ x 6′2″	2	2
3	Footing	2″ x 8″ x 1′4″	16	8
4	Top spreader	3″ x 8″ x 3′6″	2	1
5	Bottom spreader	3″ x 8″ x 4′0″	2	1
6	Scab	3″ x 8″ x 2′0″	4	2
7	Stringer*	6″ x 8″ x 5′10″	13	13
8	Bracing	3″ x 8″ x 9′6″	2**	2**
9	Driftpin	¾″ x 16″	8	4
10	Driftpin	½″ x 12″	26	24
11	Nails	60d	20 lb	15 lb

* Laminated wood roof, designed in accordance with table 3-4 may be substituted if desired.
** Change to 4 when cross bracing is required. See bracing details.

Table 4-1. Bill of Materials, Trench Cover Section, Post, Cap, and Stringer Construction Dimensioned Timber.

Suggested Construction Procedure

1. Dig holes for footers.

2. Place footers in holes making them as level as possible.

3. Nail posts to footers.

4. Place caps on top of posts and secure with driftpins (bore one-half-inch holes for pins).

5. Nail scabs in place.

6. Nail top and bottom spreaders in place.

7. Nail side braces in place.

8. Put stringers on top of caps and secure with one-half-inch driftpins.

9. Use typical overhead cover.

No.	Nomenclature	Size	Basic section as shown	Additional sections when used in series
1	Post ----------------------------------	12″ log x 7′4″	4	2
2	Cap -----------------------------------	12″ log x 7′6″*	2	2
3	Sill -----------------------------------	12″ log x 6′4″	2	1
4	Stringer*** ----------------------------	10″ log x 6′4″	8	8
5	Scab ----------------------------------	3″ x 8″ x 1′6″**	4	2
6	Bracing -------------------------------	6″ log x 9′6″	4	4
7	Top spreader --------------------------	6″ log x 3′6″	2	1
8	Driftpins ------------------------------	½″ x 16″	46	34
9	Nails ---------------------------------	60d	20 lb	18 lb

* Or larger multiples thereof.
** Scab should be dimension timber as indicated, whenever such material is available. When only logs are available the scab should be split out of the center of an 8″ log.
*** Laminated wood roof, designed in accordance with table 3–4, may be substituted if desired.

Table 4-2. Bill of Materials, Trench Cover Section, Post, Cap, and Stringer, Construction Log (fig. 4-13).

Construction Notes

1. Dig trenches for sills.
2. Place sills and level up.
3. Fasten posts to sills with one-half-inch driftpins.
4. Place caps on posts, secure with driftpins.
5. Nail scabs in place.
6. Nail in top spreaders.
7. Nail cross bracing in place.
8. Place stringers on top of caps and secure with one-half-inch driftpins.
9. Use typical overhead cover.

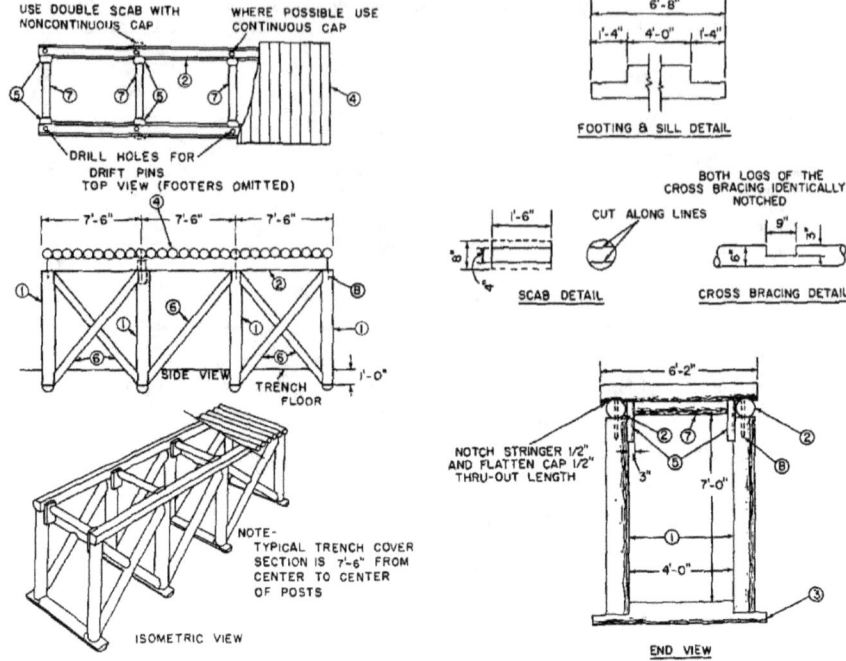

Figure 4-13. Trench section, log construction.

b. Facing Type Revetment. Facing revetment serves mainly to protect revetted surfaces from the effects of weather and damage caused by occupation. It is used when soils are stable enough to sustain their own weight. This revetment (fig. 4-15) consists of the revetting or facing material and the supports which hold the revetting material in place. The facing material may be much thinner than that used in a retaining wall. For this reason, facing type revetments are preferable since less excavation is required. The top of the facing should be set below ground level so that the revetting is not damaged by tanks crossing the emplacement.

    (1) Materials for facing. The facing may be constructed of brushwood hurdles, continuous brush, pole and dimensioned timbers, corrugated metal, or burlap and chicken wire. The method of constructing each type is described below.

    (2) Methods of support. The facing may be supported by -

      (a) Timber frames. Frames of dimensioned timber are constructed to fit the bottom and sides of the position, and hold the facing material apart over the excavated width.

90

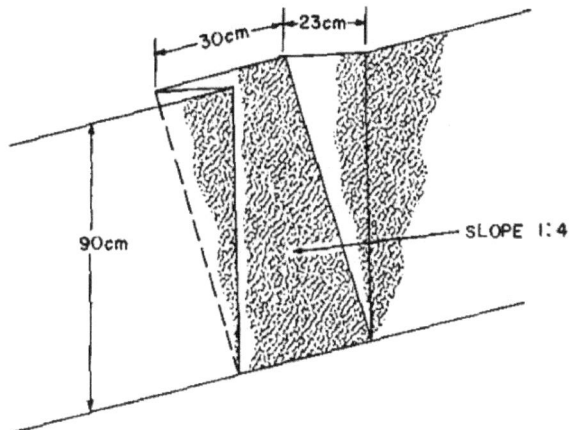

Figure 4-14. Method of sloping earth walls.

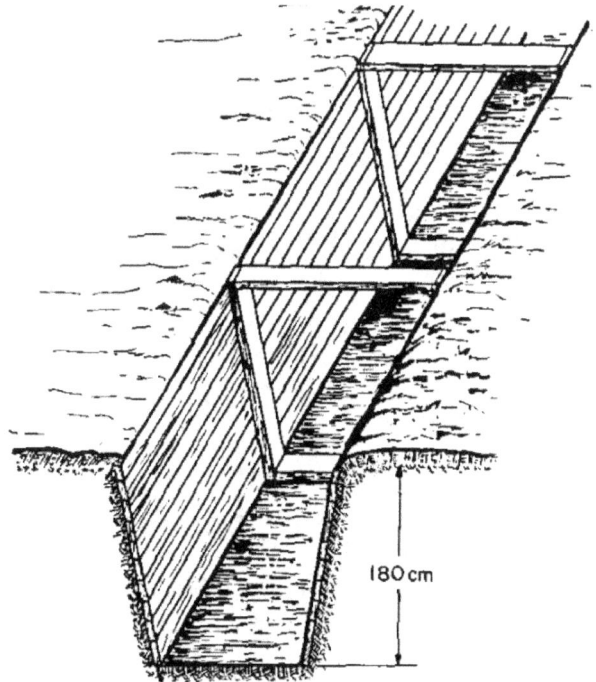

Figure 4-15. Facing revetment supported by frames,

(b) Pickets. Pickets are driven into the ground on the position side of the facing material and held tightly against the facing as shown in figure 4-16 by bracing the pickets apart across the width of the position and anchoring the tops of the pickets by means of stakes driven into the ground and tiebacks.

91

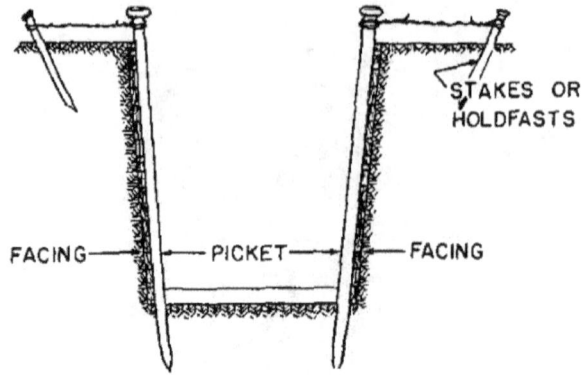

Figure 4-16. Facing revetment supported by pickets.

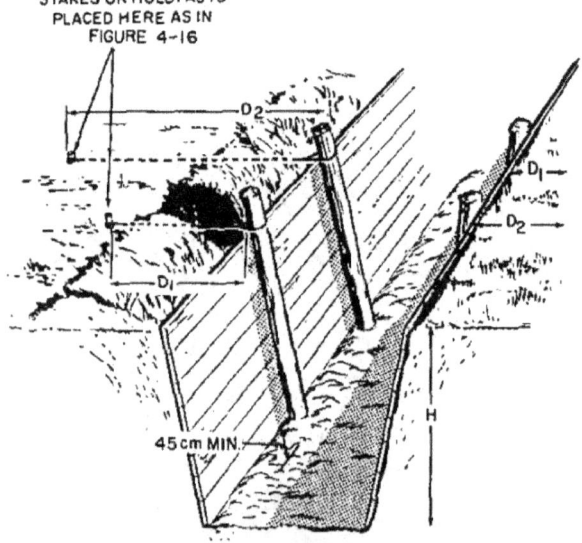

D_1 IS EQUAL TO OR GREATER THAN H
D_2 IS EQUAL TO H+2'

Figure 4-17. Method of anchoring pickets.

(3) Facing type revetments. Facing type revetments may be supported either by timber frames or pickets. The size of pickets required, and their spacing, are determined by the soil and the type of facing material used. Wooden pickets should not be smaller than 7.5 cm in diameter or in the smallest dimension. The maximum spacing between pickets should be about 2 meters. The standard pickets used to support barbed wire entanglements are excellent for use in revetting. Pickets are driven at least 45 cm into the floor of the position. Where the tops of the pickets are to be anchored, an anchor stake or holdfast is driven into the top of the bank opposite

92

each picket and the top of the picket is racked to it as shown in figure 4-17. The distance between the anchor stake and the facing is at least equal to the height of the revetted face, with alternate anchors staggered and at least 60 cm farther back. Several strands of wire holding the pickets against the emplacement walls must be straight and taut. A groove or channel is cut in the parapet to pass the wire through.

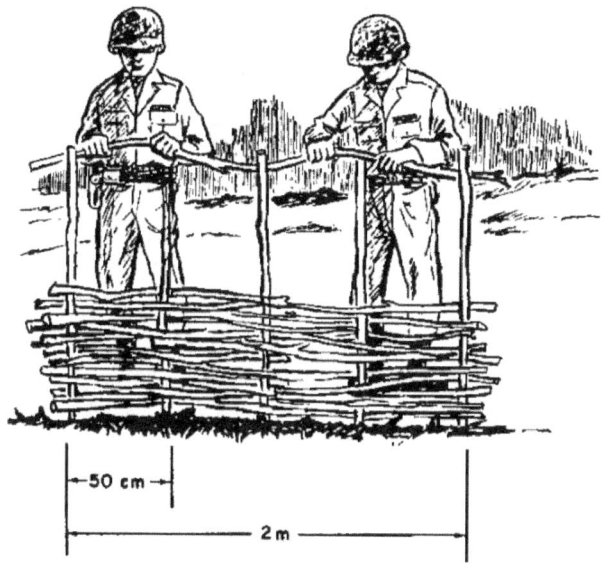

Figure 4-18. Making a brushwood hurdle.

c. Brushwood Hurdle. A brushwood hurdle is a woven revetment unit usually 2 meters long and of the required height. As shown in figure 4-18, pieces of brushwood about 2.5 cm in diameter are woven on a framework of sharpened pickets driven into the ground at 50 cm intervals. When completed, the 2-meter lengths are carried to the position, where the pickets are driven in place and the tops of the pickets are tied back to stakes or holdfasts. The ends of the hurdles are then wired together.

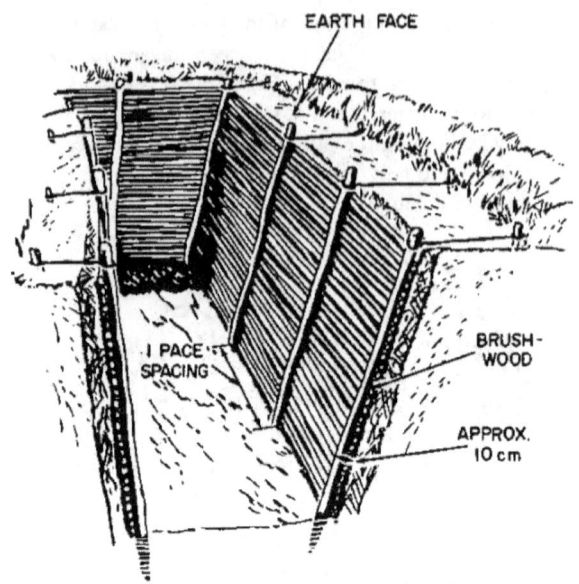

EARTH FACE

I PACE
SPACING

BRUSH-
WOOD

APPROX.
10 cm

Figure 4-19. Continuous brush revetment.

d. Continuous Brush. As shown in figure 4-19, a continuous brush revetment is constructed in place. Sharpened pickets, 7.5 cm in diameter, are driven into the bottom of the trench at 1-pace intervals and about 10 cm from the earth face to be revetted. The space behind the pickets is packed with small straight brushwood laid horizontally and the tops of the pickets are anchored to stakes or holdfasts.

e. Pole and Dimensioned Timber. A pole revetment (fig. 4-20) is similar to the continuous brush revetment except that a layer of small horizontal round poles, cut to the length of the wall to be revetted, is used instead of brushwood. Instead of poles, boards or planks are used if available; they have the added advantage of being more quickly installed. Pickets are held in place by holdfasts or struts.

f. Metal. A revetment of corrugated metal sheets, (1, fig. 4-21) or pierced steel plank may be installed rapidly and is strong and durable. It is well adapted to emplacement construction because the edges and ends of sheets or planks can be lapped as required to produce a revetment of a given height and length. All metal surfaces must be smeared with mud to eliminate possible reflection of thermal radiation and to aid in camouflage. Burlap and chicken wire revetments are installed as shown in 2, figure 4-21. When damaged, corrugated metal forms dangerous sharp edges. Prompt attention should be given to the repair of damaged revetments to prevent injuries to personnel or damage to equipment.

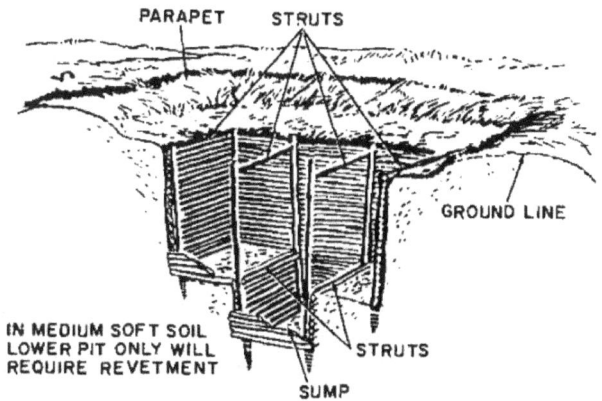

Figure 4-20. Timber revetment using small poles.

Figure 4-21. Types of metal revetment.

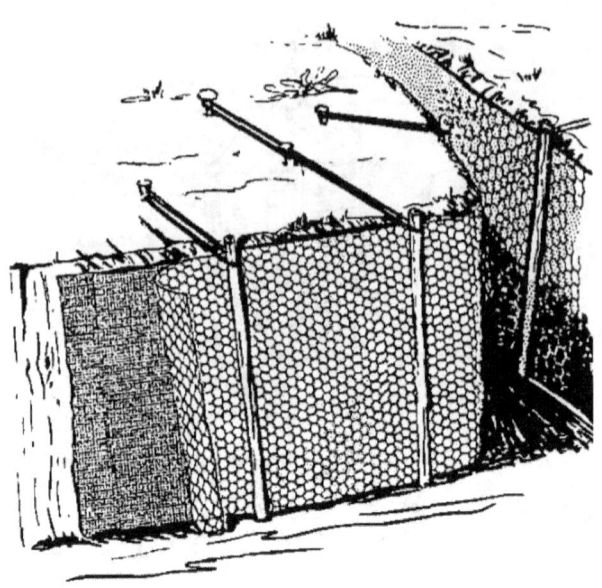

Figure 4-21 - Continued.

4-6. Repair and Maintenance of Trenches

a. Maintenance.

    (1) Drainage. It is important to keep the drainage working properly. If water is allowed to stand in the bottom of a trench, the revetment will eventually be undermined and become useless. Sumps and drains must be kept clear of silt and refuse. Trench boards should be lifted periodically so that the mud can be cleaned out from beneath them.

    (2) Berms. Berms must be kept clear and of sufficient width to prevent soil from the parapets falling into the trench.

  (4) Revetted trenches. When wire and pickets are used to support revetment material, the pickets may become loose, especially after rain. Improvised braces may be wedged across the trench at or near floor level, between two opposite pickets. Anchor wires may be tightened by further twisting. Anchor pickets may have to be driven in further to hold the tightened wires.

  (5) Sandbag revetments. Periodic inspections must be made of sandbags. Any bags that are split or damaged should be replaced.

b. Repair.

    (1) Top of trench. If the walls are crumbling at the top, making the trench wider at ground level, an elbow rest should be cut out of the full width of the berm and about 30 cm deep, or until firm soil is reached. Sandbags or sods are then used to build up the damaged area (1, fig. 4-22).

(2) Bottom of trench. If the trench walls are wearing away at the bottom, place a plank on edge, or shift brushwood as shown in 2, figure 4-22. The plank is held against the trench wall with short pickets driven into the trench floor. If planks are used on both sides of the trench, they are held in position with a piece of timber cut to the right length and wedged between the planks at floor level. Earth is placed in back of the planks.

(3) Collapsed wall. If an entire wall appears to be collapsing, the trench must be completely revetted (para 4-5) or the walls sloped (fig. 4-14) so they will stand. If the walls are permitted to cave in, the trench usually must be widened at ground level which reduces its protective value. Cave-ins should be prevented as far as possible by revetting the trench in time or by one of the remedial measures described above.

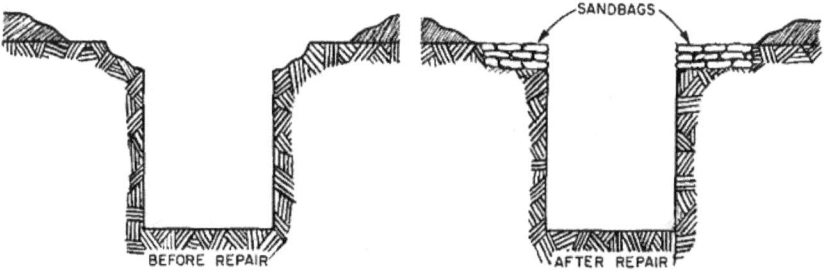

TRENCH DAMAGE AT GROUND LEVEL

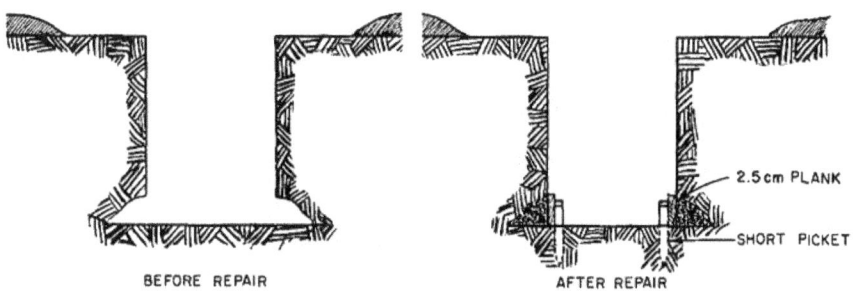

2 DAMAGE NEAR FLOOR LEVEL

Figure 4-22. Trench repair.

Section II. Fieldworks

4-7. Revetments

a. Use of sandbags. Walls are built of sandbags or sod in much the same way as bricks are used. Sandbags are also useful for temporary retaining wall type revetments, especially where silent installation is essential. The two types of sandbags in use are the cotton osnaburg and the polypropylene. Both are used in the same manner but the polypropylene bag will last approximately seven months, twice as long as the cotton osnaburg bag. Sandbags used in revetments rot in damp weather and fade in the sunlight. The useful life of sandbags can be prolonged by filling them with a mixture of dry earth and Portland cement, normally in the ratio of 1 part of cement to 10 parts of dry earth. The cement sets as the bags take on moisture. A ratio of 1 to 6 should be used for a sand-gravel mixture. The filled bags may be dipped in a cement-water slurry as an alternative method.

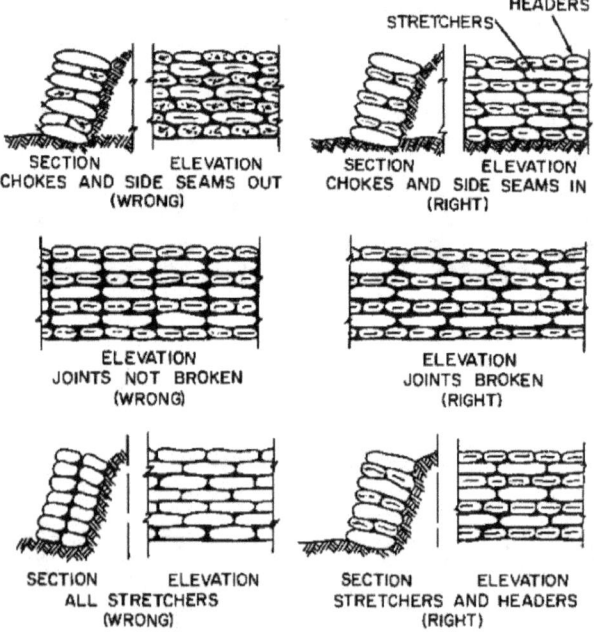

Figure 4-23. Retaining wall revetment.

(1) Construction. As a rule, sandbags are used for revetting only when the soil is very loose and requires a retaining wall to support it and for the repair of damaged trenches. A sandbag revetment will not stand with a vertical face. The face must have a slope of 1:4 and the base must be on firm ground and dug at a slope of 4:1. The sandbag wall should lean against the earth if it is to hold in place (fig, 4-23).

Figure 4-24. Use of combat entrencher to fill sandbags.

    (a) The bags are uniformly filled about three-fourths full with earth or with a dry soil-cement mixture and the choke cords are tied.

    (b) The bottom corners of the bags are tucked in after filling.

    (c) As the revetment is built, the revetted face is made to conform to this slope by backfilling or additional excavation.

    (d) Sandbags are laid so that the planes between the layers have the same pitch as the foundation, i.e., at right angles to the slope of the revetment.

    (e) The bottom row of the revetment is constructed with all bags placed as headers (fig. 4-23), The wall is then constructed using alternate rows of stretchers and headers with the joints broken between courses. The top row of the revetment wall consists of headers.

    (f) All bags are placed so that side seams on stretchers and choked ends on headers are turned toward the revetted face.

(2) Common faults. The common faults in sandbag revetments are illustrated in figure 4-23, Sandbags rot quickly, especially in wet climates. Consequently, considerable maintenance is required.

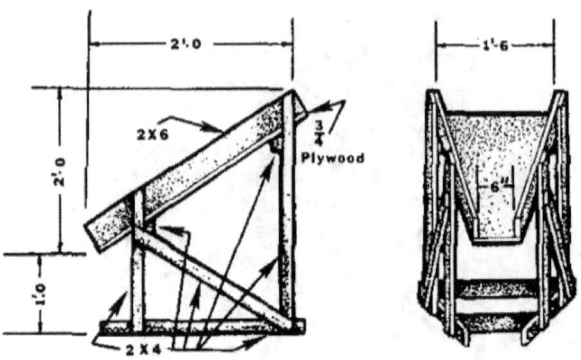

Figure 4-25. Expedient funnel for filling sandbags.

(3) Expedient means of filling sandbags. Often the requirement for filled sandbags far exceeds the capabilities of men using shovels to fill sandbags. A high-speed combat entrenching machine can be used to fill sandbags if local soil is to be used as the filler. The bag is filled by holding it under the discharge conveyor as the entrenching machine is run forward at a slow speed (fig. 4-24). This method will produce filled sandbags at a rate of one every four to five seconds. The spillage can be used to fill sandbags also since it is often loose and easily shoveled. If the sandbags are to be filled from a stockpile of sand or other material, the work can be made easier and the bags filled faster by using the funnel as shown in figure 4-25. The funnel can be constructed using either lumber or steel.

b. Sod Blocks. Thick sod with good root systems provides a satisfactory revetting material. Sod blocks cut into sections about 23 by 46 cm are laid flat, using the alternate stretcher-header method described above for use with sandbags. Sod is laid grass-to-grass and soil-to-soil, except for the top layer which should be laid with the grass upward, to provide natural camouflage. As each layer of sod is completed, wooden pegs are driven through the layers to prevent sliding until the roots grow from layer to layer. Two pegs are driven through each 23 by 46 cm sod. Sod revetment is laid at a slope of about 1 horizontal to 3 vertical.

c. Expedients. In cold weather blocks of ice may be used to construct retaining wall type revetments. They are stacked in the same manner as sandbags or sod. Water is applied to bind them together by freezing. Other expedients include earth-filled packing cases or ammunition boxes. Empty boxes or packing cases are placed in position and nailed to the lids of the layer below; the boxes are filled with earth or rock and the. lids fastened in place. This procedure is repeated for each row. The tops of the revetments are tied to pickets to prevent overturning.

4-8. Breastworks

Breastworks may be substituted for trenches, weapons emplacements, etc., when soil conditions or a high-water table makes excavation to the required depth impossible. Under these circumstances earth must be built up above ground level to form protective walls. This work requires more time and effort than digging trenches of comparable depth. Breastwork defenses are not as good protection against airbursts as excavated positions. They also have serious disadvantages against blast and nuclear radiation.

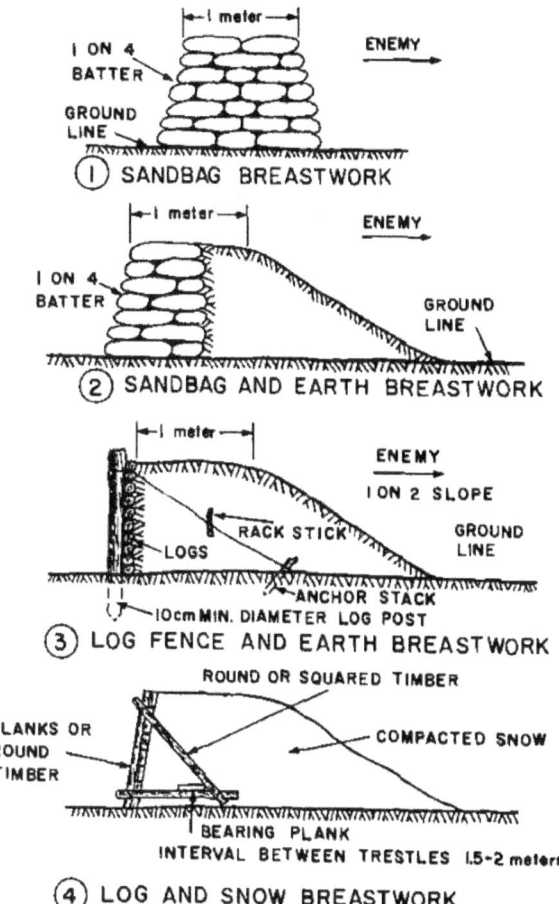

Figure 4-26. Varied types of breastworks.

a. Construction. When breastworks are constructed for fire positions and weapons emplacements their dimensions should conform to excavated positions. A front breastwork should be bulletproof, i.e., of approximately 1 meter minimum thickness. The outer face should be sloped gently; not steeper than 1:2 (fig. 4-26). The inner face should be sloped 1:4 and revetted. A rear breastwork may be similar to the front.

b. Snow Breastworks. Snow breastworks can be constructed as shown in 4, figure 426.

4-9. Snow Defenses

a. Snow as Protective Material. Snow must be packed to be effective against small arms fire. Drifted snow is usually well compacted by the wind. Loose snow has

101

only about half the value of packed snow in resisting penetration but shells and grenades bursting on impact are largely ineffective in loose snow because the fragmentation is blanketed. The thickness of snow required for protection against small arms and shell splinters is as follows:

- Newly fallen snow - At least 4 meters
- Firmly frozen snow - At least 2.5-3 meters
- Packed snow - At least 2 meters
- Ice - At least 30 cm

b. Trenches. In deep snow, trenches and weapons emplacements may be excavated in the snow to approximately normal dimensions. Unless the snow is well packed and frozen, revetment will be required (4, fig. 4-26). In shallow snow, not deep enough to permit excavation to the required depth, snow breastworks must be constructed. These should be of compacted snow, at least 2 meters thick, and revetted.

4-10. Defenses in Tropical Conditions

a. Advantages.
(1) Concealment is comparatively easy.
(2) Timber is readily available.
b. Tools. A variety of cutting tools are required to -
(1) Clear fields of fire.
(2) Cut tree roots during excavation.
(3) Cut timber for overhead cover.
c. Equipment. When large cleared areas are necessary bulldozers with winches or dozers with land clearing blades are required for grubbing trees. Bulldozers can clear from 10,000 to 12,000 square meters of heavy jungle in 8 hours. Dozers with land clearing blades can clear 15,000 to 25,000 square meters of heavy jungle in the same length of time.
d. Drainage. Good drainage is required for all excavations and should be considered in the initial siting of the position. Trenches, shelters, and emplacements are floored as soon as possible. Stone, or brushwood covered with bamboo matting may be used.
e. Overhead Cover. Waterproof material such as building paper should be included in the overhead cover for shelters or trenches and should overlap the sides of the structure about 60 cm. Material used as overhead cover must be well supported and sloped so that water will run off.

4-11. Dummy Earthworks

a. Dummy Trenches. Dummy trenches are dug so as to conceal from the air or ground the true extent of a defended area or locality. Dummy trenches should be dug about 45 cm deep, with brushwood laid in the bottom (1, fig. 4-27). The brushwood has the effect of producing an internal shadow similar to that cast by a deep trench. Parapets must be similar to those of other trenches in the position. False parapets should also be concealed.
b. Dummy Emplacements. The most noticeable feature of a roofed emplacement is the deep internal shadow of its embrasure. This appears to the enemy

from the ground as a black patch of regular shape. Usually, it will appear rectangular if the roof is flat. A rectangular embrasure can be simulated by means of a box placed in the ground, with open end to the front, and covered with earth (2, fig. 4-27). Some attempt at concealment and occasional signs of occupation will add realism.

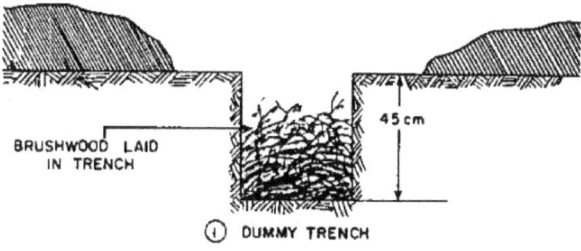

BRUSHWOOD LAID
IN TRENCH

45 cm

① DUMMY TRENCH

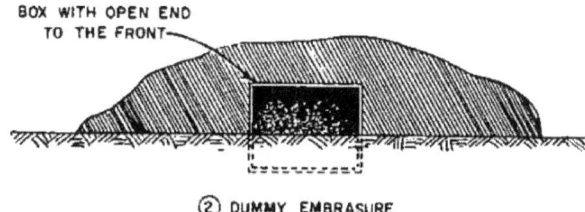

BOX WITH OPEN END
TO THE FRONT

② DUMMY EMBRASURE

Figure 4-27. Dummy earthworks.

4-12. Tunneled Defenses

a. Considerations. Tunnels are not used frequently in the defense of an area due to the time, effort, and technicalities involved; however, they have been used to good advantage. Tunneled defenses can be used when the length of time an area must be defended justifies the effort and the ground lends itself to this purpose.

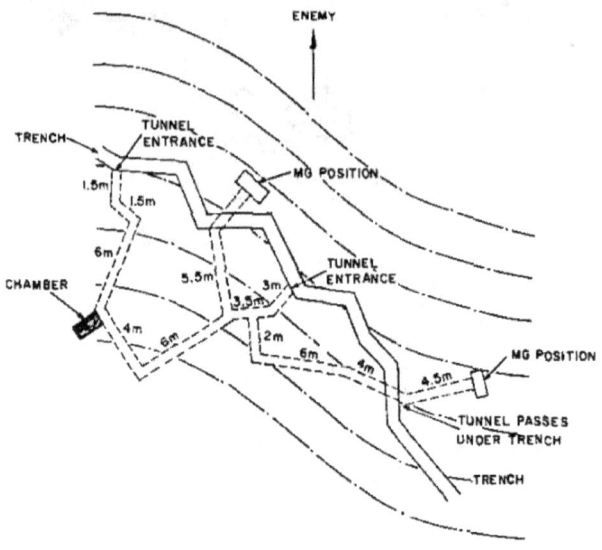

Figure 4-28. Tunneled defenses in Korea.

b. Soil. The possibility of tunneling also depends to a great extent on the nature of the soil, which can be determined by borings or similar means. Tunneling in hard rock is so slow that it is generally impractical. Tunnels in clay or other soft soils are also impractical since they must be lined throughout or they will soon collapse. Therefore, construction of tunneled defenses is usually limited to -

    (1) Hilly terrain - steep hillsides.

    (2) Favorable soil, including hard chalk, soft sandstone, and other types of hard soil or soft rock.

c. Tunnel Examples. A sketch of tunnels constructed in Korea is shown in figure 4-28. The soil was generally very hard and only the entrances were timbered. The speed of excavation, using handtools, varied according to the soil, seldom exceeding 7.5 meters per day. In patches of hard rock, as little as 1 meter was excavated in a day (24 hours). The use of power tools did not alter the speed of excavation significantly. The work was done by engineer units assisted by infantry personnel.

d. Construction. Tunnels of the type shown (fig. 2-48) are excavated about 9 meters (30 ft.) below ground level. They may be horizontal or nearly so.

    (1) Entrances. The entrances must be strengthened against collapse under shell fire and ground shock from nuclear weapons. The first 5 meters from each entrance should be framed with timber supports using 10 cm x 10 cm or comparable timbers.

104

(2) Size. Untimbered tunnels should be about 1 meter wide and 1.5 to 2 meters high.

(3) Chambers. Chambers may be constructed in rock or extremely hard soil without timber supports. If timber is not used the chamber (fig. 4-28) should not be more than 2 meters wide. If timbers are used the width may be increased to 3 meters. The chamber should be the same height as the tunnel and up to 4 meters long.

(4) Grenade trap. These should be constructed at the bottom of straight lengths where they slope. It can be done by cutting a recess about 1 meter deep in the wall facing the inclining floor of the tunnel.

(5) Disposal of soil. A considerable quantity of spoil from the excavated area must be disposed of and concealed. The volume of spoil is usually estimated as one-third greater than the volume of the tunnel. Approximately 100 tons of spoil were removed from the tunnel system shown in figure 4-28.

(6) Concealment. Tunnel entrances must be concealed from enemy observation and it may be necessary to transport spoil by hand through a hand through a trench. Cold air rising from a tunnel entrance may give away the position.

e. Precautions.

(1) Picks and shovels. There is always danger that tunnel entrances will be blocked, trapping the occupants. Picks and shovels must be kept in each tunnel so that men trapped can dig their way out.

(2) Entrances. At least two entrances are necessary for ventilation purposes; whenever possible one or more emergency exits should be provided. These last may be small tunnels whose entrances are normally closed and concealed; a tunnel may be dug from inside the system to within a few feet of the surface so that a breakthrough can be made if necessary.

CHAPTER 5 – OBSTACLE EMPLOYMENT

Section 1. Principles

5-1. Basic Considerations

a. Definition. An obstacle is any terrain feature, condition of soil, climate, or manmade object other than firepower, that is used to stop, delay, or divert enemy movement.

b. Purposes. Obstacles should be included in the overall defense plan to restrict the movement of enemy forces, delay them, or require them to regroup.

c. Tactical Obstacles. The following obstacles are commonly referred to as tactical types:

(1) Antitank obstacles intended to impede or stop the movement of track vehicles across country or on roads;

(2) Antipersonnel obstacles constructed to slow up, confuse, or divert enemy foot troops when they attempt to overrun or infiltrate a defended position or locality;

(3) Antivehicle obstacles including roadblocks, craters and other means that are used to stop or delay enemy wheeled vehicles so they can be brought under aimed fire.

(4) Beach and river line obstacles that delay, obstruct or divert enemy amphibious operations.

d. Observation. Tactical obstacles must be under observation and covered by fire for maximum benefit. An obstacle which is not covered by observed fire may be ineffective or at best lead to a false sense of security.

e. Offensive Use of Tactical Obstacles. Obstacles are used to anchor a flank or flanks of an advancing unit. They may also be used behind enemy lines to delay, disorganize, and harass troop movements and communications, especially when an enemy force is withdrawing. The wide intervals between dispersed units of company size or larger should be blocked by a combination of obstacles and firepower,

f. Nontactical Obstacles. Obstacles falling in this category may be of the same general design as obstacles constructed under tactical conditions, but the same considerations of siting and concealment do not apply. Nontactical obstacles may be used -

(1) For the protection of important installations against infiltration or sabotage.

(2) In civil policing operations to check the movements of rioters or to isolate a section of a town or city.

(3) For administrative purposes.

5-2. Characteristics of Natural Obstacles

Desirable characteristics of a natural obstacle are ease of conversion into a more effective obstacle with a minimum of effort, materials, and time; defilade from enemy observation; location where observation and defensive fires can prevent enemy breaching; and difficulty of bypassing. The most effective natural obstacles against tanks are steep slopes, unfrozen swamps, and broad, deep streams. Rice paddies, lava fields, and similar areas can also be formidable obstacles. Usually time, labor, and materials can be saved by improving natural obstacles rather than constructing artificial ones to serve the same purpose.

a. Steep Slopes. Varying degrees of steepness are required to stop different types of vehicles. Tanks can negotiate slopes as steep as 60 percent. However, trees, unfavorable soil conditions, large rocks and boulders can make slopes of less than 60 percent impassable, even though this would not be true if the same natural features were encountered on level ground. The movement of infantry is also slowed down by steep slopes since movement is slower and the troops tire more rapidly.

b. Escarpments. A steep face of rock is a formidable obstacle to both vehicles and personnel if it is over 1 ½ meters in height.

c. Ravines, Gullies, and Ditches. Ravines, gullies, and ditches are generally obstacles to wheeled vehicles. If they are over 5 meters in width, and approximately 2 meters in depth and the banks are nearly vertical, they are usually effective against tracked vehicles.

d. Rivers, Streams, and Canals. The major obstacle value of rivers, streams, and canals is that they must be crossed by special means, either deep-water fording, surface or aerial. The width, depth, velocity of the water, and bank and bottom conditions determine the ease of crossing a water obstacle by deep-water fording and floating equipment. However, a river over 150 meters wide and over 1 1 ½ meters deep is a major obstacle, limited only by the presence of bridges, favorable sites for amphibious vehicles, and fording sites. The obstacle value of fordable rivers, streams, and canals is significant when the stability of the banks and bottoms is considered. Although a few vehicles may be able to ford a water obstacle, the poor condition of the banks and bottom may prevent further use of the ford without time-consuming improvement of the crossing site. Stream velocity may likewise limit the use of a ford and enhance its value as an obstacle.

e. Frozen Streams. Antitank obstacles (fig. 5-1) can be improvised in frozen streams by cutting an opening about 3 to 4 meters wide in the ice and forcing the cut blocks of ice under the solid surface so the blocks will be carried downstream by the current. The openings are then closed with a light frame covered with cloth, brush, or tar paper with about a 10cm covering of snow. The effectiveness of this type of obstacle depends on keeping the water in the channel from freezing. A well-made trap will be effective for an extended period of time if it is inspected frequently to maintain the snow cover. If the ice freezes solid in the area of the trap, the procedure outlined above must be repeated.

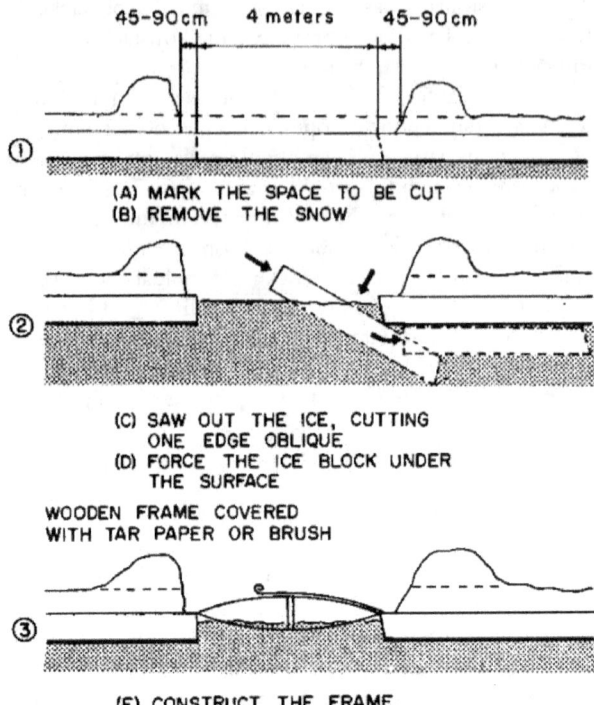

(A) MARK THE SPACE TO BE CUT
(B) REMOVE THE SNOW

(C) SAW OUT THE ICE, CUTTING
ONE EDGE OBLIQUE
(D) FORCE THE ICE BLOCK UNDER
THE SURFACE

WOODEN FRAME COVERED
WITH TAR PAPER OR BRUSH

(E) CONSTRUCT THE FRAME

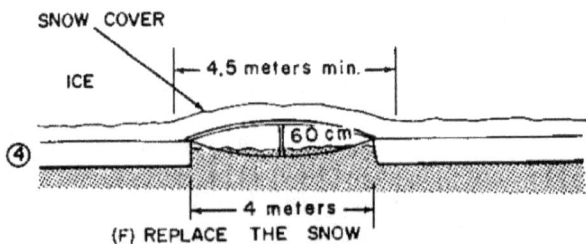

(F) REPLACE THE SNOW

Figure 5-1. Antitank trap in ice.

f. Lakes. Lakes are usually unfordable and unbridged and must be bypassed unless they are frozen solid enough to support vehicles and personnel.

g. Swamps and Marshes. The principal obstacle value of swamps and marshes is the canalization of vehicular movement onto causeways thereby exposing the columns to air or artillery attacks. Swamps and marshes over 1 meter in depth may be better obstacles than rivers, since causeways are usually more difficult to construct than bridges. The physical effort required for foot troops to cross swamps and marshes is an important factor in their usefulness as an obstacle. All roads and causeways through swamps and marshes should be extensively cratered, mined, or blocked by abatis (fig. 7-8).

108

h. Forests. Forests have the effect of canalizing movement, since the roads, trails, and fire breaks through them provide the only means for rapid movement. The obstacle value of a forest is dependent on tree size and density, soil condition, slope, and depth. If the trees are at least 20 cm in diameter and sufficiently close together, they will seriously obstruct or stop the movement of tanks. Even though the trees are seldom close enough together to stop tanks, they may prevent tank movement when they are pushed over and tangled. Much smaller trees (10cm in diameter) will slow and sometimes stop tanks on 20 percent slopes. Tree stumps that are 45 cm in diameter or larger are obstacles to tank movement. Forest undergrowth in the temperate zone is not usually dense enough to seriously obstruct foot movement, but such movement will be slowed significantly by steep slopes, adverse soil conditions, and fallen trees and branches. The most effective way of increasing the obstacle value of forests is to -

(1) Construct abatis (fig. 7-8) or craters.
(2) Place mines along the roads, trails, and firebreaks.
(3) Construct log cribs, hurdles, and post obstacles if the necessary materials are available.

i. Jungle Obstacles. Tropical jungles are important obstacles to the movement of vehicles and personnel. The ground between the trees is usually covered by interwoven vines, bushes, plants, or rotting vegetation. The ground is often swampy or marshy. The tangled undergrowth and overhead foliage limits the visibility and there are few if any paths or trails except those that permit limited foot traffic. Vehicles can seldom operate satisfactorily unless routes are prepared or extensively improved. Foot troops are required to cut trails through the dense undergrowth or move with extreme difficulty. Since the jungle is an effective obstacle to movement, any roads or trails that exist should be blocked and the stream fords and amphibian vehicle entry and exit sites should be mined. If the streams and, rivers provide the best routes, obstacles should be constructed to slow up or prevent the use of floating equipment. The following obstacles are effective against foot movement in the jungle:

(1) Punji jungle trap. Punji traps (fig. 5-2) are most effective when they merge with or resemble natural jungle obstacles. In the defense, they may be used either as barricades around camps or as barriers to impede the advance of an assault. In the offense, they may be constructed behind enemy lines to stop or hinder any retreat. Enemy patrols can be disbanded by skillful use of these traps in connection with covering snipers. A pit 1.5 to 2 meters deep, about the same length and one meter wide is dug in the middle of a jungle trail or at a stream crossing. A number of long, sharp punjis (bamboo spikes sharpened to a needle point) are placed upright in this pit, with the fire-hardened points slightly below ground level (fig. 5-2). The pit is concealed by a flimsy lid consisting of a bamboo lattice covered with a few bamboo creepers and camouflaged with mud or leaves to blend with the surrounding area. Anyone falling into the pit is instantly impaled on the spikes.

Figure 5-2. Punji jungle trap.

(2) Slit trench. A slit trench can be so placed that enemy troops will be likely to use it. Like the cover of the punji pit, the bottom of this trench is false, and underneath it are sharp punjis, which will impale anyone jumping into the trench.

j. Snow. Snow is considered deep for purposes of foot or vehicle movement when the average depth above ground elevation is 1 meter. Snow at this depth and even deeper is not unusual in the Arctic and the northernmost regions of the temperate zone. It is found at these depths also in mountainous regions. Deep snow and the accompanying ice and intense cold combine to make obstacles of major significance. Deep snow is an obstacle to movement of both foot troops and vehicles. It also blankets terrain features such as boulders, rocky areas, ditches, small streams and fallen trees so as to effectively impede movement. The obstacle value of snow can be increased by-

    (1) Erecting snow fences or breaks so that the prevailing winds will accelerate the accumulation of snow into drifts to form snow obstacles of packed snow.

    (2) Building snow walls (fig. 5-3) as obstacles against armor. The snow must be packed hard for this purpose. Walls of this type are most effective when they are sited on an upgrade.

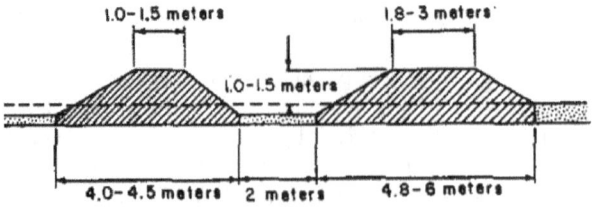

Figure 5-5. Antivehicular obstacle of packed snow.

k. Deserts. The obstacle value of deserts is that specially equipped vehicles and specially trained personnel are required to operate successfully in this

110

environment. Minefields are comparatively easy to install and relocate in the desert and the prevalent winds quickly cover up the usual signs of mine installation.

i. Built-Up Areas. The natural obstacle of built-up areas can be increased by cratering streets, demolishing walls, overturning or derailing street or railroad cars, and constructing roadblocks from steel rails, beams, and rubble. When combined with mines and barbed wire, such obstacles are effective against vehicles and personnel.

Section II. Artificial land obstacles

5-3. Basic Considerations

a. Definition. An artificial obstacle is any manmade object constructed to hinder movement. Artificial obstacles include minefields, antitank ditches, contaminated areas, hedgehogs, road craters, demolished bridges, and barbed wire. They may be constructed entirely on land or partially under water as in the case of beach and river line obstacles.

b. Use. Major types of artificial obstacles are discussed separately in subsequent chapters; however, they are normally used in conjunction with natural obstacles and in combinations of two or more types of artificial obstacles. When artificial obstacles are used in barriers, a variety of them should be used, when practicable, to increase effectiveness and as an aid to surprise and deception. Obstacles can be divided into three groups according to their uses. Seldom does an obstacle fall clearly into one of these three groups. More often than not an obstacle may be used for two or three purposes. This arbitrary classification of obstacles merely clarifies their primary uses.

(1) Protective. Protective obstacles are those obstacles used to provide security. Obstacles of this type are usually artificial and include such items as wire, minefields, and various warning devices. They are intended primarily to prevent the enemy from making a surprise assault from areas close to a position.

(2) Defensive. Defensive obstacles are obstacles used to delay the enemy force in areas where it can be engaged with heavy, intense, defensive fire. They may be either natural or artificial. A defended roadblock or an obstacle in front of a defensive position which stops or delays the enemy force once it is in range of defensive weapons are examples of this type. Defensive obstacles should be covered by appropriate fire, kept under observation, and should be employed in conjunction with protective obstacles,

(3) Tactical. Tactical obstacles are obstacles used to break up enemy attack formations and canalize the enemy force into areas where it is blocked by defensive obstacles or can be brought under intensive defensive fires. Tactical obstacles delay, harass, or demoralize the enemy by forcing him to employ dangerous or exhaustive breaching measures.

5-4. Principles of Employment

a. Coordination with Tactical Plan. Obstacles should be coordination with the tactical plan. All obstacles should contribute to the success of this plan, and all units concerned should know the location of and understand the purpose and type of obstacles employed. In addition, all concerned should know when the obstacles are to be executed, and how long they are to be defended. Only by coordination with all elements can an integrated plan be prepared that will use all defensive measures to their best advantage against the enemy.

    b. Covering by Observation and Fire.

    (1) Observation. If accurate fire is to be delivered on an obstacle or obstacle system, it must be under observation. The observation and defense of obstacles for close-in defense is the responsibility of the unit occupying the ground. However, when an obstacle system covers a large area, observation is normally the responsibility of roving patrols, an outpost system, Army aviation, or tactical air. Their final defense is a mission for mobile forces that can be brought quickly to any point of the system. At times, it is not feasible to have an obstacle under direct observation. When this is the case, warning devices or alarm systems such as trip flares, boobytraps, in connection with noisemakers should be used.

    (2) Fire. Covering an obstacle by fire usually means the difference between causing the enemy only small delay and annoyance and forcing him into a costly engagement.

    a. Both antivehicular and antipersonnel obstacles should be covered by both antivehicular and antipersonnel fire. Fire that covers antipersonnel obstacles should not only be capable of discouraging breaching, bypass, or capture by personnel but should also be capable of stopping any vehicles that may be used in the assault. Also, antivehicular obstacles must be covered by fire that will not only destroy vehicles but will prevent troops from breaching the obstacles and clearing a path for the vehicles.

    b. Obstacles are best covered by direct-fire weapons, but when this is not feasible, observed artillery fire and tactical air should be used. Artillery covering obstacles should be prepared to deliver fire that is effective against both personnel and vehicles. When it is impossible to cover obstacles by fire, they should be contaminated or heavily boobytrapped to cause the enemy to employ dangerous and exhaustive breaching measures.

    c. Employment in Conjunction with Natural and Other Artificial Obstacles. It is fundamental that an obstacle system should usually be as difficult to bypass as it is to breach except when the obstacle is intended to divert or deflect the enemy rather than to delay or stop him. Artificial obstacles must be sited to take full advantage of natural and other artificial obstacles, so as to keep logistic and construction requirements to a minimum. Natural obstacles are improved and exploited to the fullest extent as described in paragraph 5-2.

    d. Employment in Depth. Obstacles do not seriously hamper the enemy's movement until they overload or heavily tax his breaching capabilities. This cannot be accomplished unless obstacles are employed in depth. With the exception of contaminated areas, it is usually prohibitive in time and materials to construct a large deep area of continuous obstacles. The same end is accomplished by constructing successive lines of obstacles, one behind the other, as time and conditions permit. These successive lines require the enemy force to continually deploy and regroup, thus dissipating, canalizing, and dividing its effort until friendly forces can destroy it or force its withdrawal.

    e. Camouflage and Concealment.

    (1) Camouflage. Obstacles should be camouflaged or employed in such a way that they come as a surprise to the enemy. When the enemy has no prior knowledge of an obstacle, he has to reduce it without benefit of prior planning. If the obstacle is defended the defender has the advantage of the enemy's first reaction, which is usually confusion, and the enemy may be caught without the men and material to breach the obstacle.

    (2) Siting. Proper siting is often the easiest solution to obstacle camouflage problems. Large obstacle systems cannot be concealed by siting alone, but when proper advantage is taken of the terrain and the obstacles are located in folds of the ground, around blind curves in roads, or just over the tops of hills, they can be made inconspicuous from the enemy's ground observation. To help camouflage obstacles from aerial observation, regular geometric layouts of obstacles and barrier systems should be avoided and phony obstacles used to confuse the enemy as to the exact location and extent of the system.

    (3) Concealment. The best way to conceal an obstacle usually is to postpone its execution or construction as long as possible, without interfering with its readiness when needed. This cannot be done when large barrier systems are involved but is possible when preparing obstacles to block narrow avenues of approach, such as roads or bridges. Obstacles created by demolitions lend themselves readily to this procedure. When their use is contemplated they should be completely prepared for firing at the last minute.

    f. Provision for Lanes and Gaps. Whenever obstacles are employed around a defensive position or area, lanes or gaps through the system are left and concealed. These lanes are provided so that patrols, counterattacks, and friendly troops on other missions may move through the system without difficulty. Under normal circumstances the lanes or gaps necessary to mount a general offensive through the obstacle system are not provided during construction, but prepared later when the need for them arises. It is important that there be a sufficient number of lanes to allow for alternate use and that they be concealed and changed periodically to ensure that they are not discovered by the enemy. Prior plans must exist to ensure that all lanes or gaps can be blocked quickly when enemy action is expected. Lanes and gaps should be covered by fire to preclude the possibility of the enemy rushing through them before they can be closed.

    g. Affording No Advantage to the Enemy. Enemy forces may use certain obstacles to an advantage as they are breached or assaulted. Antitank ditches should be so constructed as to be useless to the enemy as fighting trenches. Log cribs should be so located that the enemy cannot deliver effective fire on defending weapons while using the crib as a breastwork. Care should be taken that obstacles are not located so that the enemy can use hand grenades against the defenders from cover or concealment provided by the obstacles. Barbed wire, mines, and boobytraps should be used extensively to deny use of any cover or concealment that might be provided to the enemy by natural or artificial obstacles. Care should be taken to guard against the inadvertent placing of an obstacle which might later hinder friendly maneuver.

5-5. Minefields

Minefields are not only an obstacle to the advance of the enemy but unlike obstacles of a passive nature, they can also inflict significant casualties; therefore, minefields are considered the best form of artificial obstacle. The installation of minefields changes favorable terrain to unfavorable terrain and materially enhances the strength of the defense system. Mines and minefields are covered in FM 5-31, FM 20-32, and TM 9-1345-200.

5-6. Caltrops

a. Description. A caltrop (fig. 5-4) has four sharpened prongs oriented so that one prong will always be vertical regardless of how the caltrop lands. The prongs are 3/32 inches in diameter and 1 ½ inches long.

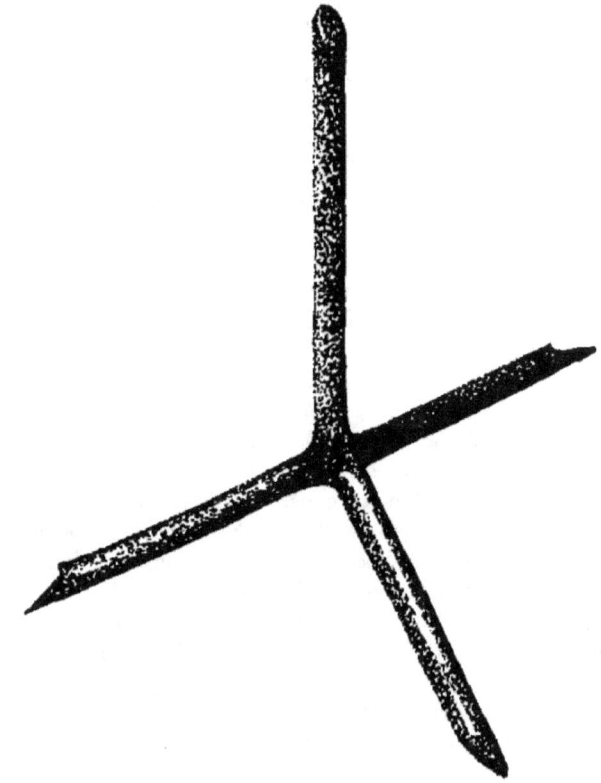

Figure 5-4. Caltrop.

b. Uses. Caltrops are employed as antipersonnel obstacles either by themselves or in conjunction with barbed wire. When emplaced with a density of 38 per meter of barrier front, an effectiveness equivalent to triple standard concertina is achieved. Caltrops are designed to cause injury by penetrating the footgear of a man who steps on one. Serious injury will result if a man quickly falls to the ground to avoid small arms or artillery fire. Caltrops can be dispensed by hand, from the rear of a truck, or from fixed and rotary winged aircraft.

5-7. Barbed Wire Entanglements

Obstacles constructed from barbed wire are simple, flexible and effective against personnel. They may also be used to impede the movement of vehicles. Barbed wire entanglements are discussed in detail in chapter 6.

5-8. Antivehicular Obstacles

In defensive positions, antivehicular obstacles are used to obstruct gaps between natural obstacles or they can be placed in a continuous line of considerable length in open terrain. Antivehicular obstacles are usually employed in conjunction with wire entanglements, minefields, and other obstacles. Under some conditions they may be continuous in areas just inland of beaches. Antivehicular obstacles are discussed in detail in chapter 7.

SECTION III. Beach & river line obstacles

5-9. Responsibility

In unilateral Army shore-to-shore amphibious operations, Army forces are responsible for the installation and removal of beach and underwater obstacles. In joint Army-Navy amphibious operations, Navy forces are normally responsible for removal of obstacles on a hostile shore seaward from the high waterline. The underwater demolition teams (UDT) of the Navy have the responsibility of removing obstacles from the high waterline to the 3-fathom (5.54 meters) line. Beyond that point Navy minesweepers clear boat and shipping lanes. The responsibility for installation of beach and underwater obstacles in friendly territory is assigned by the commander of the forces involved.

5-10. Ocean Beach Defenses

An assault across an ocean normally involves a ship-to-shore assault in which the enemy requires adequate anchorages for assault shipping and shore for beaching large landing craft. Where the overwater distance is short, however, or where the enemy can develop a nearby base in neutral or unoccupied territory, shore-to-shore operations are practicable, using smaller craft capable of landing troops and vehicles at almost any point. Against either of these types of operation, Anti-boat and antipersonnel obstacles at wading depths are desirable in most situations. Antipersonnel obstacles so located, however, are not effective against large landing craft if the latter can beach at the waterline or can side-carry floating causeways and use them to get ashore.

a. Beach Obstacles. Beach obstacles are designed to force landing craft to unload at low tide several hundred yards seaward of the high watermark. Thus, on beaches with gradual slopes assaulting infantry must cross a wide expanse of obstacle-studded beach covered by heavy defensive fire before reaching the high watermark.

At high tide, beach and underwater obstacles should be covered by just enough water so that they cannot be seen by personnel in landing craft. When landing craft strike the obstacles they are disabled and the assaulting troops are forced to disembark in deep water.

b. Anti-boat Obstacles. Anti-boat obstacles are constructed at varying heights so they are about 30 to 60 cm below the surface of the water at high tide, echeloned in depth in various arrangements of which those shown in figure 5-5 are typical.

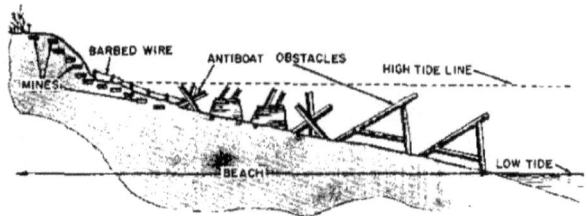

Figure 5-5. Anti-boat obstacles in beach defense.

5-11. River Line Defenses

All possible means of crossing are studied, including assault boats, footbridges, fixed and floating vehicular bridges, and the use or rehabilitation of existing bridges. In addition to Anti-boat and antipersonnel obstacles, the defender considers the use of obstacles to hamper the enemy's bridging activities and his installation of booms and other protective devices to protect bridges.

5-12. Effective Obstacles

a. Siting. The basic requirements for artificial obstacles and their employment apply equally to beach and river line obstacles. Of particular importance are the requirements that artificial obstacles be used to exploit natural obstacles, that they be inconspicuous, be kept under surveillance, and be capable of being covered by fire. Gaps and lanes are provided and are marked or referenced for the use of friendly troops, Anti-boat obstacles selected for use should be of a type which will be effective against boats which can operate in the surf, current, and various wind conditions to be expected. They are sited for maximum obstacle effect at the tide stage at which an assault is probable and for maximum effectiveness against amphibious tracked and wheeled vehicles,

b. Beach Slopes. Due to tide and current action, beaches and river lines tend to fall into two general types - those with steep slopes into deep water, and those with gradually sloping bottoms for a considerable distance offshore. Each type has advantages and disadvantages for the defense. The steep slope prevents debarkation until boats reach the beach, but it renders placing underwater obstacles more difficult. The gentle slope facilitates placing obstacles but it also allows the attacking troops to disembark while still afloat.

(1) Steep. For beaches with steeply sloping bottoms, provision should be made for stopping landing craft offshore in deep water. The obstacles may include mines of various types anchored just below the water line,

floating log booms anchored or tied to shore, which may have mines attached, and heavy chains of wire rope stretched between pile dolphins. Preferably such obstacles should be submerged so as to be out of sight but tide variations may make this impracticable. In such cases a compromise must be made between minimum visibility and maximum practicable effectiveness. Where possible, provision is made for adjusting the height of log booms and the like, to conform with water level fluctuations.

(2) Gradual. For beaches with gradually sloping bottoms, the defense attempts to prevent landing craft from reaching the beach or from reaching wading or fording depth for personnel and vehicles. In addition to obstacles of the types described above, in water of wading depth the bottom is covered thoroughly with underwater wire entanglements of all types. These must be anchored in place very securely to prevent damage from surf or currents and so that both enemy and friendly fire will tend to form tangles rather than to clear lanes. In such entanglements, channels provided for passage of friendly small boats may be closed rapidly by the use of anchored concertinas or weighted spirals.

c. Employment in Depth. Beach obstacles are typically established in bands in depth, as follows:

(1) Anti-boat obstacles. These are located from wading depth at low tide to wading depth at high tide.

(2) Barbed wire entanglements. These are placed from wading depth at high tide, inshore across the width of the beach.

(3) Antivehicular and antipersonnel obstacles. These are installed beginning at low waterline and extending inshore across the width of the beach. Mines or other obstacles are normally installed at the beach exit.

(4) Antivehicular ditches. These are dug beginning at the inshore edge of the beach, where concealment is possible.

(5) Other obstacles. These are located inshore of the beach area, in the same manner as obstacles for land defense.

CHAPTER 6 – BARBED WIRE ENTANGLEMENTS

Section I. Materials

6-1. Concept

a. Purpose. Barbed wire entanglements are artificial obstacles designed to impede the movement of foot troops and, in some cases, tracked and wheeled vehicles. The materials used in constructing barbed wire entanglements are relatively lightweight and inexpensive, considering the protection they afford. Barbed wire entanglements can be breached by fire but are rapidly built, repaired, and reinforced.

b. Siting and Layout. To be effective, barbed wire entanglements are sited and laid out to meet the following requirements.

    (1) Under friendly observation, covered by fire, and where practicable, protected by antipersonnel mines, flame mines, trip flares, and warning devices,

    (2) Concealed from enemy observation as far as practicable by incorporating terrain features such as reverse slopes, hedges, woods, paths and fence lines.

    (3) Erected in irregular and nongeometrical traces.

    (4) Employed in bands or zones wherever practicable.

    (5) Coordinated with other elements of the defense.

c Classification. Entanglements are classified according to their use and their depth and whether fixed or portable.

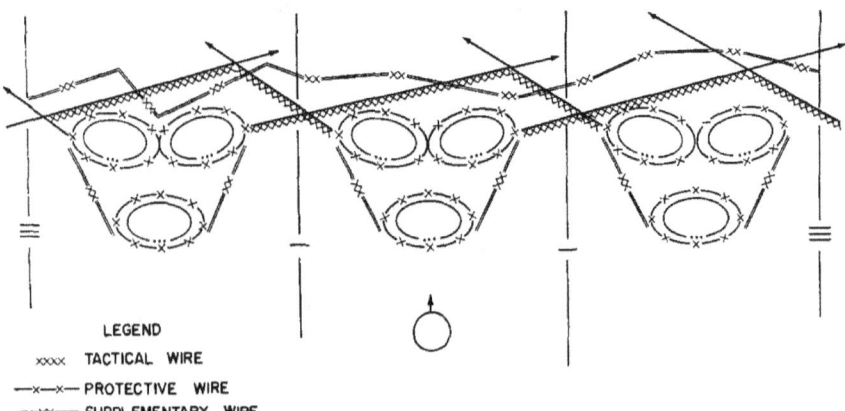

LEGEND

xxxx TACTICAL WIRE
—x—x— PROTECTIVE WIRE
—xx— SUPPLEMENTARY WIRE

Figure 6-1. Schematic layout of barbed wire entanglements in a defensive area.

    (1) Use. Entanglements are classified by use as tactical, protective, or supplementary. The employment of these types in a defensive area is shown schematically in figure 6-1.

        (a) Tactical. Tactical wire entanglements are sited parallel to and along the friendly side of the final protective line. They are

118

used to break up enemy attack formations and to hold the enemy in areas covered by the most intense defensive fire. Tactical entanglements extend across the entire front of a position but are not necessarily continuous.

(b) Protective. Protective wire entanglements are located to prevent surprise assaults from points close to the defense area. As in the case of all antipersonnel obstacles, they are close enough to the defense area for day and night observation and far enough away to prevent the enemy from using hand grenades effectively from points just beyond the obstacle, normally 40 to 100 meters. Protective wire surrounds the individual units of a command, usually the platoons (fig. 6-1). These entanglements should be connected to entanglements around other platoons by supplementary wire to enclose the entire defensive positions. Protective entanglements are erected around rear-area installations in the same manner and to serve the same purpose as protective wire around defensive positions in forward areas. Protective wire also includes the entanglements which should be installed over the tops of installations provided with overhead cover (fig. 6-2).

(c) Supplementary. Supplementary wire entanglements in front of the forward edge of the battle area are used to conceal the exact line of the tactical wire. To the rear of the FEBA, supplementary wire is used to enclose the entire defensive position by connecting the protective wire entanglements. Supplementary wire entanglements used to break up the line of tactical wire should be identical to the tactical' wire entanglements and constructed simultaneously with them whenever possible.

(2) Depth. Entanglements are classified by depth as belts, bands, or zones.

(a) Belt. A belt is an entanglement one fence in depth.

(b) Band. A band consists of two or more belts in depth, with no interval between them. The belts may be fences of the same type, or the band may be composed of two or more fences of different types.

(c) Zone. A zone consists of two or more bands or belts in depth, with intervals between them.

(3) Equivalent effectiveness. Entanglement depths are also described or specified in terms of comparative effectiveness. Tactical wire entanglements should be equivalent in effectiveness to three belts of 4and 2-pace double apron fence whenever possible. Protective wire may employ any type of entanglement provided its effectiveness is at least the equivalent of that of the 4and 2-pace double apron fence. Supplementary wire should have an effectiveness equivalent to that of the type of wire it supplements. It should be equivalent to tactical wire or equivalent to the type of protective wire being used if it connects the outer perimeters of protective wire at the flanks and rear.

(4) Portability.
    (a) Fixed entanglements are those types which must be erected in place and which cannot be moved unless completely disassembled.
    (b) Portable entanglements are those types which can be moved without complete disassembly. Portable entanglements have been developed for one of the following reasons; to permit assembly in rear areas, with ease of transportation and rapid installation in forward positions. For the temporary closing of gaps or lanes which can be reopened quickly for patrols or counterattacking forces.

    d. Lanes and Gaps. Lanes and gaps are provided for the passage of patrols, working parties, and attacking or counterattacking forces. When not in use they are kept closed by the use of portable obstacles covered by fire. In barbed wire zones, lanes and gaps are staggered on a zigzag pattern.

    e. Uses.
    (1) Outpost area. The combat outposts should be surrounded with wire entanglements. These entanglements should be carefully sited to serve as both protective and tactical wire and must be covered by small arms fire. The wire obstacle should be supplemented by antipersonnel mines, warning devices, and boobytraps.
    (2) Battle position. In the battle area, each company defense position is normally surrounded by a wire entanglement which is connected laterally across the front to the entanglements surrounding the other units in the position.
    (3) Artillery and reserve area. Wire entanglements are used in the outer protection of howitzer positions. Heavier weapons, and shelters or other installations in the reserve area, are similarly protected if justified by the situation.

    Antipersonnel obstacles. Barbed wire entanglements, trip flares, noisemakers, and antipersonnel mines are sited to warn against enemy patrol action or infiltration at night; to prevent the enemy from delivering a surprise attack from positions close to the defenders; and to hold, fix or delay the enemy in the most effective killing ground. Such obstacles should be near enough to defensive positions for adequate surveillance by the defenders by night and day and far enough away to prevent the enemy from using hand grenades against the defender from points just beyond the obstacles.

Figure 6-2. Protective wire on top of overhead cover.

f. As Roadblocks. A series of barbed wire concertinas as shown in figure 6-3 will stop wheeled vehicles. A series of these blocks placed about 10 meters apart should be used. The ends of adjacent coils are wired together and the obstacle lightly anchored at the sides of the road. The block should be sited to achieve surprise.

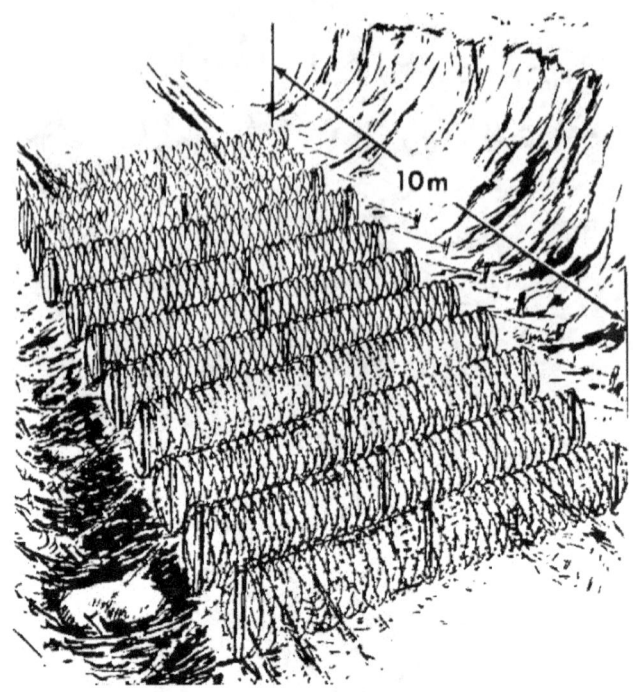

Figure 6-3. Concertina roadblock.

g. To Strengthen Natural Obstacles. Deep rivers, canals, swamps, and cliffs which form effective delaying obstacles to infantry, and thick hedgerows, fences, and woods, which are only partial obstacles, can be improved by lacing with barbed wire, by the addition of parts of standard fences on one or both sides, or by entangling with loose wire.

6-2. Standard Barbed Wire

a. Description. Standard barbed wire is 2 strand twisted No. 12 steel wire with 4-point bars at 10 cm spacing (fig. 6-4).

Figure 6-3. Standard barbed wire.

b. Handling. In handling barbed wire, the standard barbed wire gauntlets (FSN 8415268-7873) shown in figure 6-4 or heavy leather gloves are worn. They permit faster work and avoid cuts and scratches. As an added safety precaution, the wire should be grasped with the palm down.

c. Issue. Barbed wire is issued in reels (fig. 6-5) containing about 400 meters of wire. The wire weighs 40.8kgs and the reel 0.6kgs. In building a fence, two men carry one reel.

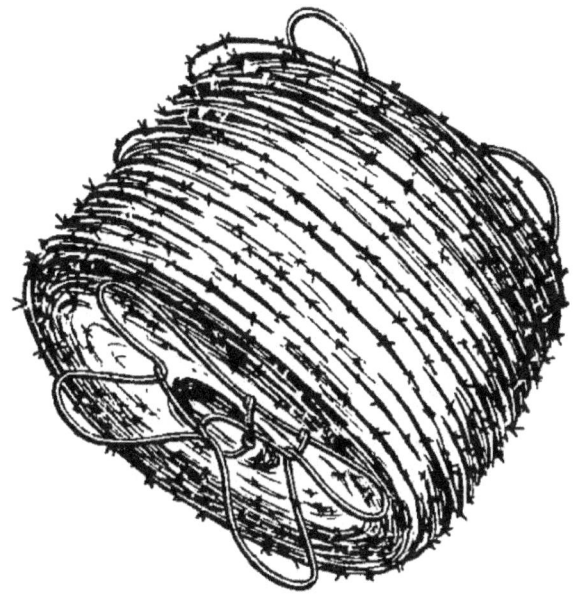

Figure 6-5. Barbed wire reel.

d. Bobbins. Bobbins (fig. 6-6) holding about. 30 meters of wire are prepared, normally in rear areas, for use in building short lengths of fence and in repairing entanglements. In use, two men handle one bobbin. One unwinds the bobbin while the other installs the wire. Two or more men may make the bobbins as follows:

(1) The bobbin sticks are prepared.
(2) The reel is rigged on an improvised trestle or other support.
(3) One man unrolls and cuts 30-meter lengths of wire, fastening one end of each to the trestle.
(4) The wire is wound in figure-of-eight shape on the bobbin sticks.

A piece of white tracing tape should be tied to the loose end of the wire to facilitate finding it.

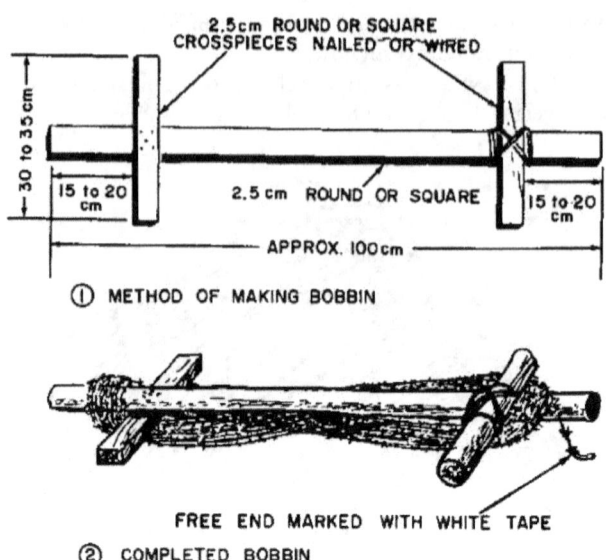

2.5cm ROUND OR SQUARE
CROSSPIECES NAILED OR WIRED

30 to 35 cm

15 to 20 cm

2.5 cm ROUND OR SQUARE

15 to 20 cm

APPROX. 100 cm

① METHOD OF MAKING BOBBIN

FREE END MARKED WITH WHITE TAPE

② COMPLETED BOBBIN

Figure 6-6. Barbed wire bobbin.

6-3. Barbed Steel Tape

a, Description. Barbed steel tape is 1.91 cm wide steel tape that is .55-mm thick with a barbed interval of 1.27 cm (fig. 6-7).

b. Handling. In handling barbed tape, heavy barbed tape gauntlets (FSN 8415-926-1674) should be used instead of the standard gauntlets. Small metal clips on the palm and fingers prevent the barbs of the tape from cutting the leather (fig. 6-8).

c. Issue. The barbed tape is issued in 50 meter reels weighing 2.4 kg. There are six reels to a cardboard carrying case.

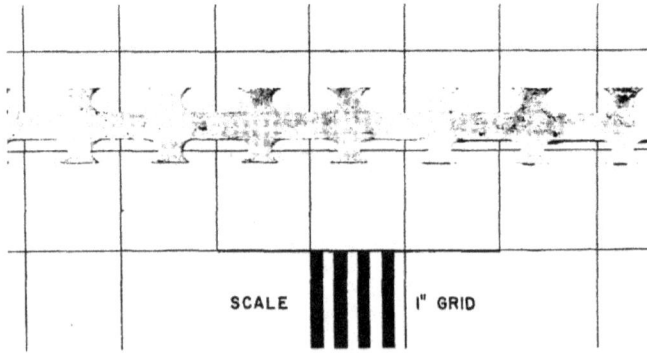

SCALE   1" GRID

Figure 6-7. Barbed steel tape.

d. Barbed Tape Dispenser. A dispenser (fig. 6-9) is required to install barbed tape. It consists of a frame to hold the 50-meter reel of barbed tape and two sets of rollers. The reel is inserted on the spindle and the tape is threaded through the two sets of parallel rollers. The outside set of rollers are then turned 90° in a clockwise direction. The hinged arm of the frame is then closed and locked in place by the

124

frame of the rotating rollers. As the tape unwinds from the reel, the two sets of rollers oriented 90° to each other impart a twist to the tape. To be effective the barbed tape must be twisted as it is installed.

Figure 6-8. Barbed tape-wire gauntlets.

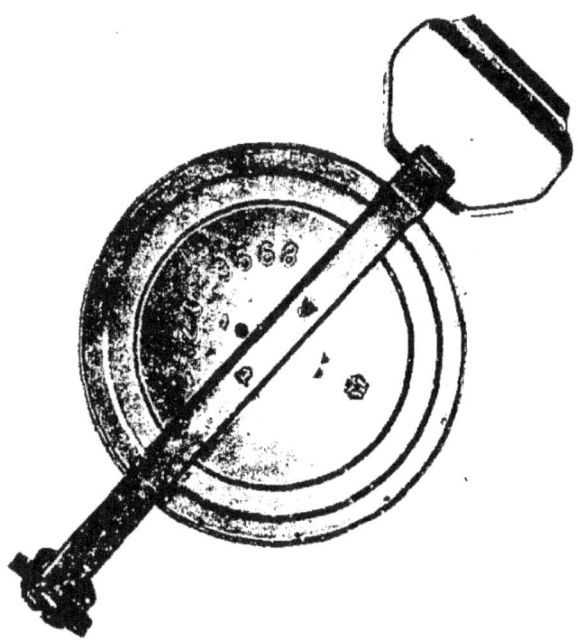

Figure 6-9. Barbed tape dispenser with 50-meter reel of tape.

e. Uses. Barbed tape can be used in place of standard barbed wire in most all cases except when it is to be repeatedly recovered and reused. The most effective fence that can be constructed using barbed tape is the double apron fence.

(1) The principal advantages of barbed tape are its size and weight. For equal lengths, barbed tape occupies a third of the space and weighs a third as much as standard barbed wire. A double-apron fence constructed with barbed tape is more difficult to breach by crawling

125

through than one constructed with standard barbed wire because the barbs of the barbed tape are closer together. Because of the flat configuration, it is more difficult to cut barbed tape with wire cutters.

(2) At the present time, the major disadvantage of barbed tape is the breaking strength. Standard barbed wire is twice as strong. Installation of barbed tape requires a dispenser. A major problem could arise if the dispenser is not available. The tape is not recoverable to its original condition. However, it may be recovered on bobbins in the twisted condition. Barbed tape is more easily cut by shell fragments than standard barbed wire. Barbed tape can also be cut with a bayonet.

6-4. Pickets

Wire entanglements are supported on metal or wood pickets.

a. Metal Pickets. Metal pickets are issued in two types, screw and U-shaped. The standard lengths are short or anchor, medium, and long (fig. 6-10). The U-shaped picket also comes in an extra-long length. Pickets that are serviceable are recovered and used again.

(1) Screw picket. The screw picket is screwed into the ground by turning it in a clockwise direction using a driftpin, stick, or another picket inserted in the bottom eye of the picket for leverage. The bottom eye is used in order to avoid twisting the picket. Screw pickets are installed so that the eye is to the right of the picket, as seen from the friendly side, so standard ties can be easily made. Screw pickets tend to be less rigid than other types but are desirable because they can be installed rapidly and silently. When silence is necessary, the driftpin used in installing the pickets should be wrapped with cloth.

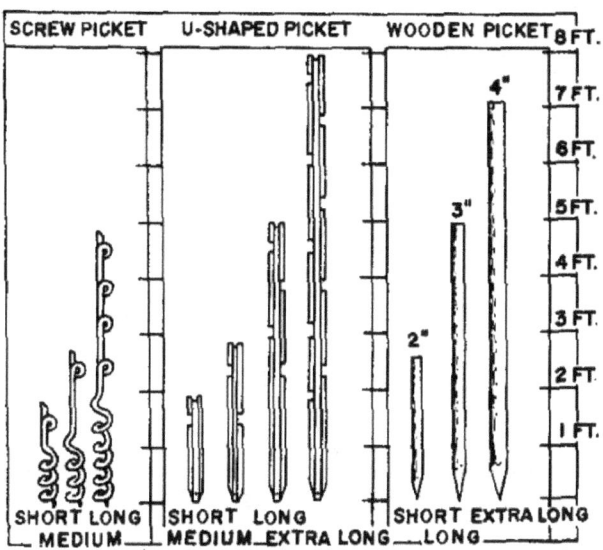

Figure 6-10. Pickets for use with barbed wire.

(2) U-shaped picket. The U-shaped picket is a cold-formed steel picket of U-shaped cross section, pointed at one end for driving. It is notched for wire ties and the pointed end has a punched hole for wires used in bundling the pickets. U-shaped pickets are driven with a sledge hammer. A stake driving cap (FSN 5340-220-8457) is used on tip of the picket to prevent a sledge from deforming it. Driving the pickets is noisier than installing screw pickets. However, noise may be cut down somewhat by placing a piece of rubber tire over the driving face of the sledge. The pickets are rigid and sturdy when properly installed and are preferable to screw pickets in situations where noise is not a disadvantage and time is available. The pickets are driven with the hollow surface or concave side facing enemy fire because small arms projectiles ricochet from the convex side. An expedient picket driver which can be locally fabricated is shown in figure 6-11. Constructed as shown it weighs approximately 12 kilograms and is operated by two men. One man holds the picket in a vertical position while the other slides the driver over the picket and starts it into the ground. Then, both men work the picket driver up and down until the required depth is reached. Short pickets can be driven by turning the picket driver upside down and using the head as a hammer. The bucket of a f front loader can be used to push U-shaped pickets into the ground if the tactical situation permits the use of equipment.

(3) Arctic adapter. For erecting barbed wire obstacles with U-shaped drive pickets under conditions where frozen ground prevents driving the pickets, an Arctic adapter is available for anchoring the pickets. The adapter is made of steel and consists of a base plate equipped with an adjustable channel receptacle and two anchor pins. It is anchored by driving the anchor pins through holes in the base plate into the ground.

127

One anchor pin drive sleeve with driving pin is provided with each 20 adapters to facilitate anchor pin emplacement. When adapters are not available, a hole can be started with a pick and the picket can be frozen in place by pouring water and snow into the hole.

b. Wooden Picket. Expedient wooden pickets of several types may be used.

(1) Round poles 10 cm in diameter are cut to standard picket lengths, sharpened on one end, and driven with a maul. The pickets are used without peeling the bark to prevent the wire from sliding on the picket and to simplify camouflage. Longer pickets are required in loose or sandy soil or when driving through a snow cover. The driving of wooden pickets is not as noisy as the driving of steel pickets, and the noise can be reduced further by fastening a section of tire tread over the face of the hammer or maul. For driving in hard earth, picket tops are wrapped with wire to avoid splitting. Pickets of hardwood, properly installed, are sturdy and rigid,

(2) Dimension lumber ripped to a square cross section may be used instead of round poles. This is equally satisfactory except that it is more difficult to camouflage. Such pickets may be dipped in camouflage paint prior to driving.

(3) Standing trees and stumps may be used as pickets when their location permits.

c. Reference. Table 6-1 lists information pertaining to materials used in the construction of barbed wire entanglements.

6-5. Concertina Fencing

(a) Standard Barbed Wire Concertina. The standard barbed wire concertina (fig. 6-12) is a commercially manufactured barbed wire obstacle made of a roll of single-strand, high strength, spring-steel wire with 4-point barbs attached at 5 cm spacing. Wires forming the coils are clipped together at intervals so that the concertina opens to a cylindrical shape 15 meters long and 90 centimeters in diameter. The concertina is easily opened and collapsed and can be used repeatedly because the wire returns to its original shape after a crushing force is applied and then removed. The wire is much harder to cut than standard barbed wire. The concertina weighs 25.4kgs.

Material	Approx weight, kg	Approx length, m	No. carried by one man	Approx weight of man-load kg
Barbed wire reel	41.5	400	½	21
Bobbin	3.5–4.0	30	4–6	14.5–24.5
Barbed tape dispenser	0.77	0.45	20	15.5
Barbed tape carrying case	14.5	300	1	14.5
Standard barbed tape concertina	14	15.2	1	14
Standard barbed wire concertina	25.4	15.2	1	25
Expedient barbed wire concertina	13.5	6.1	1	13.5
Screw pickets:				
Long	4	1.6	4	16.3
Medium	2.7	0.81	6	16.3
Short	1.8	0.53	8	14.5
U-shaped pickets:				
Extra long	7.25	2.4	3–4	21.8–29.0
Long	4.5	1.5	4	18.1
Medium	2.7	0.81	6	16.3
Short	1.8	0.61	8	14.5
Wooden pickets:				
Extra long	7.7–10.5	2.13	2	15.4–20.8
Long	5.4–7.25	1.5	3	16.3–21.7
Short	1.4–2.7	0.75	8	11.0–21.7

Table 6-1. Wire and Tape Entanglement Materials

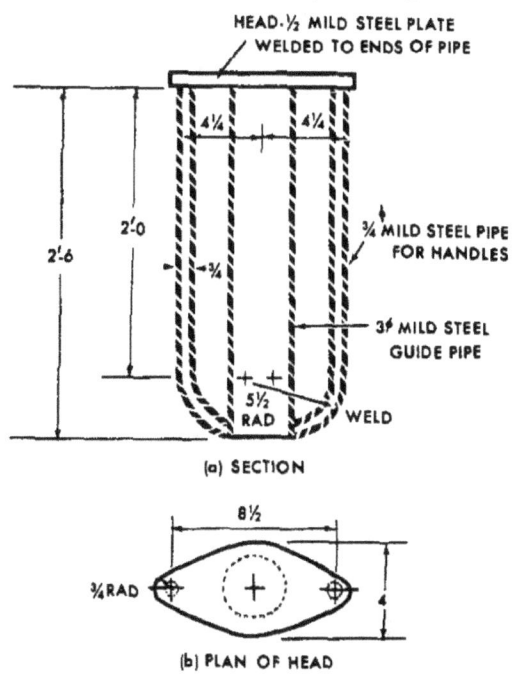

(a) SECTION

(b) PLAN OF HEAD

Figure 6-11. Expedient picket driver.

(1) Handling.

    (a) To open concertina. The collapsed concertina is tied with plain wire bindings attached to the quarter points of a coil at one end of the concertina. In opening the concertina, these bindings are removed and twisted around the carrying handle for use in retying the concertina when it is again collapsed. Four men open a concertina and extend it to the 15-meter length, with one man working at each end and others spaced along its length to ensure that it opens and extends evenly. When necessary, two men can easily open a concertina by bouncing it on the ground to prevent snagging as they open it.

    (b) To collapse concertina. Two men can collapse a concertina in the following manner: First all kinks in coils are removed. Loose clips are then tightened or replaced with plain wire. To close the concertina, one man stands at each end of it and places a foot at the bottom of the coil and an arm under the top of the coil. The two men walk toward each other closing the concertina by feeding the wire over their arms and against their feet. When closed, the concertina is laid flat and compressed with the feet. The concertina is tied with plain wire bindings.

    (c) To carry concertina. One man easily carries the collapsed concertina by stepping into it and picking it up by the wire handles attached to the midpoints of an end coil.

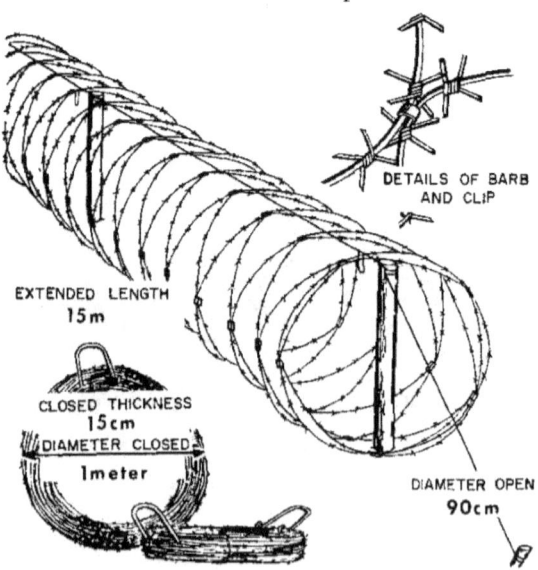

DETAILS OF BARB AND CLIP

EXTENDED LENGTH
15 m

CLOSED THICKNESS
15 cm
DIAMETER CLOSED
1 meter

DIAMETER OPEN
90 cm

Figure 6-12. Standard barbed wire concertina.

(2) Staples. Improvised staples approximately 45 cm long and made of 1/2-inch drift pins or similar material are used to fasten the bottoms of concertina fences securely to the ground.

130

b. Barbed Steel Tape Concertina. Barbed tape concertina comes in a diameter of 85 cm and an expanded length of 15.2 meters. It is formed of barbed tape wrapped around a high strength, spring steel, core wire. Its configuration, method of handling, and method of employment are similar to standard barbed wire concertina. One role weighs only 14 kg.

Section II. Construction procedures

6-6. Organization of Work

Table 6-2 gives the materials and man-hours required for entanglements of the various types. The normal sizes of work crews are given in the descriptions of the entanglements. For each construction project, the senior noncommissioned officer divides his crew into groups of approximately equal size, based on his knowledge of the skill and speed of each man. He organizes them in such a way that construction proceeds in proper order and at a uniform rate. Each individual must know exactly what his group is to do and his job in the group. Each man should have barbed wire gauntlets. The sequence of operations for each fence is given in the paragraph describing the erection of the fence. The sequence that is outlined should be followed, and as experience is gained, the size and composition of the groups may be varied. For each section of entanglement, all fence-building operations normally proceed from right to left, as one faces the enemy. It may, however, be necessary to work from left to right, and men should, if time permits, be taught to work in either direction. In case of heavy casualties, senior officer or NCO will decide what wires, if any, are to be omitted.

Type of entanglement	Pickets				Barbed wire No. of 400 m, 41.5 kg reels [1]	No. of concertinas [4]	Staples	Kgs of materials per lin m of entanglement [2]	Man-hours to erect 300 m of entanglement [3]
	Extra long	Long	Medium	Short					
Double-apron, 4- and 2-pace	..	100	...	200	14–15(19)[5]	...	...	4.6(3.5)[6]	59
Double-apron, 6- and 3-pace	.	66	...	132	13–14(18)[5]	...	...	3.6(2.6)[6]	49
High wire (less guy wires)	.	198	.	....	17–19(24)[5]	...	..	5.3(4.0)[6]	79
Low wire, 4- and 2-pace	.	...	100	200	11(15)[5]	...	...	3.6(2.8)[6]	49
4-strand fence	.	100	...	2	5–6(7)[5]	...	...	2.2(1.8)[6]	20
Double expedient concertina	..	101	...	4	3	100	295	6.9	40
Triple expedient concertina	51	101	...	7	4	148	295	10.4	99
Triple standard concertina	..	160	...	4	3(4)[5]	59	317	7.9(5.4)[5]	30

[1] Lower number of reels applies when screw pickets are used; high number when U-shaped pickets are used. Add difference between the two to the higher number when wood pickets are used.
[2] Average weight when any issue metal pickets are used.
[3] Man-hours are based on the use of screw pickets. With the exception of the triple-standard concertinas, add 20 percent to the man-hours when driven pickets are used. With experienced troops, reduce man-hours by one-third. Increase man-hours by 50 percent for nightwork.
[4] Based on concertinas being made up in rear areas and ready for issue. One expedient concertina opens to 8-meter length, as compared with 15 meters for a standard concertina; it requires 92 meters of standard barbed wire, also small quantities of No. 16 smooth wire for ties.
[5] Number of 300 m, 14.5 kg barbed tape carrying cases required if barbed tape is used in place of barbed wire.
[6] Kgs of materials required per linear meter of entanglement if barbed tape is used in place of barbed wire and barbed tape concertina is used in place of standard barbed wire concertina.

Table 6-2. Material and Labor Requirements for 800-Meter Sections of Various

a. Construction at Night. For night construction, the following additional preparations are made:
(1) Tracing tape should be laid from the materials dump to the site of work and then along the line of fence where possible.
(2) Materials should be tied together in man loads and pickets bundled tightly to prevent rattling.
(3) Wire fastenings of wire coils and pickets should be removed and replaced with string which can easily be broken.

131

(4)   A piece of tape should be tied to the ends of the wire on each reel or bobbin.

b. Supervision. Proper supervision of entanglement construction includes the following:

(1)   Proper organization of the work into tasks.

(2)   Making sure the tasks are carried out in the proper sequence.

(3)   Prevention of bunching and overcrowding of personnel.

(4)   Making sure the wires are tightened properly and spaced correctly.

(5)   Checking ties to see that they are being made correctly and at the right points.

c. Construction in Combat Areas. When working in close proximity to the enemy, the necessary precautions include -

(1)   Provision of security around the work party.

(2)   Silence.

(3)   No working on enemy side of fence unless absolutely necessary.

(4)   Use of screw pickets, if available.

(5)   Men not working should lie down near start of work until they can continue their work.

(6)   Individual weapons must be kept nearby at all times.

d. Wire Ties. Wires are tied to pickets by men working from the friendly side of the wire and picket, stretching the wire with the right hand as the tie is started. The four ties used in erecting wire entanglements are shown in figure 6-13. Barbed tape is tied in the same manner as standard barbed wire.

(1)   Top-eye tie. The top eye is used to fasten standard barbed wire to the top eye of screw pickets. It is made in one continuous movement of the left hand (fig. 6-14) while the right hand exerts a pull on the fixed end of the wire. This is a secure tie, is quickly made, and uses only a short piece of wire.

TOP EYE TIE

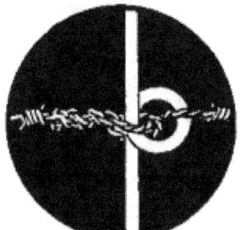
INTERMEDIATE-EYE TIE

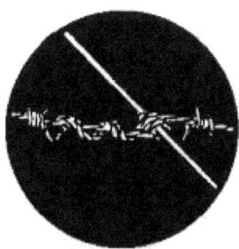
APRON TIE

POST TIE

Figure 6-13. Ties for erecting entanglements as seen from friendly side.

   (2) Intermediate-eye tie. This tie is used to fasten standard barbed wire to eyes other than the top eye, in screw pickets. It is made as shown in figure 6-15. This tie and the other ties described below require more time to make than the top-eye tie and each uses several centimeters of wire. In making the intermediate eye tie shown in figure 6-15, the following points are especially important:

      (a) The right hand reaches over the fixed wire and around the picket, with the palm down. The left hand holds the fixed end for tension.

      (b) The loops are removed from the free end and wrapped around the picket.

      (c) One side of the loop should pass above the eye and the other side below the eye.

   (3) Post tie. Standard barbed wire is fastened to wooden pickets or to the steel U-shaped picket with the post tie shown in figure 6-16. The wire should be wrapped tightly around the post to keep the barbs from sliding down. With the U-shaped picket, the wire wrapping is engaged in a notch in the picket. The method is essentially the same as that of the intermediate-eye tie.

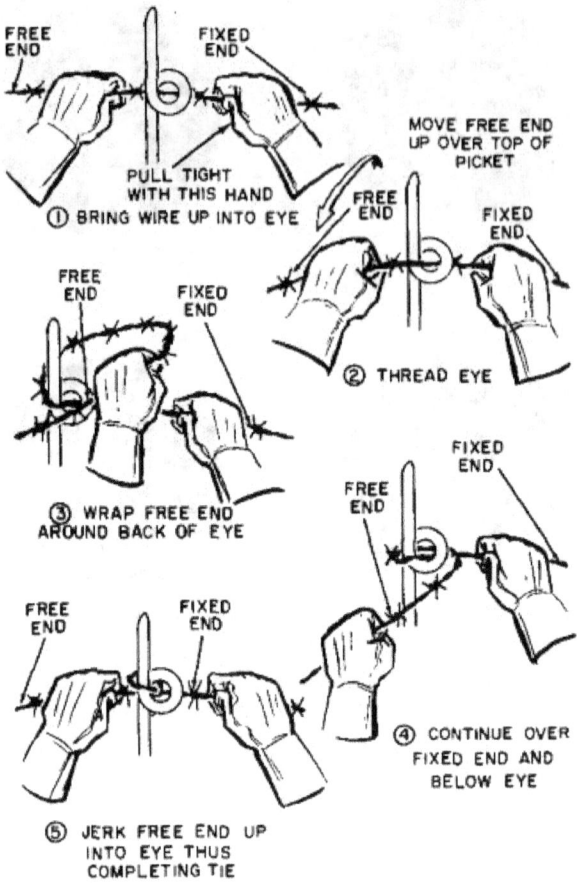

FREE END FIXED END

MOVE FREE END UP OVER TOP OF PICKET

PULL TIGHT WITH THIS HAND
① BRING WIRE UP INTO EYE

FREE END FIXED END

FREE END FIXED END

② THREAD EYE

FREE END FIXED END

③ WRAP FREE END AROUND BACK OF EYE

FREE END FIXED END

FREE END FIXED END

④ CONTINUE OVER FIXED END AND BELOW EYE

⑤ JERK FREE END UP INTO EYE THUS COMPLETING TIE

Figure 6-14. Top-eye tie.

(4) Apron tie. The apron tie is used whenever two wires that cross must be tied together. It is tied in the same manner as the post tie except that a wire is substituted for the post (fig. 6-17).

(5) Barbed tape splices. Connecting slots at each end of a 50-meter reel provide a quick method of splicing reels of barbed tape. Barbed tape may also be spliced by interlocking the twisted barbs of two separate lengths, then completing the splice by twisting a short piece of wire to each end of the area where spliced.

e. Method of Installing Wires.

(1) The end of the wire is attached to the first anchor picket. This is the picket at the right end of a section of entanglement, from the friendly side. Fences are built from right to left as this makes it easier for a right-handed man to make the ties while remaining faced toward the enemy.

(2) A bar is inserted in the reel and the reel is carried for 23 to 27 meters allowing the wire to unreel from the bottom. This is done on the friendly side of the row of pickets to which the wire is to be tied.

(3) Slack is put in the wire by moving back toward the starting point; the ties are then made by two men leapfrogging each other. If available, two men can be assigned to make the ties as the reel is unwound.

(4) Tightening Wire. After a wire is installed it can be tightened, if necessary, by racking with a driftpin or short stick (fig. 6-18). Wires should not be racked at ties or where they intersect other wires because this makes salvage of the wire very difficult. Fences are similarly racked to tighten them when they sag after having been installed for some time. Wires should be just taut enough to prevent them from being easily depressed by boards, mats, or similar objects thrown across them. If wires are stretched too tightly they are more easily cut by fragments. Barbed steel tape must never be tightened by racking.

6-7. Four-Strand Cattle Fence

a. Description. The four-strand center section of a double apron fence can be installed rapidly to obtain some obstacle effect, and aprons can be added later to develop it into a double apron fence. In country where wire fences are used by farmers, obstacles in the form of four-strand cattle fences (fig. 6-19) will blend with the landscape. Their design should follow as closely as possible the local custom, usually wooden pickets at about 2 to 4-pace intervals with four horizontal strands of barbed wire fixed to them. They should be sited along footpaths and edges of fields or crops, where they will not look out of place. If conditions permit, this fence may be improved by installing guy wires in the same manner as the diagonal wires of the double apron fence. All longitudinal wires of this fence must start and end at an anchor picket.

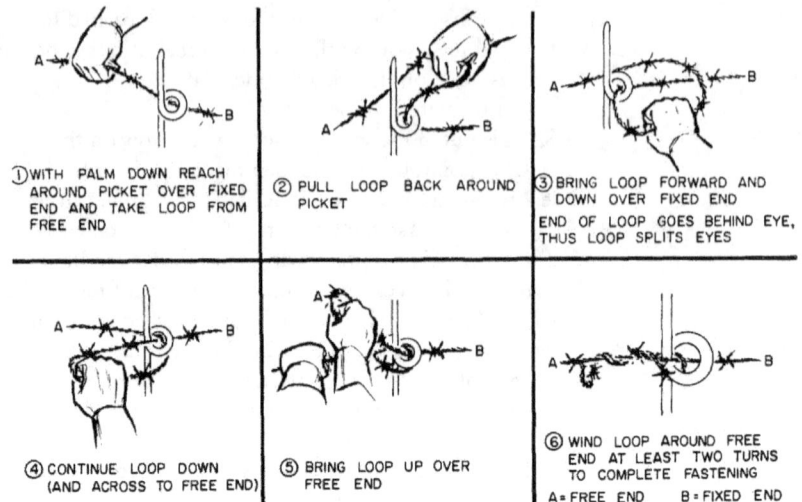

Figure 6-15 Intermediate-eye tie.

b. Construction. Eight men may be employed on short sections of this fence and up to 16 men on 300-meter sections. The two operations are laying out and installing pickets and installing wire.

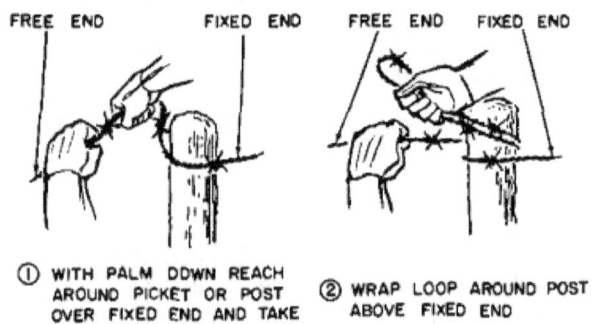

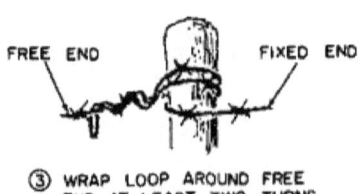

Figure 6-16. Post tie.

(1) First operation. The working party is divided into two groups of approximately equal size. The first group carries and lays out long

136

pickets at 3-meter intervals along the centerline of the fence, beginning and ending the section with an anchor picket and including anchor pickets for guys if needed. The second group installs the pickets.

(2) Second operation. As the first task is completed, men move individually to the head of the fence and are organized into teams of two or four men to install wires. For four man teams, two men carry the reel and two men make ties and pull the wire tight. For two-man teams, the wire must first be unrolled for 50 to 100 meters, then the men come back to the head of the work and make the ties, or the wire may first be made up into bobbins to be carried and unwound by one man while the other man makes the ties. The first team installs the bottom fence wire, and drawing it tight and close to the ground. Succeeding teams install the next wires in order.

6-8. Double-Apron Fence

a. Types. There are two types of double apron fence, the 4and 2-pace fence and the 6 and 3-pace fence. The 4and 2-pace fence (fig. 6-20) is the better obstacle of the two and is the type more commonly used. In this fence the center pickets are 4 paces apart and the anchor pickets are 2 paces from the line of the center pickets and opposite the midpoint of the space between center pickets. The 6 and 3-pace fence follows the same pattern with pickets at 6and 3-pace intervals. For this fence, less material and construction time are required, but the obstacle effect is substantially reduced because with the longer wire spans it is easier to raise the lower wires and crawl over or under them. Except for picket spacing, the 4and 2-pace and the 6and 3-pace fences are identical. Only the 4and 2-pace fence is discussed in detail.

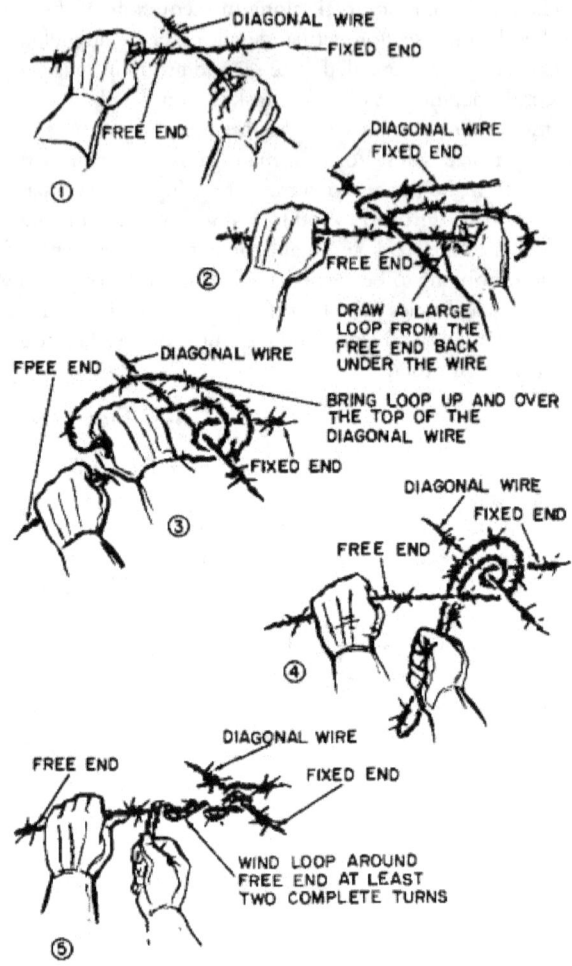

Figure 6-17. Standard barbed wire apron tie.

b. Construction. A 300-meter section of either type of double-apron fence is a platoon task normally requiring 1V6 hours, assuming 36 productive men per platoon. There are two operations in building a double apron fence: laying out and installing pickets and installing wire. The first operation is nearly completed prior to starting the second. The second operation is started as men become available and the first operation has moved far enough ahead to avoid congestion. A platoon is normally assigned to build a 300-meter section.

    (1) First operation. The working party, if not organized in three squads, is divided into three groups of approximately equal size. One squad lays out the long pickets along the center line of the fence at 4-pace intervals at the spots where they are to be installed and with their points toward the enemy. Another squad lays out the anchor pickets, with points toward the enemy and positioned 2 paces each way from the centerline

138

and midway between the long pickets (fig. 6-21). The spacing is readily checked with a long picket. The third squad installs all the pickets, with the help of the two other squads as the latter finish the work of laying out the pickets. When installed, the lower notch or bottom eye of the long pickets should be approximately 10 cm off the ground to make passage difficult either over or under the bottom wires.

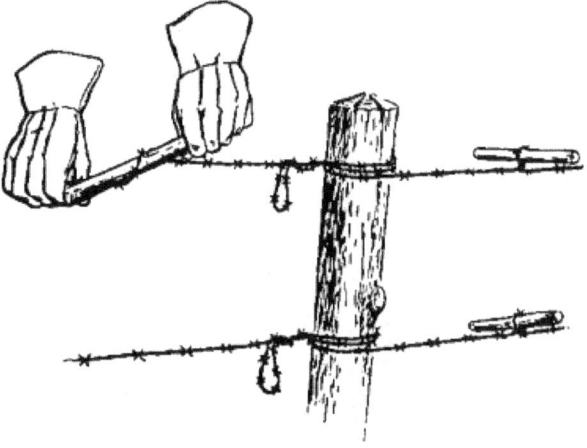

Figure 6-18. Tightening wire by racking.

(2) Second operation. As the groups complete the first operation, they return to the head of the fence and begin installing wire.

Figure 6-19. Four-strand cattle fence as viewed from the enemy side.

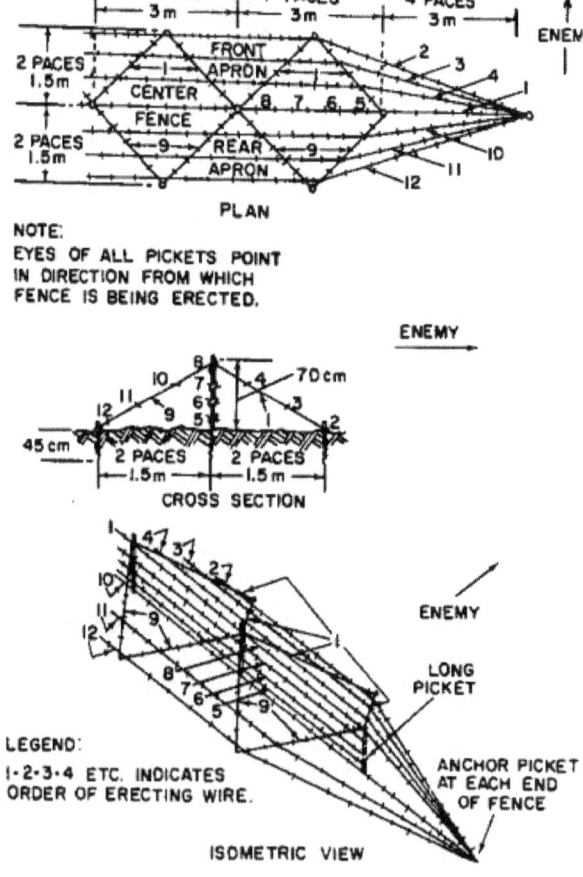

Figure 6-20. Double apron fence.

140

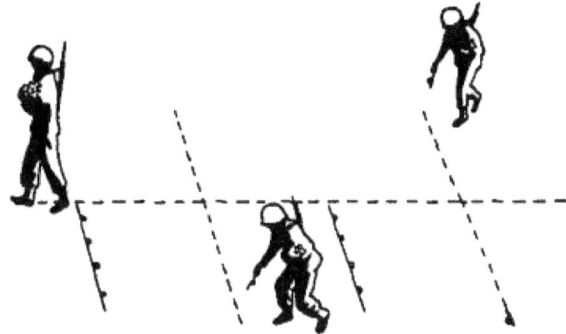

Figure 6-21. Laying out anchor pickets.

The order in which the wires are installed is shown in figure 6-20 and is further illustrated in figure 6-22. Care must be taken to avoid having any of the men cut off between the fence and the enemy. The men are divided into two or four-man groups and proceed to install the wires in numerical order; that is, as soon as the men installing one wire have moved away from the beginning of the fence and are out of the way, the next wire is started. Installation is as follows:

(a) The No. 1 wire is the diagonal wire on the enemy side and is secured with a top-eye tie to all pickets. It is important to keep this wire tight.

(b) The No. 2 wire is the tripwire on the enemy side of the fence and is secured to both diagonals just above the anchor picket with the apron tie. This wire must be tight enough and close enough to the ground to make passage over or under the wire difficult.

(c) The No. 3 wire is an apron wire on the enemy side of the fence. It is secured to the first diagonal wire, and thereafter to each alternate diagonal, and then to the last diagonal wire. The No. 4 wire is also an apron wire on the enemy side of the fence. It is secured to the first diagonal wire (No. 1), thereafter to the diagonal wires which are not tied to the No. 3 wire, and then to the last diagonal wire. Apron wires Nos. 3 and 4 are equally spaced along the diagonal wire.

(d) The No. 5 wire is the first one which is not started from the end anchor picket. It is started at the first long picket, and ended at the last long picket. It is secured with the intermediate -eye tie and is stretched tightly to prevent passage over or under it.

141

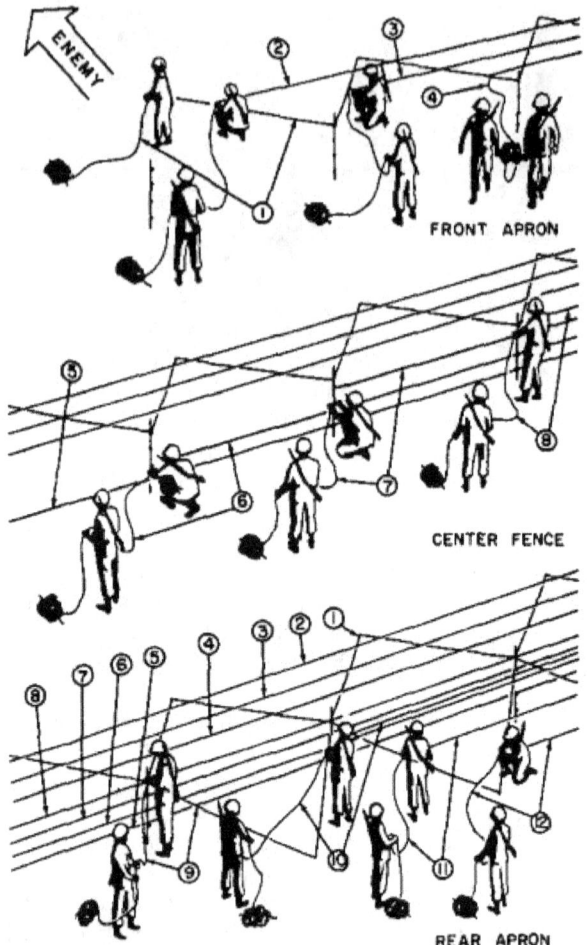

Figure 6-22. Sequence of installing wire in a double apron fence.

(e) Wires Nos. 6, 7, and 8 complete the center portion of the fence and are secured to the long pickets, Nos. 6 and 7 with the intermediate-eye tie. They also start at the first and end at the last long picket. No. 8 is secured with the top-eye tie. These wires (Nos. 6, 7, and 8) form the backbone of the fence and are drawn up tightly to hold the pickets in position.

(f) No. 9 is the diagonal apron wire on the friendly side of the fence and is secured with the top-eye tie to all pickets. Nos. 10 and' 11 are apron wires and No. 12 is the tripwire on the friendly side of the fence. Wire No. 12 is installed in the same manner as wire No. 2 ((b) above).

(g) If the fence is not satisfactorily tight when installed, wires are tightened by racking as described in paragraph 6-6/.

6-9. Standard Concertina Fences

As an obstacle, in most situations the triple standard concertina fence is better than the double apron fence. The material for it weighs about 50 percent more but it is erected with about one-half the man-hours. Every concertina fence is secured firmly to the ground by driving staples at intervals of not more than 2 meters. The staples are used on the single concertina fence and on the front concertina of the double and triple types. The two types of fence are as follows:

a. Single Concertina. This is one line of concertinas. It is erected quickly and easily but is not an effective obstacle in itself. It is used as an emergency entanglement or for the temporary closing of gaps between other obstacles. It is for such purposes that one roll of concertina may be habitually carried on the front of each vehicle in combat units.

b. Double Concertina. This consists of a double line of concertinas with no interval between lines. The two lines are installed with staggered joints. As an obstacle, the double concertina is less effective than a well-emplaced, double apron fence. It is used in some situations to supplement other obstacles in a band or zone.

6-10. Triple Standard Concertina Fence

a. Description. This consists of two lines of concertinas serving as a base, with a third line resting on top, as shown in figure 6-23. All lines are installed with staggered joints. Each line is completed before the next is started so that a partially completed concertina entanglement presents some obstruction. It is erected quickly and is difficult to cross, cut, or crawl through.

6. Detail. A 300-meter section of this fence is a platoon task normally requiring less than 1 hour. There are two operations, carrying and laying out pickets and concertina rolls and installing pickets, and opening and installing concertinas.

c. First Operation. For the first operation, the working party is divided into three groups of approximately equal size: one to lay out all pickets, one to install all pickets, and one to lay out all concertina rolls.

143

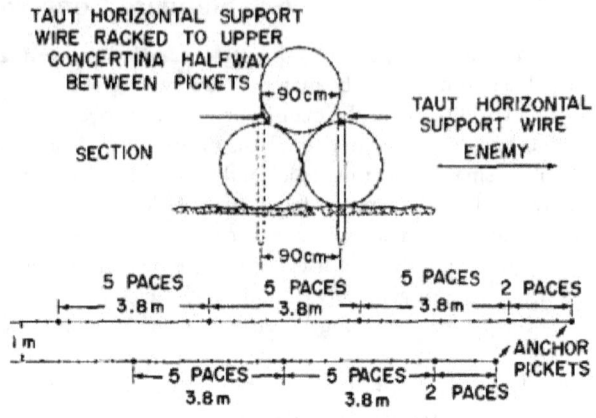

TAUT HORIZONTAL SUPPORT
WIRE RACKED TO UPPER
CONCERTINA HALFWAY
BETWEEN PICKETS

SECTION

TAUT HORIZONTAL
SUPPORT WIRE

ENEMY

PLAN SHOWING SPACING OF PICKETS

Figure 6-23. Triple standard concertina fence.

(1) The first group lays out front row long pickets at 5 pace intervals on the line of the fence (fig. 6-24) with points of pickets on line and pointing toward the enemy. The rear row long pickets are then laid out on a line 90 cm to the rear and opposite the center of interval between the front row long pickets. An anchor picket is laid out at each end of each line, 1.5 meters from the end long picket.

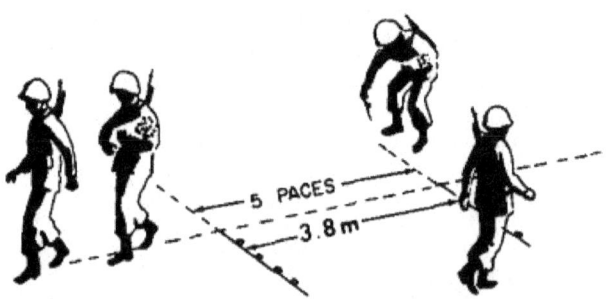

Figure 6-24. Laying out long pickets for triple concertina fence.

Figure 6-24. Laying out long pickets for triple concertina fence.

(2) The second group installs pickets beginning with the front row (fig. 6-25). As in other fences, eyes of screw pickets are to the right. Concave faces of U-shaped pickets are toward the enemy.

Figure 6-25. Installing front row pickets for triple concertina fence.

(3) The third group lays out concertinas along the rows of pickets (fig. 6-26). In the front row, one roll is placed at the third picket and one at every fourth picket thereafter. Sixteen staples accompany each front row concertina. In the second row, two rolls area placed at the third picket and two at every fourth picket thereafter. As each roll is placed in position, its binding wires are unfastened but are left attached to the hoop at one end of the roll,

d. Second Operation. As they complete the first operation, all men are organized in four man parties (fig. 6-27) to open and install concertinas, beginning at the head of the fence. The sequence, shown in general in figure 6+27 is as follows:

(1) Open the front row concertinas in front of the double line of pickets and the other two in its rear.

(2) Lift each front row concertina in turn and drop it over the long pickets, then join concertina ends as shown in figure 6-28.

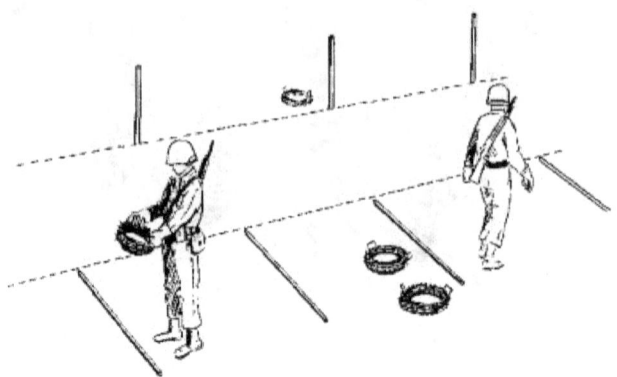

Figure 6-26. Laying out concertina.

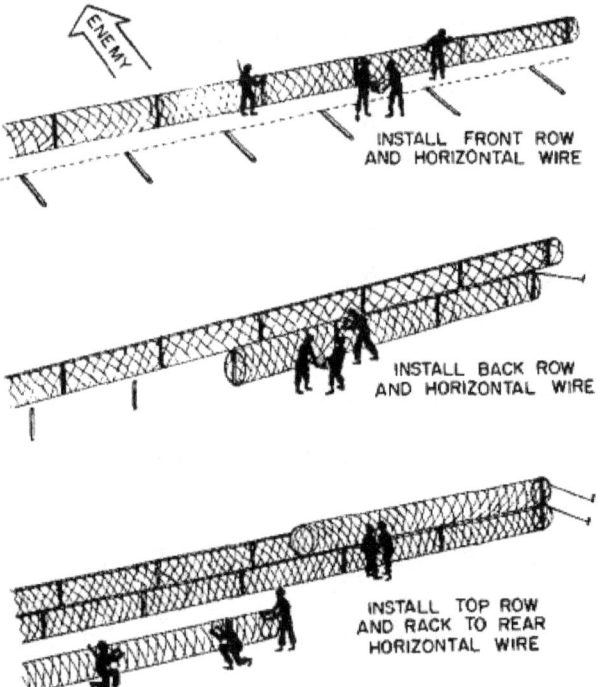

INSTALL FRONT ROW
AND HORIZONTAL WIRE

INSTALL BACK ROW
AND HORIZONTAL WIRE

INSTALL TOP ROW
AND RACK TO REAR
HORIZONTAL WIRE

Figure 6-27. Installing concertina.

(3) Fasten the bottom of the concertina to the ground by driving a staple over each pair of end hoops, one over the bottom of a coil at each long picket, and one at the and 14 points of the 3.8-meter picket spacing. Securing the front concertina to the ground is essential and must be done before installing another concertina in its rear unless the enemy side of the entanglement is sure to be accessible later.

(4) Stretch a barbed wire strand along the top of each front row and fasten it to the tops of the long pickets, using the top-eye tie for screw pickets.

These wires are stretched as tightly as possible to improve the resistance of the fence against crushing.

(5) Install the rear row concertina as described above for the front row concertina.

(6) Install the concertina in the top row (fig. 6-27), fastening the end hoops of 15meter sections with plain steel wire ties. Begin this row at a point between the ends of the front and rear of the lower rows, thus breaking all end joints.

(7) Rack the top concertina to the rear horizontal wire at points halfway between the long pickets. If there is safe access to the enemy side of the fence, similarly rack the top concertina to the forward horizontal wire.

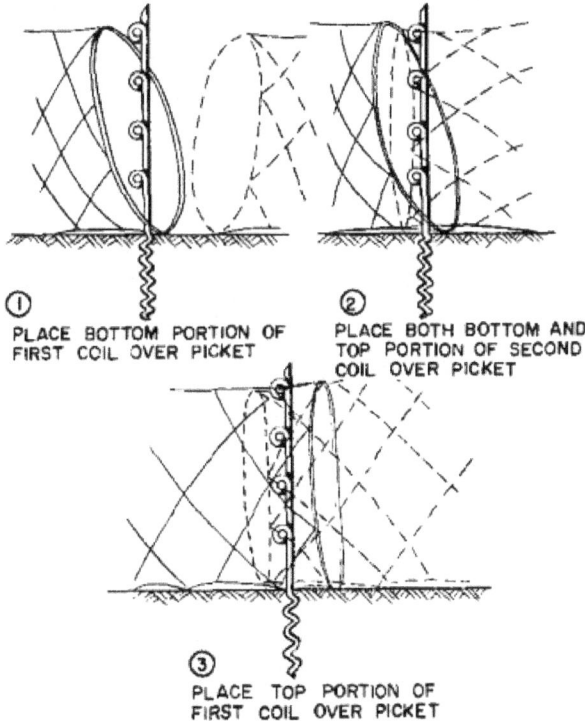

① PLACE BOTTOM PORTION OF FIRST COIL OVER PICKET

② PLACE BOTH BOTTOM AND TOP PORTION OF SECOND COIL OVER PICKET

③ PLACE TOP PORTION OF FIRST COIL OVER PICKET

Figure 6-28. Joining concertina.

6-11. Low Wire Entanglement

a. General. This is a 4- and 2-pace double apron fence in which medium pickets replace long pickets in the fence center line (fig. 6-29). This results in omission of the Nos. 6, 7, and 8 wires, and in bringing all the apron and diagonal wires much closer to the ground so that passage underneath this fence is difficult. This fence may be used advantageously on one or both sides of the double apron fence. The low wire entanglement is used where concealment is essential. In tall grass or shallow water, this entanglement is almost invisible and is particularly effective as a surprise obstacle. However, a man can pick his way through this low wire fence without much difficulty; therefore, for best results it must be employed in depth.

b. Construction. Except for the omission of three wires and the substitution of the medium pickets, this fence is constructed in the same manner as the double apron fence (para 6-8).

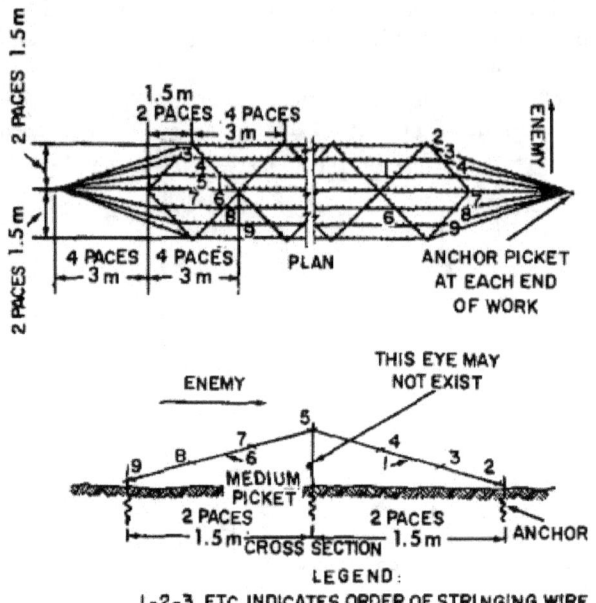

Figure 6-29. Low wire entanglement.

6-12. High-Wire Entanglement

a. Description. This obstacle consists of two parallel 4-strand fences with a third 4-strand fence zigzagged between them to form triangular cells. With two rows of pickets as shown in figure 6-30, the entanglement is classed as a belt; with one or more additional rows of fences and triangular cells it is a band. To add to the obstacle effect, front and rear aprons may be installed and spirals of loose wire may be placed in the triangular cells.

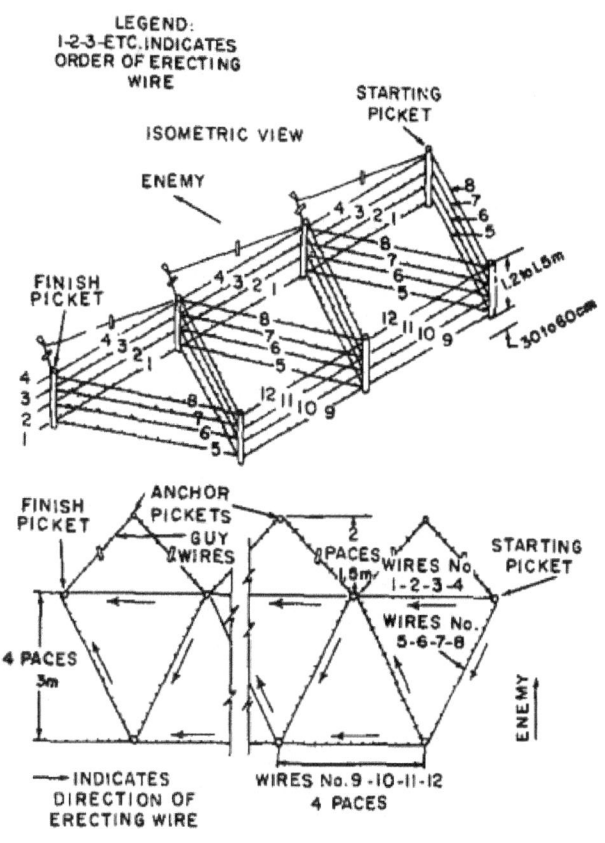

ISOMETRIC VIEW

PLAN

Figure 6-30. High wire entanglement.

b. Construction. A 300-meter section of high wire entanglement with two rows of pickets, as shown in figure 6-30, is a platoon task normally requiring about two hours, assuming 38 men per platoon. The two operations are: laying out and installing pickets, and installing wire.

(1) First operation. For this operation, the working party is divided into two groups, two-thirds of the men going to the first group and one-third to the second. The first group carries and lays out pickets, front row first and at 3-meter intervals. Second row pickets are laid out in a line 3 meters to the rear of the front row and spaced midway between them. The first group also lays out an anchor picket in line with each end of each 4-strand fence, 3 meters from the nearest long picket. If guys are needed, anchor pickets are also laid out in lines 2 paces from the lines of the front and rear fences, opposite and midpoint of spaces between the long pickets. The second group installs front row pickets, returns to the head of the fence, installs the rear row, and then installs

149

the anchor pickets. When the first group finishes laying out pickets, they begin installing wire and help finish installing the pickets.

(2) Second operation. As the first task is completed, men move individually to the head of the fence and are organized into teams of two or four men to install wires in the same manner as for the 4-strand fence. The order of installation is as shown in figure 6-30, except that if front guys are used they are installed before the No. 1 wire; rear guys after the No. 12 wire. The lengthwise wires of each 4-strand fence begin and end at an anchor picket.

6-13. Trestle Apron Fence

The trestle apron fence (fig. 6-31) has inclined crosspieces spaced at 4.8 to 6-meter intervals to carry longitudinal wires on the enemy side. The rear ends of the crosspieces are carried on triangular timber frames which are kept from spreading by tension wires on the friendly side. The crosspieces may be laid flat on the ground for tying the longitudinal wires in place and then raised into position on the triangular frames. The frames are tied securely in place and held by the tension wires. The fence should be sited in such a way that it can be guyed longitudinally to natural anchorages and racked tight.

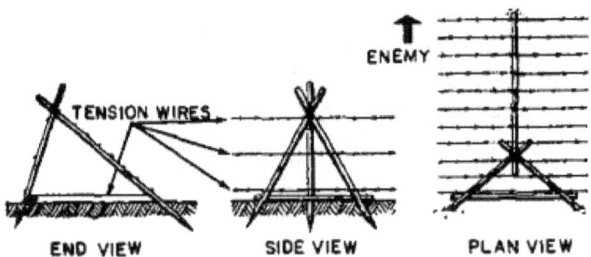

Figure 6-31. Trestle apron fence.

6-14. Lapland Fence

Figure 6-32 shows the Lapland fence which can be used equally well on frozen or rocky ground and on bogs or marshland. This fence is wired with six strands of barbed wire on the enemy side, four strands on the friendly side, and four strands on the base. In snow, the tripods can be lifted out of the snow with poles or other means to reset the obstacle on top of newly fallen snow. On soft ground, the base setting of tripods and the base wires give enough bearing surface to prevent the obstacle from sinking.

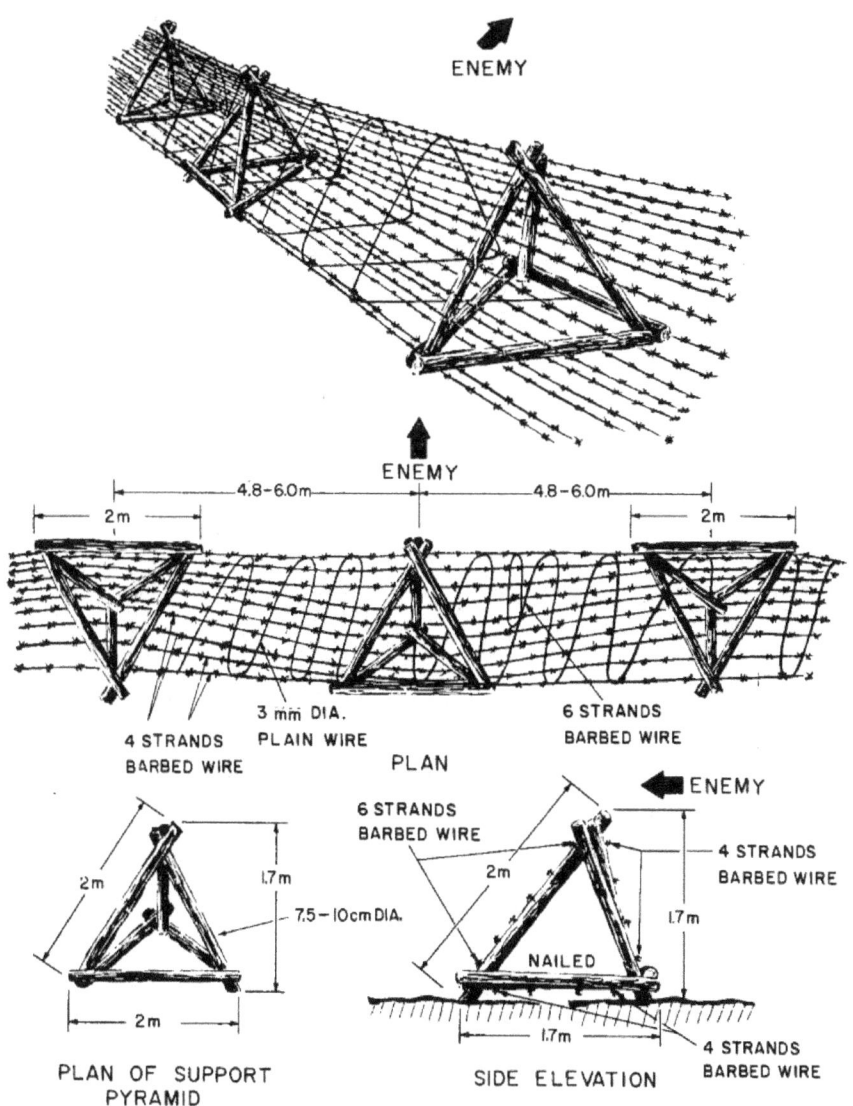

ENEMY

ENEMY

4.8-6.0m   4.8-6.0m

2m   2m

3 mm DIA.
PLAIN WIRE

6 STRANDS
BARBED WIRE

4 STRANDS
BARBED WIRE

PLAN

6 STRANDS
BARBED WIRE

ENEMY

2m

1.7m

7.5-10cm DIA.

2m

NAILED

4 STRANDS
BARBED WIRE

1.7m

2m

1.7m

PLAN OF SUPPORT
PYRAMID

SIDE ELEVATION

4 STRANDS
BARBED WIRE

Figure 6-32. Lapland fence.

6-15. Portable Barbed Wire Obstacles

Standard concertinas are readily moved and are well adapted for the temporary closing of gaps or lanes, or for adding rapidly to the obstacle effect of fixed barriers such as the double apron fence. Other portable barbed wire obstacles are described below.

a. Spirals of Loose Wire. By filling open spaces in and between wire entanglements with spirals of loose wire, the obstacle effect is substantially increased.

151

Men are tripped, entangled, and temporarily immobilized. Spirals for such use are prepared as follows:

    (1)   Drive four 1-meter posts in the ground to form a diamond 1 by V^-meter.

    (2)   Wind 75 meters of barbed wire tightly around the frame. Start winding at bottom and wind helically toward top.

    (3)   Remove wire from frame and tie at quarter points for carrying or hauling to site where it is to be opened and used. One spiral weighs less than 9.1kgs and a man can carry three or more of them by stepping inside the coils and using wire handles of the type furnished with the standard concertina.

    (4)   If spirals are needed in large quantities, mount the diamond-shaped frame on the winch of a truck and use the winch to coil the wire.

    b. Knife Rest. The knife rest (fig. 6-33) is a portable wooden or metal frame strung with barbed wire. It is used wherever a readily removeable barrier is needed; for example, at lanes in wire obstacles or at roadblocks. With a metal frame, it can be used as an effective underwater obstacle in beach defenses. Knife rests are normally constructed with 3 to 5 meters between crossmembers. They should be approximately 1 meter high. The crossmembers must be firmly lashed to the horizontal member with plain wire. When placed in position, knife rests must be securely fixed.

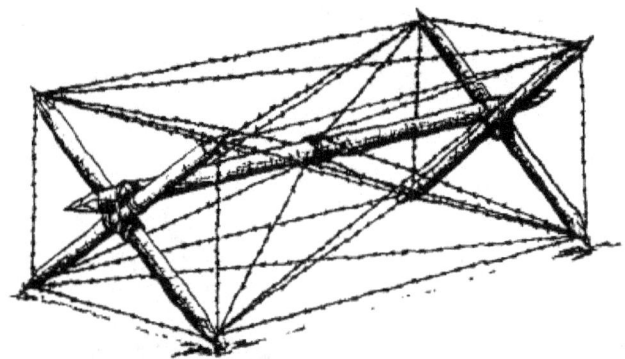

Figure 6-33. Knife rest.

    c. Tripwires. Immediately after a defensive position is occupied and before an attempt is made to erect protective wire, tripwires should be placed just outside of grenade range, usually 30 to 40 meters. These wires should stretch about 23 centimeters above the ground and be fastened to pickets at not more than 5 meter intervals. They should be concealed in long grass or crops or on a natural line such as the side of a path or the edge of a field. The tripwires should be placed in depth in an irregular pattern.

    d. Tanglefoot. Tanglefoot (fig. 6-34) is used where concealment is essential. The obstacle should be employed in a minimum depth of 10 meters. The pickets should be spaced at irregular intervals of from 75 cm to 3 meters, and the height of the barbed wire should vary between 23 to 75 cm. Tanglefoot should be sited in scrub, if possible, using bushes as supports for part of the wire. In open ground, short pickets should be used.

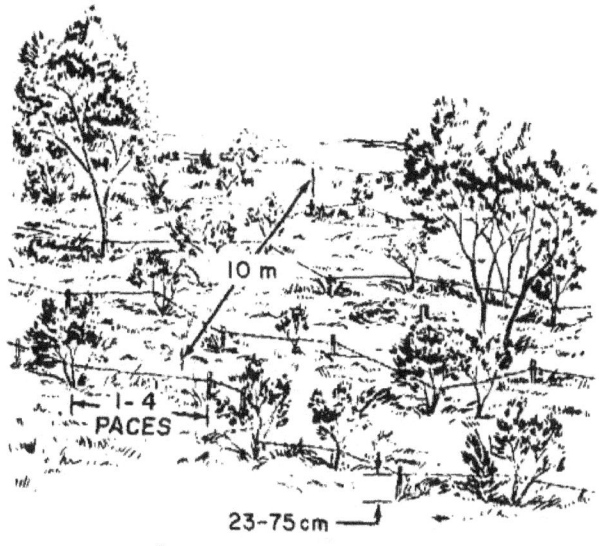

Figure 6-34. Tanglefoot.

6-16. Combination Bands

As noted in paragraph 6-12, the high wire entanglement may be built with additional rows of fences and triangular cells to form bands of any desired depth or may be made more effective by adding front and rear aprons. Other types of fences may be combined in bands to form obstacles which are much more difficult to breach than a single belt. Portable barbed wire obstacles may be added as described in paragraph 6-15. The construction of bands of varied types is desirable because this makes it difficult for the enemy to develop standard methods of passage and it permits fitting the obstacles to the situation and to the time and materials available. Six different types of effective combination bands are shown in figure 6-35. Other variations are readily developed.

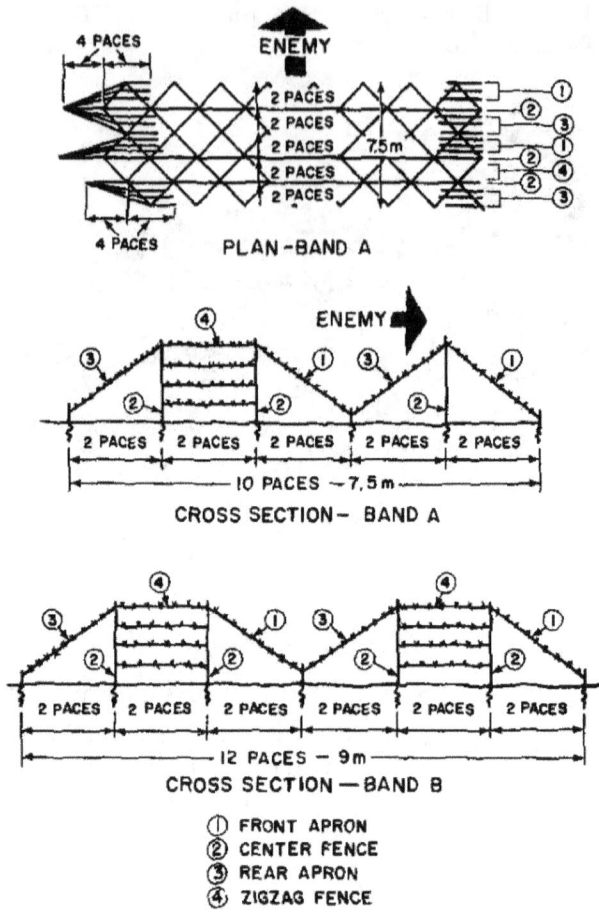

Figure 6-35. Combination bands of wire obstacles.

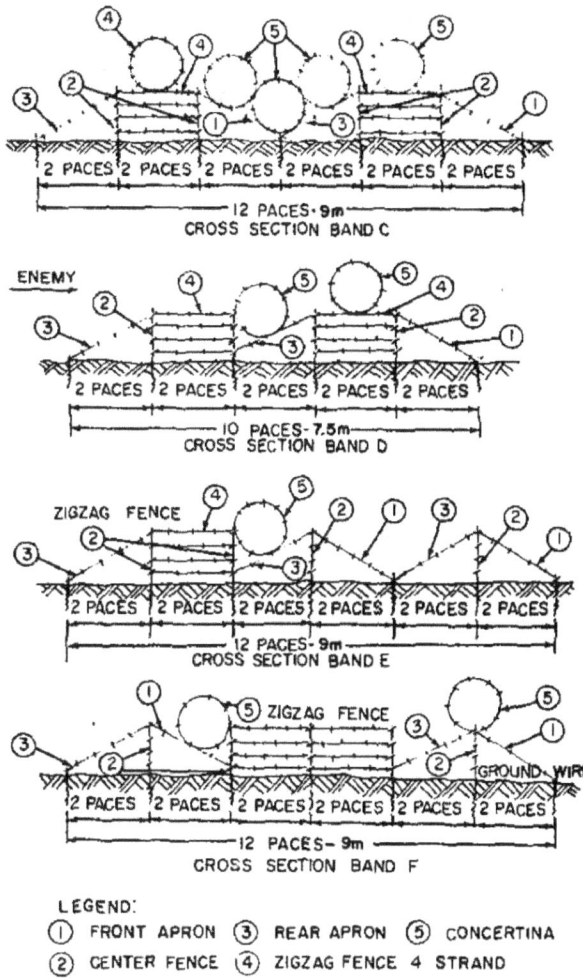

2 PACES | 2 PACES | 2 PACES | 2 PACES | 2 PACES | 2 PACES

12 PACES· 9m

CROSS SECTION BAND C

ENEMY

2 PACES | 2 PACES | 2 PACES | 2 PACES | 2 PACES

10 PACES- 7.5m

CROSS SECTION BAND D

ZIGZAG FENCE

2 PACES | 2 PACES | 2 PACES | 2 PACES | 2 PACES | 2 PACES

12 PACES- 9m

CROSS SECTION BAND E

ZIGZAG FENCE

GROUND WIRE

2 PACES | 2 PACES | 2 PACES | 2 PACES | 2 PACES | 2 PACES

12 PACES- 9m

CROSS SECTION BAND F

LEGEND:

① FRONT APRON ③ REAR APRON ⑤ CONCERTINA

② CENTER FENCE ④ ZIGZAG FENCE 4 STRAND

Figure 6-35. Combination bands of wire obstacles. Cont.

Section III. Material & Labor Estimates

6-17. Basic Considerations

Barbed wire obstacles are constructed primarily from issue materials, thus, both logistical and construction estimates are involved, Table 11 gives weights, lengths, and other data required for estimating truck transportation and carrying party requirements. Table 6-2 gives the material and labor requirements for construction of various wire entanglements. Table 6-2 is based on daylight work; for nightwork the man-hours must be increased 50 percent.

6-18. Requirements for a Defensive Position

a. Method of Estimating. Table 6-2 gives quantities and weights of material per linear meter of entanglement. If a layout to scale can be developed, the lengths of the various types of entanglements are scaled and the quantities and weights are computed. If a scaled layout cannot be prepared, rules of thumb may be used for estimating the required lengths of tactical and protective wire entanglements. If the length of front is taken as the straight-line distance between limiting points, the rules are -

(1) Length of tactical wire entanglement, is 1 ¼ times the length of front, times the number of belts regardless of the size of the unit involved.

(2) Length of protective wire entanglement for a defensive position is 5 times the length of the front being defended times the number of belts. Since protective wire encircles each platoon area of a command, the protective wire entanglement for units is 2.5 times the average platoon frontage times the number of platoons involved.

(3) Supplementary wire in front of the FEBA is used to break up the line of tactical entanglements. Its length is ¼, times the unit's frontage times the number of belts. The length of the supplementary wire entanglement behind the FEBA is approximately equal to 2 ½ times the distance from the FEBA to the rearmost reserve unit times the number of belts. This rule of thumb is adequate for all units.

b. *Example*:

GIVEN:

A defensive position with a frontage of 1,800 meters and a depth of 900 meters. The tactical wire entanglement is a band consisting of three belts of triple standard concertina fence. The protective entanglement is a band consisting of two belts of 4and 2-pace double apron fence. The supplementary entanglements are the same type and depth as the entanglements they supplement. Only screw pickets are available. The work is done during daylight hours with inexperienced personnel.

REQUIRED:

(1) Material to be requisitioned.

(2) Man-hours to construct.

(3) Number of 5-ton truck loads (to permit cross-country travel, each truck will carry only 5 tons).

SOLUTION:

Tactical

(1) Length of trace of entanglement: 1.25 × 1800 × 3 = 6,750 meters

(2) Sections of fence:
$$\frac{6,759}{300} = 22.5 \text{ sections or } 23$$

(3) Short pickets: 23 × 4 = 92

(4) Long pickets: 23 × 160 = 3,680

(5) Concertina: 23 × 59 = 1,357

(6) Staples: 23 × 317 = 7,291

(7) 400-m reels: 23 × 3 = 69

(8) Man-hours to construct: 23 × 30 = 690

(9) 5-ton truck loads:
$$\frac{6750 \times 7.9}{5 \times 2,000 \times .4536}$$
= 11.76 or *12 loads*

(1 pound = 0.4536 kilograms)

Protective

(1) Length of trace of entanglement: 5 × 1,800 × 2 = 18,000 meters

(2) Sections of fence: $\frac{18,000}{300} =$ 60 sections

(3) Short pickets: 60×200 = 12,000

(4) Long pickets: 60×100 = 6,000

(5) 400-meter reels: 60×14 = 840

(6) Man-hours to construct: $60 \times 59 = 3,540$

(7) 5-ton truck loads:
$$\frac{18,000 \times 4.9}{5 \times 2,000 \times .4536}$$
= 19.4 or *20 loads*
Supplementary (in front of FEBA)
Same as tactical.
Supplementary (behind FEBA)

(1) Length of trace of entanglement: $2.5 \times 900 \times 2$ = 4,500 meters

(2) Sections of fence: $\frac{4,500}{300}$ = 15 sections

(3) Short pickets: 15×200 = 3,000

(4) Long pickets: 15×100 = 1,500

(5) 400-meter reels: 15×14 = 210

(6) Man-hours to construct: $15 \times 59 = 885$

(7) 5-ton truck loads:
$$\frac{4,500 \times 4.9}{5 \times 2,000 \times .4536}$$
= 4.8 or *5 loads*

CHAPTER 7 – ANTIVEHICULAR OBSTACLES

7-1. Defense

Antivehicular obstacles should not be continuous across the front of a position, but should have gaps which can be kept under observation and fire and at which flares and other warning devices can be kept in operational condition. Such gaps tend to canalize vehicular movement. With observation and effective covering fire placed on these gaps, an attack with vehicles can be stopped. If enemy forces are equipped with short gap bridging, the effectiveness of antivehicular obstacles under 20 meters in width is materially decreased. A narrow ditch will halt a unit so equipped only until this organic bridging can be brought into use.

7-2. Siting

Antivehicular obstacles are sited to take advantage of trees, brush, or folds in the ground for concealment and surprise effect. If they can be sited to permit flooding with water, the obstacle becomes more effective and helps to deny its use to the enemy as a protected firing position for infantry. In some situations, antivehicular obstacles may also be sited for close in protection in front or to the rear of the main line of resistance and as adjuncts to other obstacles. In such locations, vehicles may be separated from their infantry support and are vulnerable to antivehicular weapons.

7-3. Ditches

a. Types (fig. 7-1).

(1) Triangular ditches. These are relatively easy to build, but a vehicle stopped in a ditch of this type can usually back out and try another route.

(2) Side hill cuts. Side hill cuts are variations of the triangular ditch adapted to side hill locations and have the same advantages and limitations.

(3) Trapezoidal ditches. These require about double the construction time of triangular type ditches, but they are more effective obstacles. In a trapezoidal ditch, as the center of gravity of the vehicle crosses the edge, and if the ditch depth exceeds the height of the vehicle wheels or treads, vehicles are trapped. Sections of ditch longer than 100 meters are not normally camouflaged. In winter, a trapezoidal ditch may be camouflaged by snow to resemble a standard trench (fig. 7-2).

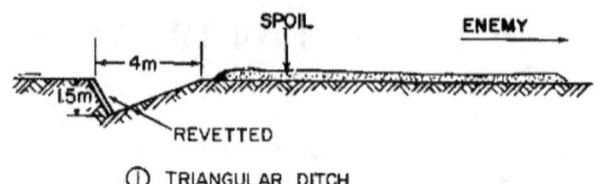

① TRIANGULAR DITCH

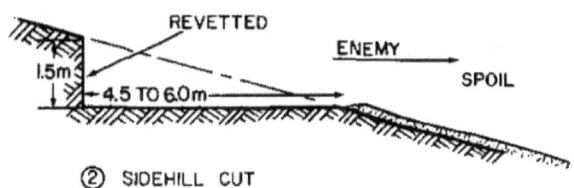

② SIDEHILL CUT

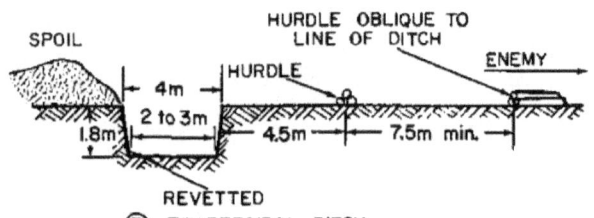

③ TRAPEZOIDAL DITCH

Figure 7-1. Antivehicular ditches.

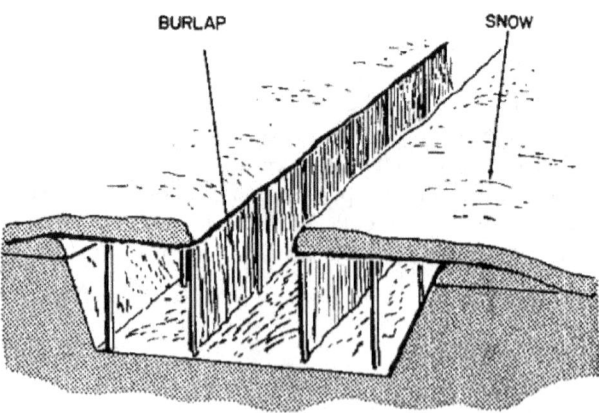

Figure 7-2. Antivehicular ditch camouflaged to resemble a trench.

b. Construction Procedures.

(1) Excavation. Ditches are excavated by earthmoving equipment, by explosives as described in FM 5-25, or by handtools. To be effective, ditches made by explosives must be dressed to true surfaces by

excavating equipment or handtools. Triangular and side hill cut ditches are constructed rapidly by a combination of explosives and motorized graders and angle-dozers. The actual time required varies widely in different types of soils. If available and if it can be used at the site of the ditching, the standard %-yard shovel is used in ditch excavation. Estimating factors for construction time in average soil are shown in table 7-1.

(2) Revetting. The face of the ditch, or both faces in the case of a trapezoidal ditch, should be revetted as soon as possible after it has been dug. Facing type revetting is used almost exclusively, with pole type or brushwood hurdles preferred because of their durability. For revetting techniques, refer to chapter 4. It is particularly important that the top of the revetment be about 20 cm below the top of the ditch and that the anchor stakes and tieback wires be buried under 30 cm of earth.

Method of construction	Dimensions of ditch		Crew size	Construction rate (meters/hr)
	Depth (meters)	Width at top (meters)		
Handtools	2	4	Platoon [1]	4 (triangular) 2 (trapezoidal)
Explosives [3]	3	9	Squad [2]	7.5
Earthmoving equipment (% yd shovel, w/2 operators and 3-10 hand laborers)	2	4	Platoon [1]	7 (triangular) 3 (trapezoidal)

[1] 40 men.
[2] 13 men.
[3] 36 pounds of ammonium nitrate per meter of length of crater.

Table 7-1. Estimating Data on Ditch Construction

7-4. Craters

a. Use. Crater type obstacles are used for blocking roads, trails, or defiles, preferably at points where the terrain prevents bypassing the obstacle or where terrain suitable for bypassing can be mined and covered by antivehicular fire. Craters should be improved wherever possible by steepening the sides, flooding or mining.

b. Preparation. As in the case of bridge demolitions, craters are formed by explosive charges placed in advance and prepared for later detonation. The weights of charges, depths, and arrangement are given in detail in FM 5-25. The methods normally employed include -

(1) Placement of charges in a culvert under the road and concealed and wired for detonation from a safe distance.

(2) If a culvert is not available at the point selected, charges are placed in the bottoms of holes excavated in the road. Truck mounted earth augers, if available, are used for digging the holes. The charges are placed, and wired for detonation at a safe distance. The holes are backfilled in such a way that they are not readily noticed. The use of ADM to produce craters is covered in FM 5-26.

7-5. Log Hurdles and Cribs

a. Hurdles. Log hurdles formed of 25to 45 cm logs as shown in figure 7-3 may be used to add to the obstacle effect of a crater, or other type of roadblock. The hurdles force vehicles to reduce speed as they approach the obstacles or they may act as an additional means of trapping vehicles in the vicinity of antitank ditches. Each hurdle consists of one 45 cm or three 25 cm logs firmly staked in place on a roadway or on ground suitable for use as a bypass. A hurdle of this size stops or damages most types of wheeled vehicles. Tanks can cross them at reduced speeds on reasonably level ground but are stopped by hurdles on uphill grades which approximate the critical grade of the vehicle. To stop a tank on such a slope, the size and location of the pole or log hurdle must be such that the ground line of the tank will be tilted to a slope of 1 to 1. The poles must be firmly tied between strong stakes at not more than 1.5 meter intervals. To determine the height of the hurdle required, a stick 3.5 meters long is held at an angle of 45° above horizontal, with one end of the ground downhill from the hurdle location. The distance between the upper end of the stick and the ground gives the required height of the hurdle. The hurdle should be sited on the steepest part of the slope and as near the top as possible.

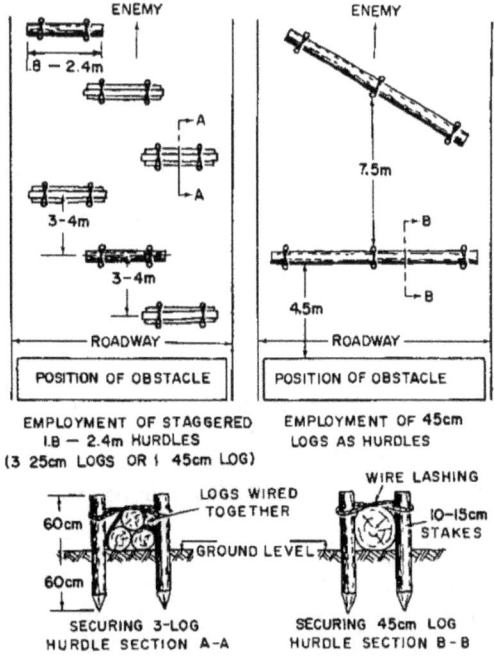

Figure 7-3. Types of log hurdles.

b. Cribs. Rectangular or triangular log cribs (figs. 7-4 through 7-6) are used effectively as roadblocks where standing timber is available and where such an obstacle cannot be bypassed readily. Unless substantially built, obstacles of this type are not effective against heavy tracked vehicles. Cribs are strengthened by filling them with earth; and preferably the earth is obtained by digging a shallow ditch in front of the obstacle. Log hurdles in front of a log crib force vehicles to reduce speed and add

162

to the effectiveness of the roadblock. An engineer platoon equipped with platoon tools can build 6 meters of this obstacle in 4 to 8 hours.

Figure 7-4. Rectangular log crib used as roadblock.

7-6. Posts

a. Use. Posts are among the most effective antivehicular obstacles because each post presents a breaching problem to the attacker. There is no fast method of breaching a belt of posts. Normally, the attacker will seek to bypass such an obstacle. Post obstacle belts may be constructed using either steel, log, or concrete posts.

b. Steel Posts. These posts are usually sections of rail, heavy pipe or structural members. Due to their small cross-sectional area, steel posts are installed over footings to prevent their being driven into the earth by the weight of a tank.

c. Log Posts. These posts should be hard wood with a minimum diameter of 40 cm. Footings are used under log posts only where the soil has exceptionally poor load-bearing characteristics. Figure 7-7 depicts a belt of log post obstacles.

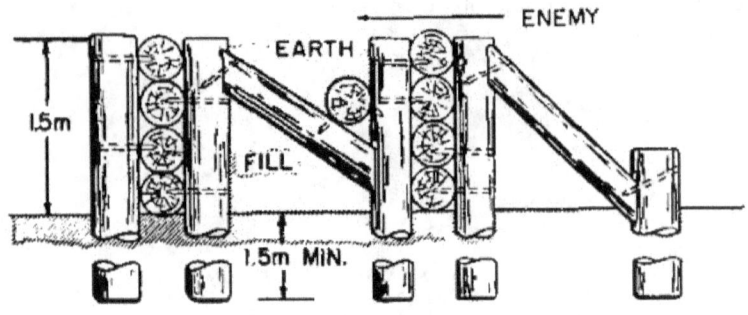

CROSS SECTION

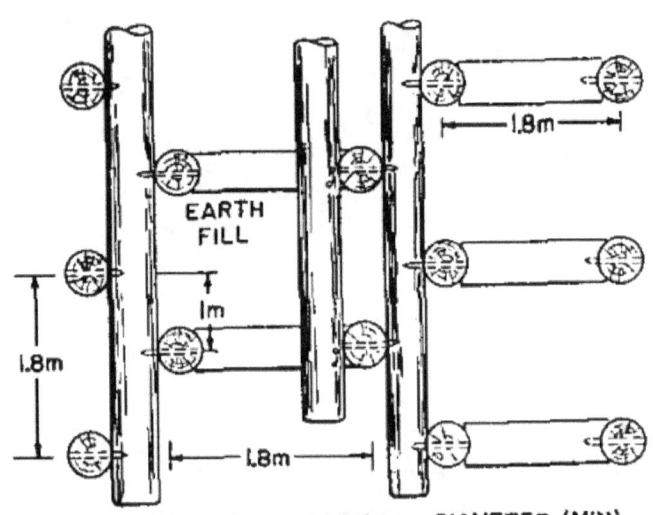

NOTE: ALL LOGS 20cm DIAMETER (MIN)

PLAN

Figure 7-5. Details of log crib used as roadblock.

164

Figure 7-6. Triangular log crib used as roadblock.

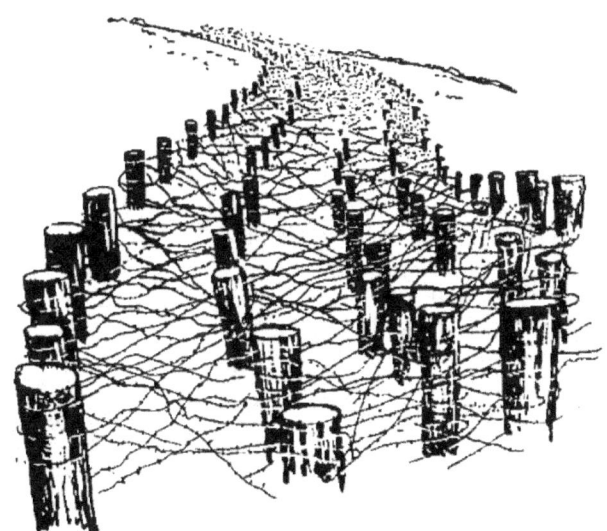

Figure 7-7. Belt of log post obstacles.

d. Concrete Posts. Precast concrete posts may be emplaced either vertically or angled in the direction of the enemy line of approach using lengths, spacing, and arrangements as described for wood or steel post obstacles.

(1) Concrete posts should be square in cross section and 3 meters or more in length. They can be readily precast in horizontal open-top boxes with plank bottoms and removable sides and ends. Two lifting rings are set in the top surface at the quarter points of the length, for loading and unloading, and a similar ring is positioned at the top end for raising it into position. A chisel-shaped point can be easily formed at the bottom end if the concrete posts are to be driven in with pile driving equipment. Lengthwise reinforcement is provided several centimeters inside the surface near each corner of the square post with a transverse wrapping of wire at each 30 cm of length. Round reinforcing bars of 1.25 cm diameter are adequate for the longitudinal reinforcement. Reinforcement can be improvised by using 4 to 6 strands of barbed wire at each corner, attached to the form ends and racked tightly, preferably to almost the breaking strength of the wire. After curing for 1 week or more under wet burlap, such posts are installed in the same manner as described for wood posts or steel posts. If piledriving equipment is to be used, a steam or air hammer may be required for driving heavy posts of this type depending on the type of soil.

(2) Round concrete posts may be improvised from corrugated metal pipe of small sizes filled with concrete. Because of the time required to funnel concrete into pipe held vertically and because of the expenditure of the pipe, this method is less efficient than the use of square precast concrete posts.

e. Placing.

(1) All posts are buried 1.5 meters in the ground either vertically or at a slight angle toward the enemy, and project above ground level between 75 and 120 cm. The height should vary from post to post. The minimum acceptable density for posts is 200 per 100 meters of front. The spacing should be irregular, with at least 1 meter and not more than 2 meters between post.

(2) Posts are equally useful whether employed in long belts or in short sections as roadblocks. By pre-digging holes, lining them with pipe, and covering them for later rapid installation of posts, the road may be kept open for use until the roadblock is needed. The rate of construction of such roadblocks is approximately as follows, based on a 6-meter road width:

(a) Using pile driving equipment, 2 NCO's and 16 men: 4 to 6 hours.

(b) Using power earth auger or demolitions (shaped charges), 1 NCO and 8 men: 2 to 2 ½ hours.

(c) Using handtools, one combat engineer platoon: 3 to 5 hours.

(3) Use of spirals of wire, with posts. The effect of post type obstacles can be improved, and the obstacles made more difficult to breach, by weaving spirals of barbed wire among the posts as shown in figure 7-7. The belt illustrated is an antipersonnel as well as an antivehicular obstacle.

166

a. Use. Trees felled as shown in figure 7-8 can be used to block a road or defile. To stop tracked vehicles the trees should be at least 60 cm or more in diameter and at least 6 meters tall. To effectively block a road through a heavily wooded area, an abatis at least 75 meters deep is required.

b. Construction. Abatis may be constructed using handtools, by the use of explosives alone, or by a combination of notching and explosives as shown in figure 7-9. Using only handtools, one engineer platoon can build 75 meters of abatis in 8 hours. Information on the use of explosives for the construction of abatis is contained in FM 5-25. Bushy-top trees with heavy branches and thick foliage should be used for abatis wherever possible since the branches reduce the momentum of the vehicle and the foliage sets up a screen. The trees should be felled as shown in figure 7-8 so that the trunk remains attached to the stump. To ensure that the trunk remains attached, no cut is made on the side of the tree toward which it is to fall, the tree is strained to fall in the required direction, and the butt is cut two thirds through on the opposite side. The effectiveness of an abatis is increased by interlacing barbed wire in the branches of the trees.

Figure 7-8. Abatis used as roadblock.

Figure 7-9. Preparing explosive charges for abatis construction,

7-8. Steel Obstacles

a. Hedgehogs. Steel hedgehogs as shown in figure 7-10 are relatively lightweight for the obstacle effect they provide, and they are quickly installed or removed. They are designed to revolve under wheeled vehicles and puncture them or to belly up tracked vehicles. Unless kept under observation and covered with fire, the enemy can readily move them aside. They are well adapted for use in vegetation high enough to afford complete or partial concealment. Exposed parts should be painted to blend with the background. Hedgehogs are made up in rear areas, using three angles about 10 cm by 10 cm by 1 cm, 120 cm long, and a 1 cm steel plate about 50 cm square. A hedgehog of this size weighs about 160 pounds. Hedgehogs are used in rows, with at least 150 hedgehogs to each 100 meters of front which is to be protected in this manner.

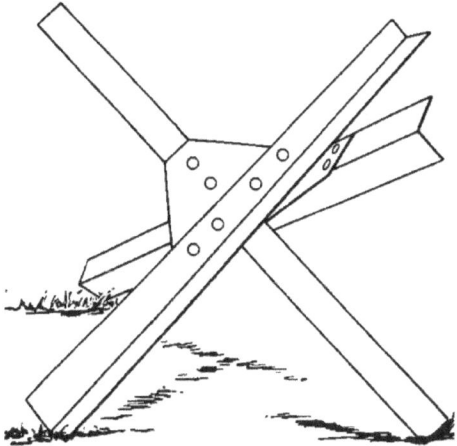

Figure 7-10. Steel hedgehog.

b. Tetrahedrons. Steel tetrahedrons shown in figure 7-11 are employed in a manner similar to that of hedgehogs. They are usually made of 10 cm by 10 cm by 1.5 cm angles, the base and sides in the shape of equilateral triangles, 1.5 meters on a side. Their finished height is approximately 1.2 meters.

Figure 7-11. Steel tetrahedron.

7-9. Concrete Obstacles

a. Cubes. Cubes are concrete obstacles of approximately cubical shape, set in irregular rows. A typical size and arrangement is shown in figure 7-12. Because of the weights involved and the simplicity of erecting forms for cubes, these obstacles are best cast in place if the situation permits. A cube of the size shown in figure 7-12 requires about 1.8 cubic meters of concrete and weighs slightly less than 5 tons.

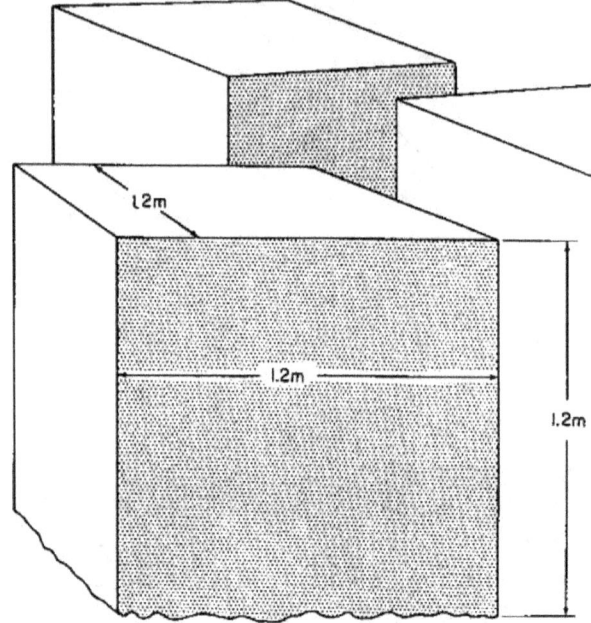

Figure 7-12. Concrete cubes.

b. Cylinders. Concrete obstacles of cylindrical shape are usually smaller than cubes and are light enough to be precast. Their use is similar to that of cubes, and they may be preferable in situations in which precast obstacles are the type required. Cylinders may be precast in forms made of lightweight sheet metal which need not be removed. A cylinder of the size shown in figure 7-13 requires 1 cubic meter of concrete and weighs a little less than 3 tons.

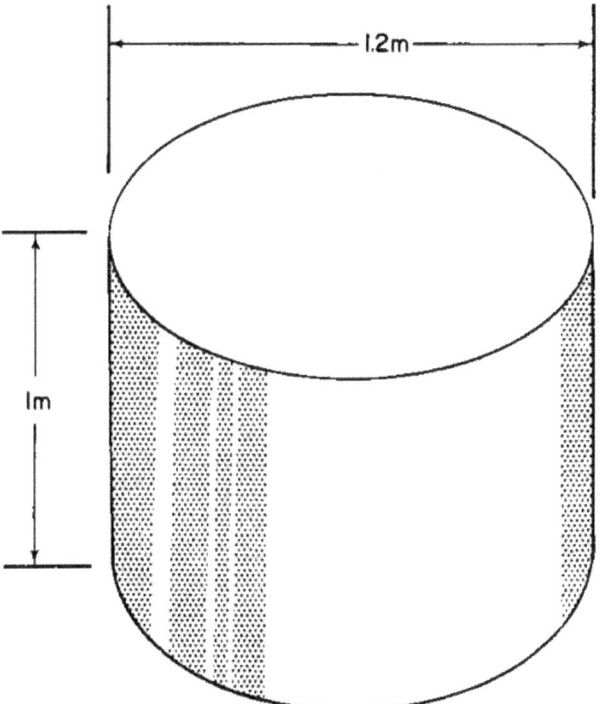

Figure 7-13. Concrete cylinder.

c. Tetrahedrons. Concrete tetrahedrons are pyramids with base and sides of equilateral triangles, 1.5 meters on a side. They are set in irregular rows as shown in figure 7-14. A tetrahedron of this size has a vertical height of about 1.2 meters, requires 0,9 cubic meter of concrete, and weighs about 1.1 tons. They may be precast in trough-shaped forms between triangular divisions, with a lifting ring embedded in the center of the top surface of each tetrahedron,

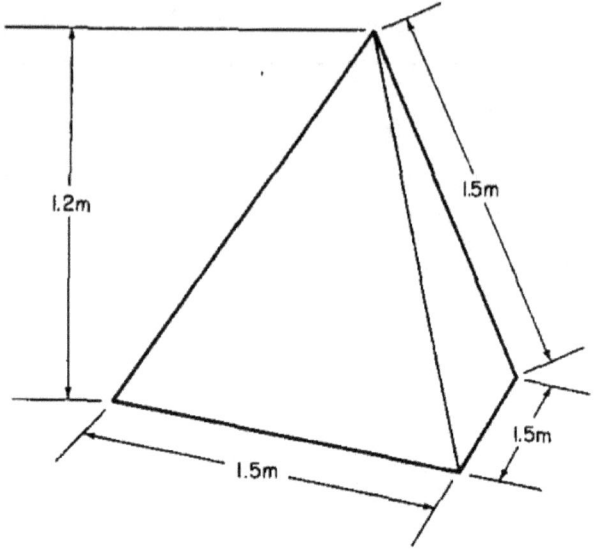

Figure 7-14. Concrete tetrahedron.

7-10. Expedients

a. Roadblocks may be improvised from farm carts, automobiles, and trucks, which are loaded with rock, concrete, or other heavy material. When placed in position their wheels should be damaged or removed, and the vehicles should be firmly anchored.

b. Vehicles can be moved to close a gap that has been left to keep the road open.

c. A roadblock which may be effective in some situations is constructed quickly by the method shown in figure 7-15. A heavy tree at one side of a road is cut almost through and its trunk is attached by a wire rope to a tree across the road in such a way that if a passing vehicle strikes the rope the tree will fall and damage the vehicle or pin it in place.

Figure 7-15. Wire-rope roadblock.

7-11. Use of Screens and Dummy Obstacles

a. Purpose. Wherever possible, antivehicular obstacles, particularly roadblocks, should be concealed by screens for the following reasons:

(1)   To conceal the true nature of the obstacle.

(2)   To prevent fire from being directed at the most vulnerable part.

(3)   To confuse the crew of the vehicle. Screens should also be erected in front of dummy obstacles and at sites where no obstacle exists, causing delay and expenditure of valuable ammunition. The enemy force will not know with any certainty what form of obstacle or defense opposes it or whether any real obstacle exists. If the force stops to investigate, the defense will have an opportunity to destroy it; if it goes ahead, it runs the risk of running into mines or of being held on an obstacle under fire.

h. Siting. Screens should be sited not more than 3 meters from the obstacles which they are concealing. If a vehicle goes through a screen at this distance, it will encounter the obstacle before it can halt. Therefore, it will not be in position to fire at the obstacle. Screens must not obscure the fields of fires of the defenders.

c. Construction. A form of screen suitable for concealing a roadblock consists of two horizontal strips of canvas, garnished netting, or blankets, the lower part suspended from wires about 120 cm from the ground, and the upper part at a height of 2 to 2.5 meters. The upper part should overlap the lower part by 15 to 33 cm.

d. Dummy Obstacles. Dummy obstacles should be used extensively to confuse and delay tanks and cause them to waste ammunition. They should be carefully made in order to present a realistic appearance. They can be made of plaster, wood, or asbestos sheets. Wooden obstacles can be used to represent steel obstacles. Antitank and antipersonnel mines should be interspersed extensively between dummy obstacles.

173

CHAPTER 8 – BEACH & RIVER LINE OBSTACLES

8-1. Principles

Most of the types of obstacles described in paragraphs 7-10 and 7-11 can be used as anti-boat obstacles for some types of boats in water depths for which they are adapted and in which they can be sited and anchored. The tide range determines the water depths for which it is practicable to position obstacles on the bottom above the low waterline. Outside this line, heavy obstacles may be sunk from boats or lowered by cranes operating from the beach or afloat in small landing craft. Posts of timber, steel, or concrete are effective Anti-boat obstacles, readily placed except in rocky or coral bottoms. Posts are preferably emplaced or driven with a slope or batter toward deep water. Wooden obstacles of other types should be filled with rock or otherwise anchored in position. Anti-boat obstacles may be connected with wire rope or. may have barbed wire or other types of obstacles anchored between them. In rivers or other locations where the water level is constant or the tide range is minor or negligible, standard cased antitank mines tied to posts or other obstacles under the surface provide effective obstacles.

8-2. Timber Obstacles

Unpeeled round logs provide the types of anti-boat obstacles described and shown, but sawed timbers may be used if more readily available. In addition to the uses of wooden posts described in paragraph 7-6, timber obstacles of the following types are used effectively under various conditions:

a. Rock-Filled Cribs and Pillars. Rock-filled timber cribs (fig. 8-1) are normally 2 to 3 meters long by 1 meter wide, and have stability at heights up to 2 meters. The logs are drift pinned at the corners. Cribs may be installed on a beach at low water or may be dragged or lowered into water before completing the rock fill. For lower heights, smaller cribs; triangular in shape and known as pillars (fig. 8-2), are built with less material and effort. Both types may be connected by barbed wire, wire rope, or a combination of both.

Figure 8-1. Rock-filled cribs.

Figure 8-2. Rock-filled pillars.

b. Tetrahedrons. Timber tetrahedrons (fig. 8-3) are pinned and wired to a triangular bottom frame which is weighted in place with rocks. A post may be driven through the obstacle for improved anchorage. Tetrahedrons are normally spaced at intervals of 5 to 10 meters and may be connected with wire rope or incorporated in a barbed wire fence.

Figure 8-3. Timber tetrahedrons.

c. Log Scaffolding, in suitable water depths, log scaffolding, as shown in figure 8-4, is effective in impeding small boats. Wooden posts driven into the bottom are reinforced by diagonal braces extending inshore and have horizontal stringers attached to the offshore face.

Figure 8-4 Log scaffolding.

d. Braced Wooden Posts. This obstacle, (fig. 8-5) may be built in relatively shallow water in which there is little or no tide range. The posts are driven approximately to water level in two rows. They are staggered so that diagonal braces can extend from each rear post to two of the front posts to provide a structure of exceptional rigidity. The bottom ends of the braces may be fastened to the rear posts before the latter are fully driven and before the work is so deep as to require diving equipment. The front posts may be connected with wire rope or barbed wire to further improve the rigidity of the structure and to add to the obstacle effect. The efficiency of this obstacle is further enhanced by the liberal use of barbed wire tangles securely fastened to and between the posts.

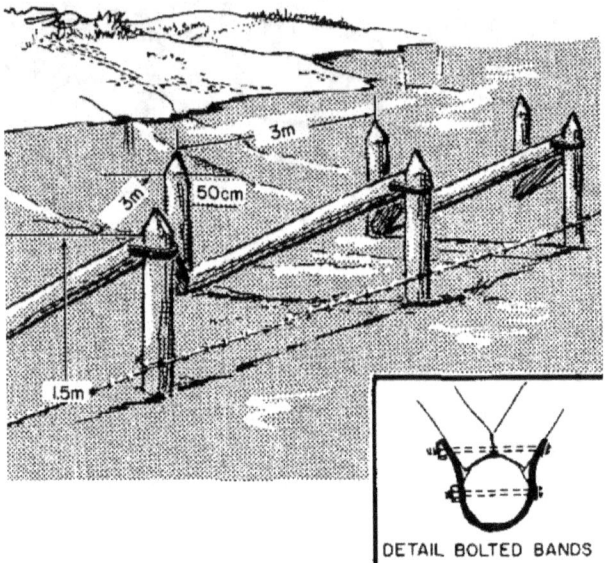

Figure 8-5. Braced wooden posts.

e. Log Tripods. Braced log tripods, constructed of logs at least 20 centimeters in diameter, as shown in figure 8-6, are effective Anti-boat obstacles. The obstacle is positioned with its longest leg facing the direction of expected assault; this leg may be capped with a standard antitank mine or sharpened to a point. Constructed in varying sizes so they are covered by 30 to 60 cm of water at high tide, these obstacles are placed on beaches from the low-tide mark back to about halfway to the high tide line.

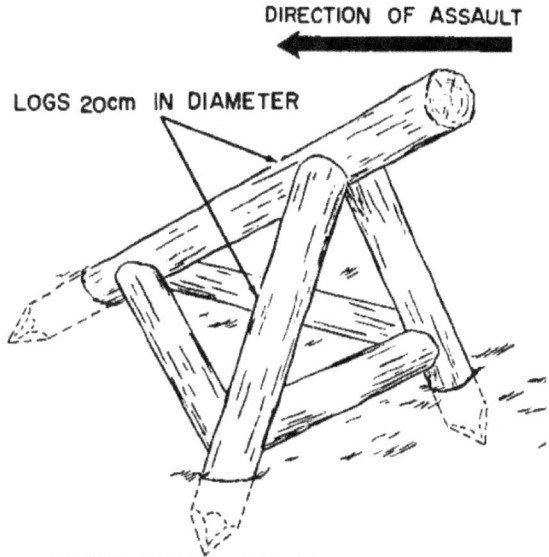

Figure 8-6. Log tripod.

f. Log Ramps. Log ramps are constructed as shown in figure 8-7. They are used to tear the bottoms out of assault craft riding up on them, and to upset such craft. They are effective obstacles with or without mines fastened to the high end of the ramp. Ramps may be placed either in an irregular pattern or in a continuous belt spaced at approximately 3meter intervals.

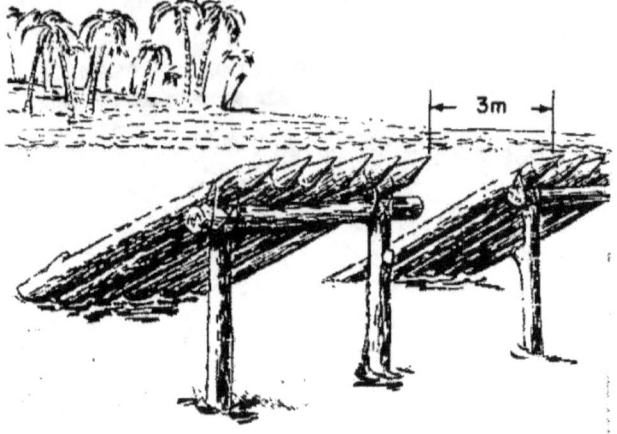

Figure 8-7. Log ramps.

g. Nutcrackers. Nutcrackers are constructed as shown in figure 8-8. The .9m x .9m x .6m base has a center well or recess large enough to house one or two antitank mines, depending on whether a one-way or two-way obstacle is desired. It also has a built-in socket for the bottom end of the activating rail or pole. Shear pins, usually of one-half cm soft iron, hold the rail erect and prevent detonation of the mines by wave action. A landing craft striking the pole will break or bend the shear pin sufficiently to detonate the mines. Nutcrackers are normally employed in an irregular pattern interspersed with plain steel and log posts.

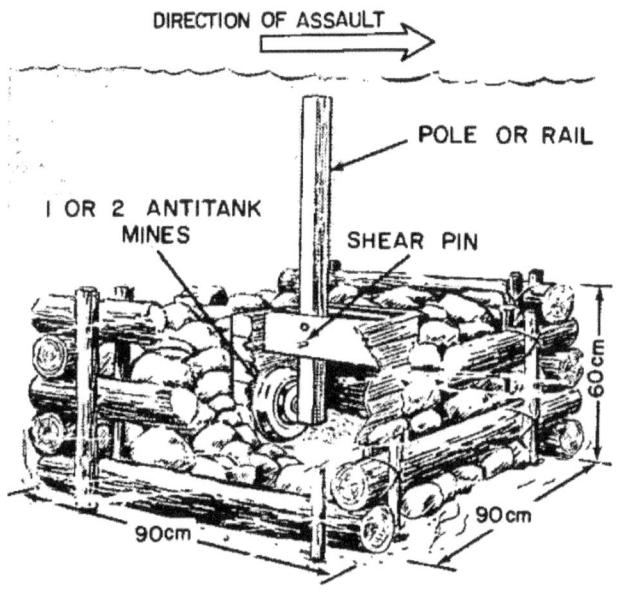

Figure 8-8. Nutcracker.

8-3. Steel Obstacles

Steel beams, piles, and rails provide simple and effective Anti-boat obstacles of the post type. Steel rails can be driven in rocky or coral bottoms in which wood piles would be splintered. Steel obstacles of portable types are advantageous for underwater use because of high unit weight of steel; they remain in position without anchorage against wave or currents. Steel obstacles intended for field fabrication for Anti-boat use are described in a and b below.

a. Scaffolding. On beaches having considerable tidal range, 5-cm steel pipe may be driven into the bottom and welded together to form a structure of the scaffolding type, as shown in figure 8-9. Floating mines may be. attached below the normal water level, to be detonated if scraped by a vessel.

181

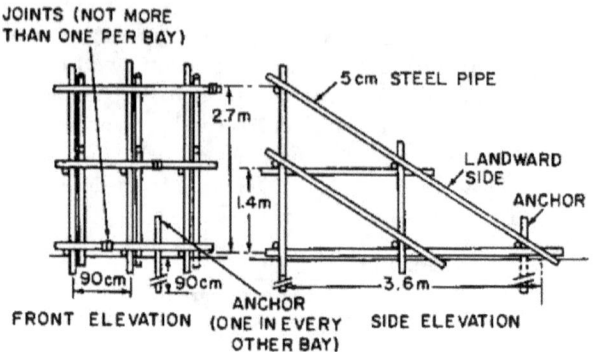

Figure 8-9. Steel scaffolding.

b. Hedgehogs. Steel hedgehogs of the type shown in figure 7-10 are fabricated in rear areas, shipped knocked down, and quickly assembled with bolted connections. The angles used are usually about 2 meters long, making the obstacle about 1 meter high. The hedgehog is emplaced without anchorage so that it revolves under a boat or amphibious vehicle, holes it, and anchors it as it sinks. Normally hedgehogs are installed in several rows, using about 150 hedgehogs to each 100 meters of beach.

8-4. Concrete Obstacles

As with obstacles of other materials, all types of concrete obstacles described in paragraph 7-9 may be used as beach obstacles under certain conditions. Concrete obstacles of post type are particularly useful if heavy piledriving equipment is available. Some types are improved for Anti-boat use by embedding rails in their tops to form horned scullies. The cylinder modified in this manner is shown in figures 8-10 and 8-11. By setting the rails at an angle of about 45° with the vertical, a fast-moving boat is holed and may be sunk as its momentum carries it down over the length of the horn. The horns may be improved by pointing them, using oxyacetylene cutting equipment.

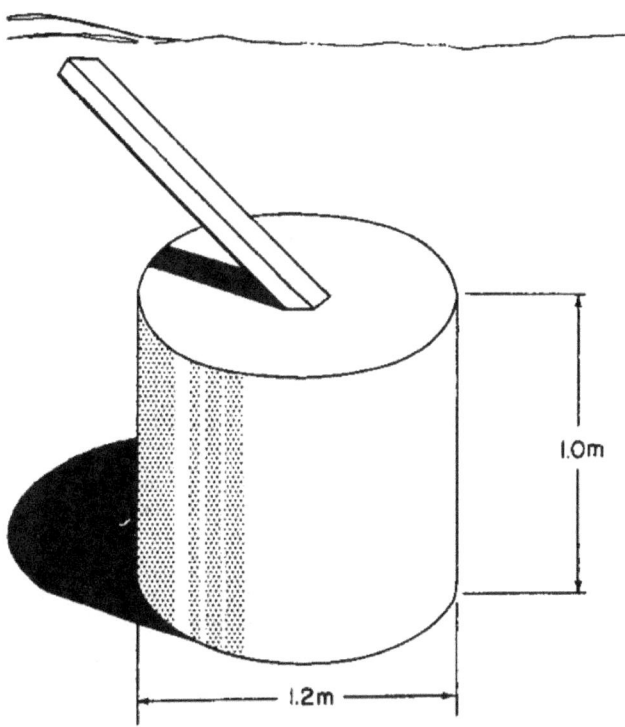

Figure 8-10. Horned scully based on concrete cylinder.

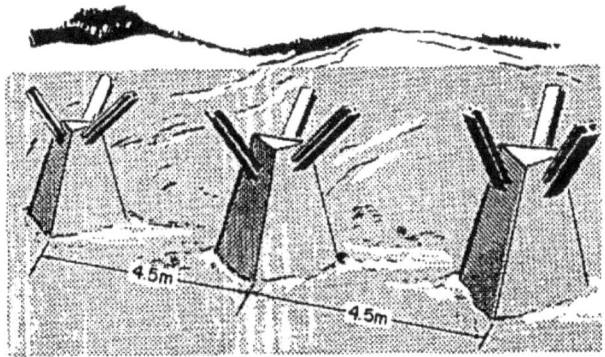

Figure 8-11. Horned scullies based on small dragon's teeth.

8-5. Barbed Wire Beach Obstacles

Wire entanglements are used as antipersonnel obstacles but will also stop light landing craft. They are placed inshore of scaffolding or sunken obstacles and, if possible, are covered by machinegun fire. Entanglements normally are built at low tide. They require constant maintenance, particularly if placed in surf. Wire also is erected on beaches or riverbanks, often in connection with antitank and antipersonnel minefields. Almost all of the types of wire obstacles described in chapter 6 may be used in conjunction with other types of beach and underwater obstacles.

8-6. Expedient Underwater Obstacles

The obstacles described in a and b below are made with native materials, some supplemented with barbed wire, and are difficult to reduce. Wherever possible, mines should be used with the obstacles to increase their effectiveness and to hinder removal by enemy underwater demolition teams.

a. Rock Mounds. These consist simply of mounds of rock about 1-meter high and 3.5meters square and staggered at intervals of 3 to 5 meters on the outer edges of reefs or likely landing beaches.

b. Rock Walls (fig. 8-12). Rock walls are about 1 meter high and 1 meter wide, in sections or continuous lines. They should be mined and topped with concertinas. They should be sited so that the top of the wire is just under the surface at high tide.

Figure 8-12. Rock walls.

APPENDIX A - REFERENCES

A-1. DA Pamphlets (DA PAM)

108-1 Index of Army Films, GTA Charts and Recordings
310-Series Military Publications Indexes (as applicable)

A-2. Army Regulations (AR)

320-5 Dictionary of U.S. Army Terms
320-50 Authorized Abbreviations and Brevity Codes

A-3. Field Manuals (FM)

5-1 Engineer Troop Organizations and Operations
5-20 Camouflage
5-21 Camouflage of Fixed Installations
5-22 Camouflage Materials
5-23 Field Decoy Installations
5-25 Explosives and Demolitions
5-26 Employment of Atomic Demolition Munitions (ADM)
5-31 Boobytraps
5-34 Engineer Field Data
5-35 Engineer's Reference and Logistical Data
5-36 Route Reconnaissance and Classification
20-32 Landmine Warfare
21-5 Military Training Management
21-6 Techniques of Military Instruction
21-10 Military Sanitation
21-26 Map Reading
21-30 Military Symbols
21-40 Chemical, Biological, and Nuclear Defense
21-75 Combat Training of the Individual Soldier and Patrolling
23-65 Browning Machinegun, Caliber .50, HB, M2
23-67 Machinegun, 7.62-mm, M60
24-20 Field Wire and Field Cable Techniques
30-5 Combat Intelligence
31-10 Barriers and Denial Operations
31-50 Combat in Fortified and Built-up Areas
31-60 River-Crossing Operations
31-72 Mountain Operations
54-2 The Division Support Command
61-100 The Division
100-5 Field Service Regulations; Operations
100-10 Field Service Regulations; Administration
101-5 Staff Officers' Field Manual: Staff Organization and Procedure
101-10-1 Staff Officers' Field Manual: Organization, Technical, and
Logistical Data, Unclassified Data

101-31-1 Staff Officers' Field Manual; Nuclear Weapons Employment, Doctrine and Procedures

A-4. Technical Manuals (TM)

5-200 Camouflage Materials

5-286 Semipermanent Highway and Railway Trestle Bridges

5-302 Construction in the Theater of Operations

5-311 Military Protective Construction {Nuclear Warfare and Chemical and Biological Operations)

5-312 Military Fixed Bridges

5-330 Planning, Site Selection, and Design of Roads, Airfields and Heliports in the Theater of Operations

5-331 Management; Utilization of Engineer Construction Equipment

5-360 Port Construction and Rehabilitation

5-725 Rigging

9-1345-200 Landmines

9-1300-214 Military Explosives

9-1950 Rockets

(C) 23-200 Capabilities of Nuclear Weapons (U)

30-246 Tactical Interpretation of Air Photos

APPENDIX B – CONVERSION FACTORS – ENGLISH-METRIC SYSTEMS

Basic Metric Relationships

Length

One Unit (below) Equals →	mm	cm	meters	km
mm (millimeter)	1.	0.1	0.001	0.000,001
cm (centimeter)	10.	1.	0.01	0.000,01
meters	1,000.	100.	1.	0.001
km (kilometer)	1,000,000.	100,000.	1,000.	1.

Length Conversion Tables—English-Metric Systems

km → miles	miles → kilometers	meters → yards	yards → meters	meters → feet	feet → meters	cm → inches	inches → centimeters
1	0.62	1.61	1.09	0.91	3.28	0.30	0.39	2.54
2	1.24	3.22	2.19	1.83	6.56	0.61	0.79	5.08
3	1.86	4.83	3.28	2.74	9.84	0.91	1.18	7.62
4	2.49	6.44	4.37	3.66	13.12	1.22	1.57	10.16
5	3.11	8.05	5.47	4.57	16.40	1.52	1.97	12.70
6	3.73	9.66	6.56	5.49	19.68	1.83	2.36	15.24
7	4.35	11.27	7.66	6.40	22.97	2.13	2.76	17.78
8	4.97	12.87	8.75	7.32	26.25	2.44	3.15	20.32
9	5.59	14.48	9.84	8.23	29.53	2.74	3.54	22.86
10	6.21	16.09	10.94	9.14	32.81	3.05	3.93	25.40
12	7.46	19.31	13.12	10.97	39.37	3.66	4.72	30.48
20	12.43	32.19	21.87	18.29	65.62	6.10	7.87	50.80
24	14.91	38.62	26.25	21.95	78.74	7.32	9.45	60.96
30	18.64	48.28	32.81	27.43	98.42	9.14	11.81	76.20
36	22.37	57.94	39.37	32.92	118.11	10.97	14.17	91.44
40	24.85	64.37	43.74	36.58	131.28	12.19	15.75	101.60
48	29.83	77.25	52.49	43.89	157.48	14.63	18.90	121.92
50	31.07	80.47	54.68	45.72	164.04	15.24	19.68	127.00
60	37.28	96.56	65.62	54.86	196.85	18.29	23.62	152.40
70	43.50	112.65	76.55	64.00	229.66	21.34	27.56	177.80
72	44.74	115.87	78.74	65.84	236.22	21.95	28.35	182.88
80	49.71	128.75	87.49	73.15	262.47	24.38	31.50	203.20
84	52.20	135.18	91.86	76.81	275.59	25.60	33.07	213.36
90	55.92	144.84	98.42	82.30	295.28	27.43	35.43	228.60
96	59.65	154.50	104.99	87.78	314.96	29.26	37.80	243.84
100	62.14	160.94	109.36	91.44	328.08	30.48	39.37	254.00

Example: 2 inches = 5.08 cm

Fractions of an Inch

Inch	1/16	1/8	3/16	1/4	5/19	3/8	7/16	1/2
cm	0.16	0.32	0.48	0.64	0.79	0.95	1.11	1.27

Inch	9/16	5/8	11/16	3/4	13/16	7/8	15/16	1.
cm	1.43	1.59	1.75	1.91	2.06	2.22	2.38	2.54

Units of Centimeters

cm	0.1	0.2	0.3	0.4	0.5	0.6	0.7	0.8	0.9	1.0
Inch	0.04	0.08	0.12	0.16	0.20	0.24	0.28	0.31	0.35	0.39

Basic Metric Relationships
Weight

One Unit (below) Equals →	gm	kg	metric ton
gm (gram)	1.	0.001	0.000,001
kg (kilogram)	1,000.	1.	0.001
metric ton	1,000,000.	1,000.	1.

Weight[1] Conversion Tables—English-Metric Systems

metric ton → short ton	short ton → metric ton	kg → pounds	pounds → kilograms	grams → ounces	ounces → grams
1	1.10	0.91	2.20	0.45	0.04	28.4
2	2.20	1.81	4.41	0.91	0.07	56.7
3	3.31	2.72	6.61	1.36	0.11	85.0
4	4.41	3.63	8.82	1.81	0.14	113.4
5	5.51	4.54	11.02	2.67	0.18	141.8
6	6.61	5.44	13.23	2.72	0.21	170.1
7	7.72	6.35	15.43	3.18	0.25	198.4
8	8.82	7.26	17.64	3.63	0.28	226.8
9	9.92	8.16	19.84	4.08	0.32	255.2
10	11.02	9.07	22.05	4.54	0.35	283.5
16	17.68	14.51	35.27	7.25	0.56	453.6
20	22.05	18.14	44.09	9.07	0.71	567.0
30	33.07	27.22	66.14	13.61	1.06	850.5
40	44.09	36.29	88.18	18.14	1.41	1134.0
50	55.12	45.36	110.23	22.68	1.76	1417.5
60	66.14	54.43	132.28	27.22	2.12	1701.0
70	77.16	63.50	154.32	31.75	2.47	1984.5
80	88.18	72.57	176.37	36.29	2.82	2268.0
90	99.21	81.65	198.42	40.82	3.17	2551.5
100	110.20	90.72	220.46	45.36	3.53	2835.0

Example: Convert 28 pounds to kg
    28 pounds = 20 pounds + 8 pounds
    From the tables: 20 pounds = 9.07 kg and 8 pounds = 3.63 kg
    Therefore, 28 pounds = 9.07 kg + 3.63 kg = 12.70 kg
[1] The weights used for the English system are avoirdupois (common) weights.
[2] The short ton is 2000. pounds.
[3] The metric ton is 1000. kg.

cu. ft → cu. yd	cu. yd → cu. meters	cu. meters → cu. ft	cu. meters → cu. ft	cu. ft → cu. ft	cu. ft → cu. yd
	cu. yd	cu. meters	cu. ft	cu. meters	cu. ft	cu. yd

	cu. yd	cu. meters	cu. ft	cu. meters	cu. ft	cu. yd
1	0.037	0.028	27.0	0.76	35.3	1.31
2	0.074	0.057	54.0	1.53	70.6	2.62
3	0.111	0.085	81.0	2.29	105.9	3.92
4	0.148	0.113	108.0	3.06	141.3	5.23
5	0.185	0.142	135.0	3.82	176.6	6.54
6	0.212	0.170	162.0	4.59	211.9	7.85
7	0.259	0.198	189.0	5.35	247.2	9.16
8	0.296	0.227	216.0	6.12	282.5	10.46
9	0.333	0.255	243.0	6.88	317.8	11.77
10	0.370	0.283	270.0	7.65	353.1	13.07
20	0.741	0.566	540.0	15.29	706.3	26.16
30	1.111	0.850	810.0	22.94	1059.4	39.24
40	1.481	1.133	1080.0	30.58	1412.6	52.32
50	1.852	1.416	1350.0	38.23	1765.7	65.40
60	2.222	1.700	1620.0	45.87	2118.9	78.48
70	2.592	1.982	1890.0	53.52	2472.0	91.56
80	2.962	2.265	2160.0	61.16	2825.2	104.63
90	3.333	2.548	2430.0	68.81	3178.3	117.71
100	3.703	2.832	2700.0	76.46	3531.4	130.79

Example: 3 cu. yd = 81.0 cu. ft
Volume: The cubic meter is the only common dimension used for measuring the volume of solids in the metric system.

APPENDIX C – FORTIFICATION PROTECTION FACTORS

C-1. Purpose

Fortifications Protection Factors (FPF's) provide a means of determining, within specified limits, the relative value of field fortifications. FPF's give simple meaningful numbers for comparison of the protection afforded by fortifications against nuclear weapons. Their use does not require detailed nuclear weapons effects training, classified data, or graphs. FPF's are not substitutes for detailed weapons effects analysis.

C-2. Definition

The Fortification Protection Factor (FPF) of a fortification is a measure of the chance of injury to a man in the fortification from a nuclear burst in his vicinity compared to the chance of injury to a man in the open at the same place. FPF's are based on the size of the area in which the ground zero of a nuclear burst must lie in order to have at least a 50 percent probability of causing injury to a person in the center of the area which is equal to the area of damage for the weapon in question. The FPF's of fortifications are determined by the ratio of the areas of damage for protected and unprotected troops for the same weapon and conditions.

C-3. Application

The FPF applies to a fortification under a wide range of conditions. As the ratio of damage is always less than 1, it is multiplied by 100 to avoid the use of fractions. FPF's are always between and 100; the greater the FPF of a fortification, the less protection is afforded.

For example: a man in the open has an FPF of 100, but if he moves to a one-man foxhole he has a FPF of 65, or 35 percent more protection than he had while exposing himself.

APPENDIX D – USE OF EXPLOSIVES IN EXCAVATION OF EMPLACEMENTS

Section I. Introduction

D-1. Application

a. This appendix describes a method of using explosives to reduce the amount of pick work required to excavate weapon emplacements, thus making their construction faster and easier. Since blasting craters causes a wide dispersion of soil which is difficult to camouflage, this appendix is concerned chiefly with a procedure for loosening soil with explosives so it can be shoveled easily.

b. The method applies only to types of soil normally excavated with pick and shovel and not to rock or unusual ground structure. Use of explosives is not recommended for excavations extending less than 2 feet (60 cm) below ground level. The charges used are small and placed at such depth and spacing that spoil dispersion is confined to a small radius. This confinement is insured by placing a tarpaulin over the tamped charges.

     c. The desirability of using explosives as described depends on the availability of explosives and personnel trained in their use, and upon the possibility of the emplacement's location being disclosed to the enemy by the sound of explosion.

D-2. Tools and Materials

     Tools required are earth augers, crowbars, pick handles or other tamping sticks, picks, and shovels. Materials required are explosive, electric blasting caps, firing wire, galvanometer, blasting machine or battery, and a tarpaulin, or blasting mat large enough to extend 4 feet (1.2 meters) beyond the edges of the emplacement.

Section II. General procedure

D-3. Depth and Spacing of Boreholes

     a. Depth. Boreholes are dug to the depth of the desired floor level. If this depth is greater than 4 feet (1.2 meters), the entire area is excavated to a depth of 4 feet (1.2 meters), and the procedure is repeated to obtain the desired depth. Boreholes for ramps are dug while the loosened soil is being shoveled from the emplacement. Crowbars often are necessary to loosen the earth so holes can be dug with augers.

     b. Spacing, Boreholes are spaced at not more than V/-> times the depth and, when possible, in such a pattern that they are equidistant from each other. Typical layouts are described in paragraphs D-6 through D-9.

D-4. Placing Explosive Charges

     a. Test Charge.
(1) Because effectiveness of explosives varies greatly in different soils, and confinement of spoil is desired, the size of charges used is determined from a test shot. For this shot, one-half pound of explosive per foot of depth is placed in one of the interior holes. The hole is filled, thoroughly tamped, covered with the tarpaulin, and fired electrically.
(2) A complete breaking and loosening of the soil halfway to adjoining holes, without dispersion of the spoil, is desired. Unless the test results are entirely unsatisfactory, additional test shots are not needed. The results of the test give the basis for determining the quantity of explosive desired for the other holes. Usually, the original charge need not be increased or decreased by more than one-half pound block of explosive.

     b. Main Charge. The proper amount of explosive, as determined in a above, is placed and tamped in each hole, and the cap wires are connected in series. Detonating cord is not used because of resulting damage to the tarpaulin. The tarpaulin is spread and the charges are exploded electrically. If charges are of proper strength, the tarpaulin will be lifted a few feet into the air with most of the spoil confined beneath it, and both spoil and canvas will fall back to their original location. Normally, the tarpaulin will not be damaged unless the ground surface contains rocks, or is frozen or otherwise crusted.

D-5. Completion of Emplacement

The loose earth is removed (fig. D-1), the hole is shaped by pick and shovel to the desired dimensions, and the spoil is used to form a parapet. The potholes blown directly beneath the charges are filled and tamped thoroughly. Ramps are constructed as described in paragraphs D-10 and D-11.

Figure D-1. Emplacement after excavation of all loose earth.

Section III. Rectangular Emplacements

D-6. Layout of Boreholes

Boreholes for rectangular emplacements are laid out in parallel rows of equally spaced holes (fig. D-2). A row of holes of proper depth is spaced along the sides 2 feet (60 cm) inside the edge of the emplacement. Since the distance between rows should not exceed 1 ½ times the depth of holes, one or more additional rows may be required between the outside rows.

D-7. Layouts of Charges

a. Outer Rows. The outer rows of charges are located as follows:

(1) Mark outline of emplacement on ground, and locate a hole inside each corner 2 feet (60 cm) from both side lines.

(2) Space additional holes equidistantly along both sides, at distances not exceeding 1 ½ times the depth of holes.

b. Inner Rows. To locate charges of inner rows properly, proceed as follows:

(1) Space inner rows equidistantly from outer rows, at distances not exceeding 1 ½ times the depth of holes.

(2) Locate holes the same distance apart as in outer rows, but staggered with respect to them.

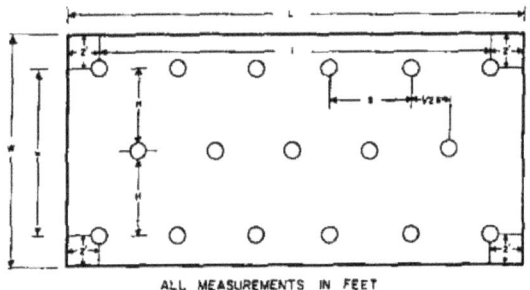

ALL MEASUREMENTS IN FEET

L = LENGTH OF EMPLACEMENT
W= WIDTH OF EMPLACEMENT
I = L-4 =LENGTH BETWEEN CORNER HOLES
× = W-4=WIDTH BETWEEN CORNER HOLES
S = DISTANCE BETWEEN HOLES IN ROW (NOT MORE THAN $1\frac{1}{2}$ × DEPTH OF HOLES)
H = DISTANCE BETWEEN ROWS (NOT MORE THAN $1\frac{1}{2}$ × DEPTH OF HOLES)

Figure D-2. Layout of boreholes for rectangular emplacements.

Section IV. Circular emplacements

D-8. Layout of Boreholes

Circular emplacements are prepared best by a circular arrangement of boreholes surrounding a borehole at the center of the emplacement (fig. D-3). Several concentric rings of holes will be required in large emplacements, whereas only one ring or only one charge may be required for small emplacements (fig. 4).

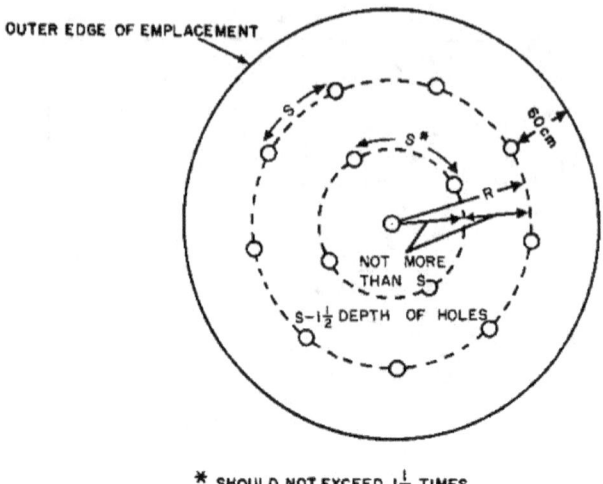

Figure D-3, Layout of boreholes for large circular emplacements.

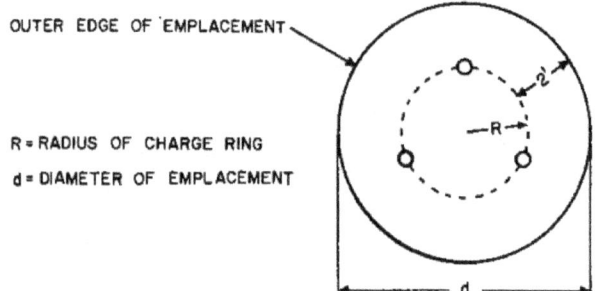

Figure D-4. Layout of boreholes when diameter of emplacement exceeds 1 ½ but not more than 3 times the depth of the boreholes.

D-9. Layouts of Charges

Table D-1 gives radii of rings and number of holes per ring for circular emplacements of various sizes. This table is based on the following steps:

a. Location of Rings,

(1) Using a length of cord, inscribe on the ground a circle 2 feet (60 cm) less in radius than the desired emplacement,

(2) Divide the above radius by 1 ½ times the depth of holes to determine the number of rings.

(3) Locate additional rings at equal distances between the outer ring and the center of the ring.

b. Location of Holes. Space holes equidistantly along each circumference at distances not exceeding 1 ½ times the depth of holes.

c. Small Emplacements.

(1) When the diameter does not exceed 1 ½ times the depth, a single charge placed at the center is sufficient. In this emplacement, size of charge is based upon diameter rather than depth of borehole. For a test hole use one-half pound of explosive per 1 ½ feet (45 cm) of diameter.

(2) When the diameter is between IV2 and 3 times the depth, three holes are spaced equidistantly around the ring and the center hole is omitted (fig. D-4).

Section V. Ramps

D-10. Construction Procedure

Ramps for emplacements are built on a slope of 4:1, hence, the length of the ramp depends on the depth of the excavation. Holes increasing in depth down the ramp are laid out as illustrated in figure D-5. Since no explosive is used in an excavation less than 2 feet (60 cm), the upper end of the ramp is excavated by pick and shovel. When ramps reaching a depth greater than 4 feet (1.2 meters) are to be constructed, the portion to be greater than 4 feet (1.2 meters) deep is excavated by the method used for rectangular emplacements, then sloped as described in paragraph D-ll.

D-1 1: Layouts of Charges for Ramps

a. Outside Rows. Boreholes are located in the position and to the depth indicated in figure

Feet / Meters

Depth of Borehole	Ring No.†	3' (.9) R*	N†	4' (1.2) R	N	5' (1.5) R	N	6' (1.8) R	N	7' (2.1) R	N	8' (2.4) R	N	9' (2.7) R	N	10' (3.0) R	N	11' (3.3) R	N	12' (3.6) R	N	13' (3.9) R	N	14' (4.2) R	N	15' (4.5) R	N
2'/.6 meters	1	1 (.3)	3	2 (.6)	5	3 (.9)	7	4 (1.2)	9	5 (1.5)	11	6 (1.8)	13	7 (2.1)	15	8 (2.4)	17	9 (2.7)	19	10 (3.0)	21	11 (3.3)	24	12 (3.6)	26	13 (3.9)	28
	2					2 (.6)		2.5 (.75)	6	3 (.9)	6	4.75 (1.4)	7	5.3 (1.6)	10	6 (1.8)	12	7.5 (2.3)	13	8.25 (2.5)	16	9 (2.7)	18	10.5 (3.2)	19		22
	3													2.3 (.7)	5	2.75 (.8)	6	3 (.9)	7	5 (1.5)	11	5.5 (1.7)	12	6 (1.8)	13	7.8 (2.2)	17
	4																			2.5 (.8)	6	2.8 (.8)	6	3 (.9)	7	5.25 (1.6)	11
	5																									2.8 (.8)	6
3'/1.8 meters	1	1 (.3)	3	2 (.6)	3	3 (.9)	5	4 (1.2)	6	5 (1.5)	7	6 (1.8)	9	7 (2.1)	10	8 (2.4)	12	9 (2.7)	12	10 (3.0)	13	11 (3.3)	14	12 (3.6)	16	13 (3.9)	19
	2											2.5 (.75)	4	3.5 (1.1)	5	4.5 (1.4)	6			6.5 (2.0)	10	7.3 (2.2)	11	8 (2.4)	12	8.8 (2.6)	13
	3																			3.3 (1.)	5	3.8 (1.1)	6	4 (1.2)	6	4.3 (1.3)	7
4'/1.2 meters	1			2 (.6)	3	3 (.9)	4	4 (1.2)	5	5 (1.5)	6	6 (1.8)	7	7 (2.1)	8	8 (2.4)	10	9 (2.7)	11	10 (3.0)	12	11 (3.3)	13	12 (3.6)	13	13 (3.9)	14
	2											3 (.9)	4	3.5 (1.8)	4	4.5 (1.2)	5			5 (1.8)	5	5.5 (1.1)	6	6.5 (1.7)	6	8.8 (2.6)	10
	3																									4.3 (1.3)	5

*Number does not include center-hole charge.
† Rings are numbered from outside toward center.
* R = Radius of ring of boreholes.
† N = Number of boreholes in ring.

Table D-I. Number of Charges Required for Circular Emplacements.

D-5. Lay out these holes as follows:

(1) Trace an outline of the ramp on the ground, with 4 feet (1.2 meters) of length for every foot (30 cm) of depth.

(2) Two feet (60 cm) inside the edge of the ramp and 10 feet (3 meters) from its outer end, place a borehole 2 feet (60 cm) deep. In line, 4 feet (1.2 meters) nearer the emplacement, place a second hole 3 feet (90 cm) deep.

(3) Place a similar pair of charges 2 feet (60 cm) inside the opposite edge of the ramp.

b. Inner Rows. Space inner rows equidistantly between outer rows at distances not exceeding 4 feet (1.2 meter). Holes in inner rows have the depths and locations shown in figure D-5.

Section VI. Craters

D-1 2, Blasting Craters for Emplacements

When camouflage is not required, craters of approximately the desired shape of the emplacement may be blown with explosives. The shovel work required to complete the excavation is considerably less than that required for the method described in preceding sections. The center of the crater will be too deep and must be filled with spoil from the sides and tamped.

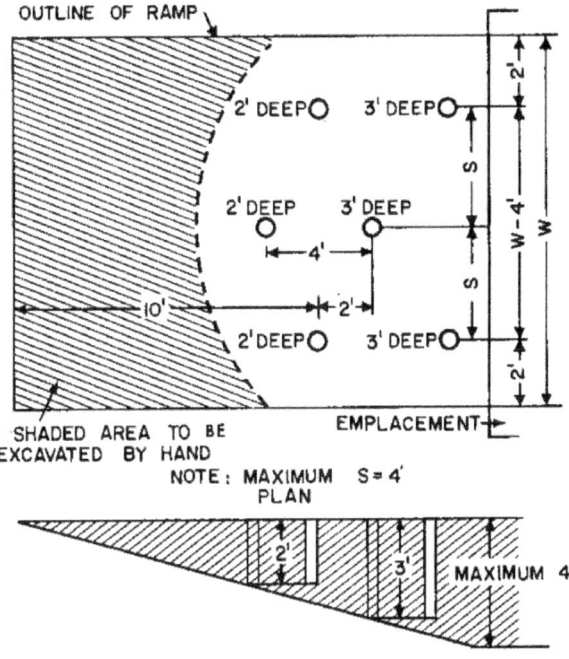

SECTION THROUGH OUTSIDE ROW OF HOLES

Figure D-5. Layout of boreholes in preparing a ramp.

D-13. Layouts of Charges

The layout of holes for both circular and rectangular craters is similar to that used in the methods described in paragraphs D-6 through D-9 except that the following general rules govern the dimensions:

a. The depth of boreholes is two-thirds the desired depth of excavation.

b. Maximum spacing between rows, and between holes in the same row, is twice the depth of boreholes.

c. The distance between the desired boundary of emplacement and outer boreholes is equal to the depth of boreholes.

d. Two-thirds of the charge is placed at the bottom of the borehole, and one-third is placed halfway down.

e. Charges in the center hole of a circular emplacement, and in interior holes of a rectangular emplacement, are twice those used in outer boreholes.

f. Table D-2 is a guide in determining proper charges based on sandy clay soil. If a number of emplacements are to be constructed, it is desirable to use one of them as a test before boreholes of remaining emplacements are charged.

197

Depth of borehole (feet/meters)	Half-pound blocks of explosive
2'/.6m	5
3'/.9m	10
4'/1.2m	15
5'/1.5m	25

Table D-2. Quantity of Explosive for Blasting Craters.

Section VII. Foxhole digger explosive kit

D-14. Characteristics

a. Case.

Material	Shape	Size	Wt
Plastic with screw cap.	Tubular with truncated top.	7.38 x 2.28 in.	1.0 lb

b. Shaped Charge.

Material	Shape	Size	Explosive Charge			
			Type	Det Vel	Wt	Booster
Copper cone with 60° angle; and plastic.	Tubular with truncated top.	7.37 x 2.0 in	Octol	27,559 fps	118g (4.16 oz)	RDX

c. Cratering Charge.

Material	Shape	Size	Explosive Charge			
			Type	Det Vol	Wt	Booster
2 segments of pressed explosive; connecting sleeve.	Tubular	8.21 x 1.0 in	PBXN-1	24,606 fps	162g (5.71 oz)	RDX

d. Fuzes.

Material	Shape					
Stainless steel body; steel coupling.	Tubular	4.25 x 0.56 in	Mechanical with spring-driven striker	Push button	Cotter pin	RDX and primer.

e. Auxiliary items. Piece of No. 9 nylon twine 36 in. long; steel stability rod 4.25 x 0.1in.; two strips adhesive-coated foam tape; and lug on side of case with hole for stability rod and ring for attaching kit to soldier's clothing or equipment.

f. Remark. Outer case of kit serves also as standoff for shaped charge.

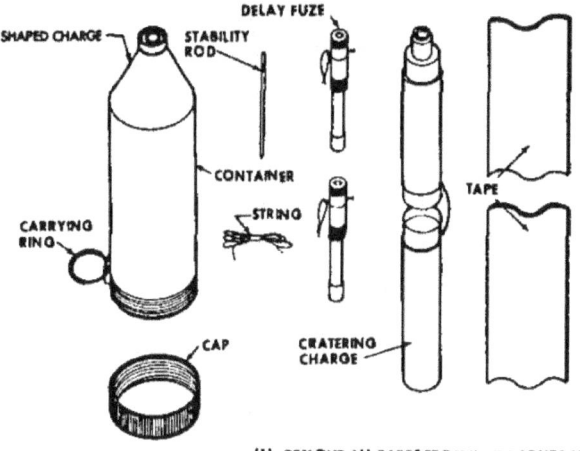

DELAY FUZE

SHAPED CHARGE

STABILITY ROD

CONTAINER

CARRYING RING

STRING

TAPE

CAP

CRATERING CHARGE

(1) REMOVE ALL PARTS FROM INSIDE CONTAINER
(2) LEAVE CAP OFF

FOXHOLE DIGGER EXPLOSIVE KIT

Figure D-6. Foxhole digger explosive kit.

D-15. Arming and Placement

See figure D-7.

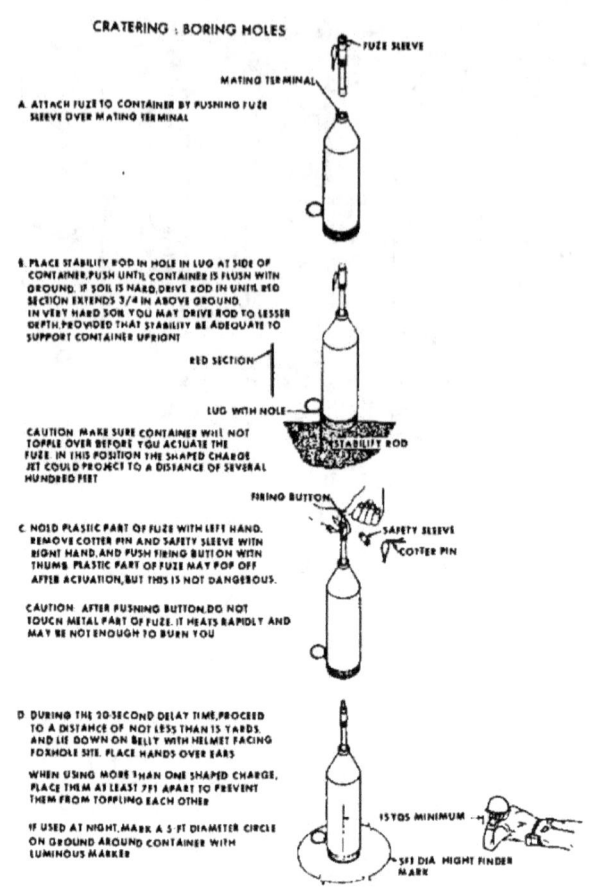

CRATERING : BORING HOLES

FUZE SLEEVE

MATING TERMINAL

A. ATTACH FUZE TO CONTAINER BY PUSHING FUZE
SLEEVE OVER MATING TERMINAL

B. PLACE STABILITY ROD IN HOLE IN LUG AT SIDE OF
CONTAINER, PUSH UNTIL CONTAINER IS FLUSH WITH
GROUND. IF SOIL IS HARD, DRIVE ROD IN UNTIL RED
SECTION EXTENDS 3/4 IN ABOVE GROUND.
IN VERY HARD SOIL YOU MAY DRIVE ROD TO LESSER
DEPTH, PROVIDED THAT STABILITY BE ADEQUATE TO
SUPPORT CONTAINER UPRIGHT

RED SECTION

LUG WITH HOLE

STABILITY ROD

CAUTION MAKE SURE CONTAINER WILL NOT
TOPPLE OVER BEFORE YOU ACTUATE THE
FUZE IN THIS POSITION THE SHAPED CHARGE
JET COULD PROJECT TO A DISTANCE OF SEVERAL
HUNDRED FEET

FIRING BUTTON

SAFETY SLEEVE

COTTER PIN

C. HOLD PLASTIC PART OF FUZE WITH LEFT HAND.
REMOVE COTTER PIN AND SAFETY SLEEVE WITH
RIGHT HAND. AND PUSH FIRING BUTTON WITH
THUMB. PLASTIC PART OF FUZE MAY POP OFF
AFTER ACTUATION, BUT THIS IS NOT DANGEROUS.

CAUTION AFTER PUSHING BUTTON, DO NOT
TOUCH METAL PART OF FUZE. IT HEATS RAPIDLY AND
MAY BE HOT ENOUGH TO BURN YOU

D DURING THE 20 SECOND DELAY TIME, PROCEED
TO A DISTANCE OF NOT LESS THAN 15 YARDS.
AND LIE DOWN ON BELLY WITH HELMET FACING
FOXHOLE SITE. PLACE HANDS OVER EARS

WHEN USING MORE THAN ONE SHAPED CHARGE,
PLACE THEM AT LEAST 7FT APART TO PREVENT
THEM FROM TOPPLING EACH OTHER

IF USED AT NIGHT, MARK A 5 FT DIAMETER CIRCLE
ON GROUND AROUND CONTAINER WITH
LUMINOUS MARKER

15 YDS MINIMUM

5FT DIA NIGHT FINDER
MARK

Figure D-7. Arming and placement of foxhole digger kit for cratering.

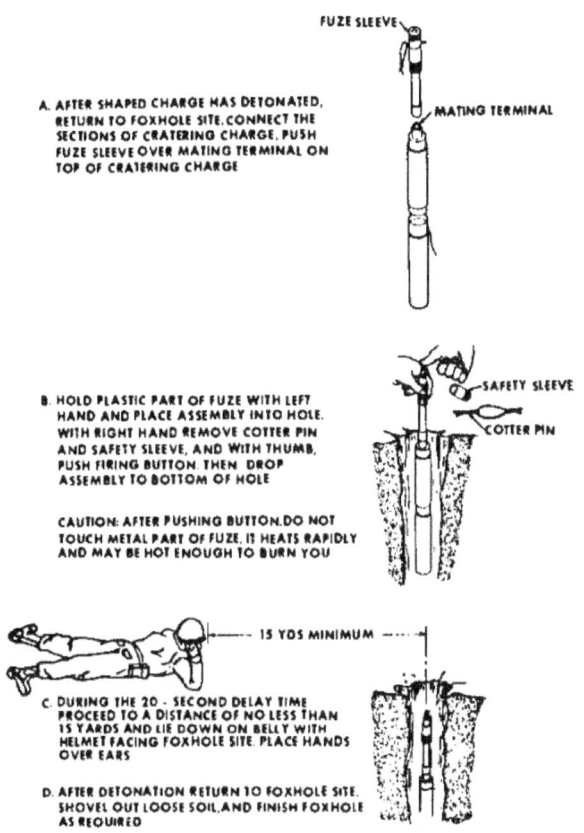

FUZE SLEEVE

MATING TERMINAL

A. AFTER SHAPED CHARGE HAS DETONATED, RETURN TO FOXHOLE SITE, CONNECT THE SECTIONS OF CRATERING CHARGE. PUSH FUZE SLEEVE OVER MATING TERMINAL ON TOP OF CRATERING CHARGE

SAFETY SLEEVE

COTTER PIN

B. HOLD PLASTIC PART OF FUZE WITH LEFT HAND AND PLACE ASSEMBLY INTO HOLE. WITH RIGHT HAND REMOVE COTTER PIN AND SAFETY SLEEVE, AND WITH THUMB, PUSH FIRING BUTTON. THEN DROP ASSEMBLY TO BOTTOM OF HOLE

CAUTION: AFTER PUSHING BUTTON, DO NOT TOUCH METAL PART OF FUZE. IT HEATS RAPIDLY AND MAY BE HOT ENOUGH TO BURN YOU

15 YDS MINIMUM

C. DURING THE 20 - SECOND DELAY TIME PROCEED TO A DISTANCE OF NO LESS THAN 15 YARDS AND LIE DOWN ON BELLY WITH HELMET FACING FOXHOLE SITE. PLACE HANDS OVER EARS

D. AFTER DETONATION RETURN TO FOXHOLE SITE. SHOVEL OUT LOOSE SOIL, AND FINISH FOXHOLE AS REQUIRED

Figure D-7. Arming and placement of foxhole digger kit for cratering. Cont.

D-16. Effect

a. The shaped charge will penetrate soil, depending on the density, to depths varying from 50 to 85 centimeters, forming a tapered hole 6 centimeters in diameter at the top and 1.5 centimeters at the bottom.

b. The cratering charge will form a crater in soil about 107 centimeters in diameter and about 80 centimeters deep.

INDEX

www.ingramcontent.com/pod-product-compliance
Lightning Source LLC
Chambersburg PA
CBHW070109290526
45789CB00005B/1978